THE GLOSSARY OF
USER
RESEARCH

Compiled & Edited By:
Manasi Pathak

Rhythm

Independent
Publication

THE GLOSSARY OF USER RESEARCH

Compiled & Edited By:
Manasi Pathak

ISBN:9798861651202

9798861651202

Published by:
Rhythm Independent Publication,
Jinkethimmanahalli, Varanasi, Bengaluru, Karnataka, India - 560036

For all types of correspondence, send your mails to the provided address above.

The information presented herein has been collated from a diverse range of sources, comprehensive perspective on the subject matter.

A/B Testing

A/B Testing is a user-research method used to compare two or more versions of a design or experience to determine which one performs better. It involves creating two (or more) variants, A and B, that differ in only one aspect, such as color, layout, or content, and then randomly splitting users into groups to experience each variant.

The purpose of A/B Testing is to gather data and insights on user behavior and preferences to make data-driven decisions for improving the user experience. By comparing the metrics and performance of different variants, researchers can identify the most effective design elements or features that lead to desired outcomes, such as increased conversions, engagement, or user satisfaction.

Acceptance Testing

Acceptance testing is a formal evaluation process conducted in the context of user-research (UXR) to validate and assess a product or system's compliance with specified requirements and user expectations. It aims to ensure that the product or system meets the necessary standards and functionality as defined by the intended users.

During acceptance testing, the primary focus is on the end-users' perspectives and experiences. It involves testing the product or system in real-world scenarios, simulating real-life situations, and taking into account the users' feedback and observations. The purpose is to determine whether the product or system is user-friendly, efficient, and capable of fulfilling the intended purpose effectively.

Accessibility Audits

Accessibility audits in the context of user research (UXR) refer to the evaluation of digital products or services to assess their compliance with accessibility guidelines and standards. These audits involve a detailed examination of various components and functionalities of a website or application to identify any barriers or limitations that may hinder access for individuals with disabilities. The ultimate goal of accessibility audits is to ensure that digital products are inclusive and provide equal access to all users, regardless of their abilities or impairments. During an accessibility audit, a user researcher conducts a comprehensive review of the design, layout, and content of a digital product. This evaluation may include assessing the color contrast of text and background, evaluating the readability of content, analyzing the organization and structure of information, examining the functionality of interactive elements (such as links, buttons, and forms), and verifying the compatibility with assistive technologies (e.g., screen readers, keyboard navigation). User researchers follow established accessibility guidelines, such as the Web Content Accessibility Guidelines (WCAG), which provide specific criteria and techniques for making digital products accessible. These guidelines cover various aspects related to accessibility, including perceivability, operability, understandability, and robustness. By conducting accessibility audits, user researchers can identify accessibility gaps and recommend improvements to enhance the overall user experience for individuals with disabilities. These audits contribute to the development of more inclusive digital products, promoting equal access and participation for everyone.>

Accessibility Compliance Testing

Accessibility compliance testing in the context of user research (UXR) involves evaluating a website, application, or digital product against established accessibility guidelines to ensure it can be accessed and used by people with disabilities. The objective of accessibility compliance testing is to identify barriers or obstacles that may prevent individuals with disabilities from engaging with the digital product effectively.

This testing typically involves conducting various assessments and evaluations based on WCAG (Web Content Accessibility Guidelines) criteria, which provide standards and recommendations for making digital content accessible to people with disabilities. User researchers will often perform manual inspections and tests, as well as use assistive technologies like screen readers, keyboard-only navigation, or voice recognition software to simulate the experiences of individuals with disabilities.

Accessibility compliance testing aims to uncover potential issues such as insufficient color contrast, missing alt text for images, inaccessible forms or navigation, inadequate labeling or descriptions, and other elements that may hinder the usability and overall accessibility of the digital product. Identifying these barriers allows user researchers to recommend improvements or modifications to ensure compliance with accessibility standards and enhance the user experience for individuals with disabilities.

Accessibility Surveys

Accessibility surveys in the context of user-research (UXR) are a systematic and structured method used to gather data and insights on the accessibility of a digital product or service. These surveys are specifically designed to assess how well the product or service meets the needs of individuals with disabilities and other accessibility challenges. By conducting accessibility surveys, UXR professionals aim to understand the barriers and challenges experienced by users with disabilities when interacting with the digital interface. The surveys typically include a series of questions and prompts that cover various dimensions of accessibility, such as visual, auditory, and motor impairments. The questions in accessibility surveys are carefully crafted to elicit detailed and specific feedback from participants. They may cover topics like the effectiveness of alternative text for images, the availability of captions for videos, the ease of navigation using keyboard shortcuts, and the adaptability of font size and color contrast. These questions help UX researchers identify areas of improvement and prioritize accessibility enhancements. The data collected from accessibility surveys can help inform the design and development process to ensure that digital products and services are more inclusive and accessible to a broader range of users. It provides valuable insights that allow UX teams to make informed decisions and implement necessary changes to meet accessibility standards and guidelines. Overall, accessibility surveys play a crucial role in advocating for user-centric design practices and improving the usability and inclusivity of digital experiences for people with disabilities.>

Accessibility Testing

Accessibility testing in the context of user research (UXR) refers to the process of evaluating and assessing the usability and inclusiveness of a digital product or service for individuals with disabilities. It involves systematically examining the design, functionality, and user experience of a website, application, or digital content to ensure that it can be accessed, understood, and used by all users, including those with visual, auditory, cognitive, or motor impairments.

During accessibility testing, researchers conduct various tests and evaluations to identify potential barriers or challenges that people with disabilities may encounter while interacting with the digital product. This may include testing with assistive technologies such as screen readers, magnifiers, or voice recognition software, as well as conducting manual assessments and usability studies with individuals from diverse disability groups.

The goal of accessibility testing is to uncover any barriers or issues that prevent individuals with disabilities from fully accessing and using the digital product or service. Through this process, user researchers aim to ensure that the product meets international accessibility standards, such as the Web Content Accessibility Guidelines (WCAG), and provides an inclusive user experience for all individuals.

By conducting accessibility testing, user researchers can gather valuable insights and feedback from users with disabilities, allowing them to make informed design decisions and improvements to enhance the overall usability and inclusiveness of the digital product. This process not only promotes equal access to information and services but also helps organizations comply with legal requirements and create a more user-centered and inclusive user experience.

Accessibility

Accessibility in the context of user research (UXR) refers to the practice of designing and evaluating digital products and services in a way that ensures they can be used by as many people as possible, regardless of their abilities or disabilities.

It involves taking into consideration the diverse range of users and their specific needs, such as those with visual impairments, hearing impairments, motor impairments, cognitive impairments, or other disabilities. Accessibility aims to remove barriers and provide equal access and usability for all individuals, regardless of their limitations.

Adjourning Technique

The adjourning technique, in the context of user research (UXR), refers to the process of formally concluding a research study or project and disseminating the results to relevant stakeholders. It involves summarizing the findings, evaluating the research process, and determining the next steps for the project.

During the adjourning phase, the UXR team collates and analyzes the data collected during the research study. They identify patterns, trends, and insights that can inform decision-making and drive improvements in the user experience. The team documents their findings in a comprehensive report, using visuals such as charts and graphs to present the data effectively.

Once the research findings have been compiled, the UXR team conducts a formal presentation or workshop to share the results with key stakeholders, including designers, developers, product managers, and executives. The goal of this presentation is to ensure that the research findings are understood and to facilitate discussions around potential design or product changes.

After the presentation, the UXR team evaluates the effectiveness of the research process, reflecting on the methods used, the challenges encountered, and the learnings gained. They identify areas for improvement and note any changes or adjustments that need to be made for future research projects.

The adjourning technique is critical in the field of user research as it ensures that research findings are effectively communicated, understood, and utilized by relevant stakeholders. It also allows the UXR team to reflect on their work and continuously improve their research practices.

Advocacy

Advocacy in the context of user research (UXR) refers to the act of representing and promoting the needs, interests, and perspectives of users within a product development process. It involves being a vocal and active advocate for the users, ensuring that their needs and concerns are properly considered and addressed.

The role of an advocate in user research is to gather and present compelling evidence and insights about users' experiences, preferences, and pain points. This may involve conducting user interviews, surveys, usability tests, and other research methods to gain a deep understanding of the target users. The advocate then uses this research data to highlight the users' needs and experiences to the product team, stakeholders, and decision-makers.

Affinity Diagrams

Affinity diagrams are a user research technique commonly used in UX research to organize and analyze qualitative data gathered from user interviews, observations, or surveys. This technique helps researchers identify patterns, themes, and relationships within the data, allowing for a deeper understanding of user needs, concerns, and preferences.

The process of creating an affinity diagram involves grouping related data points or insights into clusters based on their similarities or affinities. This is done through a collaborative exercise with a group of stakeholders or researchers. Data points can be written on sticky notes or index cards, and participants are encouraged to group them together based on common themes or connections they see.

Affinity diagrams promote a participatory and inclusive approach to data analysis, as they allow multiple perspectives to be considered. By involving different stakeholders in the process, a broader range of insights and viewpoints can be captured, leading to more comprehensive findings.

Once the affinity diagram is completed, researchers can visually observe the emerging patterns or themes, which can then inform design decisions or potential areas for further investigation. It helps in synthesizing and organizing a large amount of qualitative data into meaningful categories, making it easier to identify trends and actionable insights.

Agile Retrospectives

Agile retrospectives in the context of user research (UXR) refer to the practice of reflecting and evaluating the strengths and areas of improvement in the user research process within an Agile framework. It is a collaborative and iterative approach that allows the UXR team to continuously adapt and enhance their practices based on their experiences and feedback.

During agile retrospectives, the team gathers to review the user research activities and outputs, including techniques used, data collected, insights generated, and any challenges encountered. The focus is on identifying what worked well, what needs improvement, and what actions can be taken to enhance the future user research endeavors.

The primary objective of agile retrospectives in UXR is to foster a culture of learning, experimentation, and improvement. By regularly reflecting on their work, the UXR team can make adjustments to their research methods, collaboration processes, and communication strategies. This ensures a user-centered approach and helps to deliver more accurate and valuable insights, ultimately leading to the creation of user-centric products and services.

Agile retrospectives in the UXR context typically follow a structured format, such as the "What Went Well, What Could Be Improved, and What Actions to Take" (WWW) approach. This format encourages open and honest discussions among team members, allowing everyone to contribute their observations, suggestions, and action items.

In conclusion, agile retrospectives in user research enable teams to reflect on their practices, identify areas for improvement, and take action to enhance their user-centered approach. By continuously learning and adapting, the UXR team can provide more valuable insights and contribute to the development of successful user experiences.

Agile User Interviews

Agile User Interviews, in the context of user-research (UXR), refer to a dynamic and iterative approach to gathering insights and feedback from users. This method involves conducting interviews with users throughout the entire product development process, from early stages to post-launch evaluations.

The main objective of Agile User Interviews is to understand users' needs, expectations, and frustrations in order to inform and shape the design and development of digital products or solutions. These interviews follow the principles of the Agile methodology, which involves continuous learning, adaptation, and collaboration.

Alpha Testing

Alpha testing in the context of user research (UXR) refers to the early stage of testing a product or service with a small group of targeted users. This type of testing is typically conducted by the development team, allowing them to gather valuable feedback and identify any usability issues or formative insights.

During alpha testing, the primary objective is to assess the overall user experience, usability, and functionality of the product or service. The selected group of users, often a representative sample, interact with the system in real-world scenarios to uncover any potential flaws or areas for improvement. This testing phase occurs before the product or service is finalized and prepared for wider distribution or beta testing.

Amplitude

Amplitude is a user research (UXR) tool used to collect, analyze, and interpret data regarding user behavior and interactions with a digital product or service. It provides powerful analytics and insights that help understand user journeys, identify trends, and make informed decisions for product improvement.

As a UXR tool, Amplitude helps researchers measure and quantify various user actions, such as clicks, taps, searches, and transactions, across different platforms and devices. It tracks and records user events and data, providing valuable information about user engagement, retention, and conversion rates.

Analysis

User research (UXR) is a systematic approach to understanding users and their needs, motivations, and behaviors in order to inform the design and development of products and services. It employs a variety of qualitative and quantitative methods to gather data and insights, which are then used to improve the user experience and ensure that products meet users' expectations and goals.

UXR involves conducting studies and interviews with users, observing their interactions with products, and analyzing data to identify patterns and trends. This research helps uncover pain points, challenges, and opportunities for improvement in the user journey. By understanding users' preferences, habits, and expectations, designers and developers can create more user-centric solutions and make informed decisions about the features, functionality, and user interface of a product.

Analytics

Analytics is the systematic process of gathering and analyzing data to gain insights and make informed decisions. In the context of user research (UXR), analytics refers to the practice of using data to understand user behavior, preferences, and patterns in order to improve the user experience.

Through analytics, UX researchers collect and analyze various types of data such as user interactions, click-through rates, time spent on specific tasks or pages, and demographic information. These data points provide valuable information about how users engage with a product, website, or application.

Appcues

Appcues is a user onboarding and product adoption platform that helps businesses improve their user experience. It offers a toolset that enables product teams to create and implement interactive onboarding flows, tooltips, and feature announcements without requiring coding expertise.

As a user-research (UXR) tool, Appcues helps UX researchers gather valuable insights about user behavior and preferences. Its features allow researchers to create and A/B test different onboarding experiences to better understand user engagement and conversion rates. By tracking user interactions and analyzing data, Appcues provides researchers with the ability to identify pain points in the onboarding process and make data-driven decisions to improve the overall user experience.

Appsee

Appsee is a user research tool specifically designed for User Experience Researchers (UXR), which helps them monitor, analyze, and optimize user interactions with mobile apps and websites. It provides detailed insights into user behavior, navigation patterns, and engagement levels, enabling UXR professionals to make informed decisions and improve the overall user experience.

With Appsee, UXR teams can gain valuable insights into how users interact with their app or website by capturing and recording every user session. This allows researchers to observe actual user behavior firsthand, identifying any usability issues or pain points that may be hindering the user experience. By analyzing session recordings, heatmaps, and touch heatmaps, UXR teams can understand where users are encountering difficulties, where they are spending most of their time, and which areas of the app or website are most engaging.

Apptentive

Apptentive is a user research tool used in the field of User Experience Research (UXR). It allows businesses to gather valuable feedback and insights from their users, helping them make informed decisions to improve the user experience of their products or services.

With Apptentive, researchers can interact with users through various channels such as in-app messaging, surveys, and app store reviews. This tool enables businesses to proactively engage with their users, understand their needs, and identify any pain points or areas for improvement.

AxiomUX

AxiomUX is a user-research methodology that aims to inform the design and development of user-centered products and experiences. It involves gathering qualitative and quantitative data through various research techniques to gain insights into user behaviors, needs, and preferences. By understanding the target audience, AxiomUX helps to uncover valuable insights that guide the decision-making process throughout the design and development lifecycle.

This methodology encompasses a range of research activities, including user interviews, surveys, observation, and usability testing. Through these research methods, AxiomUX seeks to uncover user motivations, pain points, and expectations. The data collected is analyzed to identify patterns and trends, which are then used to inform design decisions and create user-centered solutions.

Behavioral Analytics

Behavioral analytics in the context of user research (UXR) refers to the analysis of user behavior and interactions with a product or service to gain insights and improve the user experience. It involves the collection, measurement, and interpretation of data related to user actions, patterns, and preferences.

By studying user behavior, researchers can understand how users engage with a product, what features they use the most, and where they encounter difficulties or obstacles. This information helps UX designers and developers make informed decisions to enhance the usability, functionality, and overall satisfaction of the product.

Behavioral Economics Testing

Behavioral economics testing refers to the systematic evaluation and analysis of human behavior and decision-making processes within the context of user research (UXR). It aims to understand and predict how individuals make choices and respond to stimuli, particularly in relation to economic and financial matters.

Within the field of UXR, behavioral economics testing involves examining how users interact with digital products or services and how their behaviors are influenced by various psychological and cognitive factors. By conducting experiments, observations, and interviews, researchers can uncover the underlying behavioral tendencies that drive users' decision-making processes.

Benchmark Testing

Benchmark testing is a user-research method used to evaluate the performance and usability of a website or application by comparing it against established standards or competitors. It provides quantitative data that can be used to measure the effectiveness and efficiency of a product, and to identify areas for improvement.

In benchmark testing, a group of participants is given a set of tasks to complete on a website or application. Their performance is measured based on various factors such as task completion time, error rates, and subjective satisfaction ratings. These measurements are then compared to established benchmarks, which can be industry standards or the performance of competing products.

Benchmarking Studies

A benchmarking study in the context of user research (UXR) refers to a systematic evaluation and comparison of a product or service against industry standards or competing offerings. The goal of benchmarking studies is to assess and measure the performance, usability, and user experience of a product or service, allowing designers and researchers to identify areas for improvement and make informed decisions based on data.

During a benchmarking study, researchers typically identify relevant metrics and criteria to evaluate the product or service under investigation. These can include factors such as task completion rates, error rates, user satisfaction ratings, and efficiency measures. Researchers may use a combination of qualitative and quantitative methods to collect data, including user interviews, surveys, observation, and usability testing.

Best Practices

User research (UXR) refers to the practice of collecting and analyzing data about users and their experiences to inform the design and development of products and services. UXR aims to understand users' behaviors, needs, and motivations in order to create solutions that meet their expectations and improve their overall experience.

It involves various methods, such as interviews, surveys, observations, and usability testing, to gather qualitative and quantitative data. Qualitative data provides insights into users' thoughts, feelings, and attitudes, while quantitative data offers measurable information, such as demographics and usage metrics.

By conducting user research, organizations gain valuable insights that help them make informed design decisions, identify pain points in existing experiences, and uncover opportunities for innovation. It helps bridge the gap between the user's perspective and the design team's goals, resulting in user-centered designs that are more intuitive, effective, and enjoyable to use.

Throughout the design process, UXR is iterative and involves continuous feedback and validation from users. Designers and researchers collaborate to analyze the collected data, identify patterns, and derive actionable insights. These insights guide the design and development decisions, leading to user experiences that align with users' needs and preferences.

In summary, user research (UXR) is the systematic practice of gathering and analyzing user data to inform the design and development of products and services. It plays a crucial role in creating user-centered solutions by understanding user behaviors, needs, and motivations and applying these insights throughout the design process.

Beta Testing

Beta testing is a method of user research performed during the final stages of software development. It involves releasing a test version of a product to a limited number of real users, who then provide feedback on the product's usability, functionality, and overall user experience.

The purpose of beta testing is to gather insights and uncover issues that may have been overlooked in earlier stages of development, helping to ensure that the final product meets the needs and expectations of its intended users. This feedback not only helps to identify bugs and technical glitches, but also highlights areas where the user interface may need improvement, or where features may be unclear or confusing to users.

Brand Equity Testing

Brand equity testing is a user research process conducted in the field of user experience research (UXR) that aims to evaluate the perceived value and strength of a brand among its target audience. It involves gathering insights and feedback from users to assess the brand's influence, reputation, and overall impact on user behavior and decision-making processes.

During brand equity testing, researchers employ various qualitative and quantitative methods to measure users' perception of the brand, including their emotional connection, trust, familiarity, and loyalty towards the brand. This may involve conducting surveys, interviews, and focus groups to collect subjective opinions and thoughts, as well as analyzing quantitative data such as web analytics, purchase behavior, and brand recognition metrics.

Brand Image Testing

Brand Image Testing is a user-research method employed to evaluate and analyze the perception and reputation of a brand among its target audience. It aims to understand how customers perceive a brand, how they associate it with specific values or attributes, and how the brand is positioned in the marketplace.

During brand image testing, user researchers collect qualitative and quantitative data to assess the overall brand image. This data is gathered through various research techniques, such as surveys, interviews, focus groups, and observations. Through these methods, researchers gain insights into consumers' emotions, attitudes, opinions, and experiences related to the brand.

The primary objectives of brand image testing are to assess whether the brand aligns with its intended image, identify areas where the brand needs improvement, and measure the impact of marketing efforts or changes in brand messaging. It helps businesses make informed decisions about brand positioning, messaging, and strategy by providing valuable insights into consumer perceptions and preferences.

This research method can also be used to understand how a brand is perceived in relation to its competitors. By comparing the brand image of different companies in the same industry, businesses can identify their competitive advantage or weaknesses and develop strategies to stand out in the market.

Overall, brand image testing plays a crucial role in shaping a brand's identity and reputation. It provides businesses with valuable insights into their target audience's perception of their brand, allowing them to make data-driven decisions to improve and strengthen their brand's image in the marketplace.

Brand Loyalty Testing

Brand loyalty testing is a user-research methodology used to evaluate the extent to which customers are committed and devoted to a particular brand. It involves assessing the level of trust, satisfaction, and emotional connection that customers have with a brand, as well as their likelihood to repeat purchases and recommend the brand to others.

This type of testing helps organizations understand the factors that contribute to brand loyalty and identify areas for improvement. It provides insights into customer preferences, expectations, and perceptions, and assists in the development of strategies to enhance customer loyalty and retention.

CTA (Call-To-Action) Testing

CTA (Call-to-Action) Testing refers to the process of evaluating and analyzing the effectiveness of the call-to-action elements on a website or digital platform. This form of user research, often conducted by UX researchers, aims to understand how users respond to different CTAs and identify areas for improvement.

During CTA testing, researchers typically design experiments or conduct usability tests to gather data on user behavior and perception. This may involve presenting participants with various CTAs (such as buttons, links, or banners) and observing their actions and feedback. The objective is to determine which CTAs are most effective in guiding users towards desired actions, such as making a purchase, signing up for a newsletter, or completing a form.

Canny

The Canny method is a computer vision algorithm commonly used in user research (UXR) to detect and enhance edges in images. It was developed by John F. Canny in 1986 and has since become one of the most widely used edge detection techniques.

The Canny algorithm involves several steps to accurately identify and highlight edges in an image. These steps include:

1. Noise reduction: The algorithm applies a Gaussian filter to the image to reduce unwanted noise and create a smoothed grayscale version of the original image.

2. Gradient calculation: The algorithm calculates the intensity gradients of the smoothed image using techniques such as the Sobel operator. This step identifies regions of significant intensity change, which often correspond to edges.

3. Non-maximum suppression: The algorithm then examines the gradient magnitude and direction to thin out the detected edges. Only the local maxima in each direction are retained, resulting in a thin, continuous line along each edge.

4. Double thresholding: The Canny algorithm applies two thresholds, a high and a low threshold, to classify the remaining edge pixels. Pixels with gradient magnitudes above the high threshold are considered strong edges, while those between the low and high thresholds are considered weak edges.

5. Edge tracking by hysteresis: The final step connects the weak edges to the strong edges by analyzing connectivity. Only edges that are connected to strong edges are retained, forming the final edge map.

The Canny algorithm is particularly useful in user research as it helps identify and analyze the visual boundaries in images. This information can be utilized to understand user interactions, improve user interfaces, and optimize the overall user experience.

Card Sorting

Card sorting is a user research technique used in the field of user experience (UX) research to understand how users organize and categorize information. It involves presenting users with a set of cards, each representing a piece of content, and asking them to group the cards into categories that make sense to them. The goal of card sorting is to uncover users' mental models and thought processes when organizing information.

During a card sorting session, participants are typically given a stack of cards and asked to organize them into groups that they find meaningful. They may also be asked to label the groups they create. By observing how users group the cards, researchers can gain insights into how users conceptualize and organize information in relation to the given content. This information can then be used to inform the organization and structure of websites, apps, or other digital products.

Case Studies

A case study is a type of research method used in user research (UXR) to investigate a particular phenomenon or situation in depth. It involves the analysis and examination of a specific individual, group, or organization over a given period of time to gain insights and understanding of their experiences, behaviors, and interactions within a given context.

Typically, a case study in UXR focuses on studying the holistic perspective of the user and their interactions with a product, service, or system. It aims to provide a detailed and comprehensive understanding of the user's needs, motivations, and pain points, resulting in actionable insights for design and development.

Certification

A certification in the context of user research (UXR) refers to a formal recognition or qualification that validates an individual's knowledge, skills, and expertise in the field of conducting user research. It serves as evidence of one's competency and proficiency in applying research methods and techniques to gather insights into user behaviors, needs, and preferences.

Obtaining a certification in user research typically involves completing a structured program or course of study, which may include a combination of theoretical learning, practical exercises, and assessments. These programs are designed to equip individuals with the necessary knowledge and practical skills to effectively plan, execute, and analyze user research studies.

By earning a UXR certification, professionals demonstrate their commitment to maintaining high standards of quality and ethics in their research practices. It enhances their credibility and marketability within the user experience (UX) industry, as it provides potential employers or clients with assurance of their expertise in conducting user research. Additionally, a certification can help individuals differentiate themselves from others in a competitive job market and potentially increase their earning potential.

In conclusion, a certification in user research is a formal recognition of an individual's knowledge and skills in conducting user research. It signifies their competency and expertise in applying research methods to gather insights into user behaviors, needs, and preferences. Obtaining a UXR certification can enhance career prospects and credibility within the UX industry.

Chalkmark

Chalkmark is a user-research tool primarily used in the field of User Experience Research (UXR). It helps UX researchers gather quick and valuable feedback on the effectiveness of website designs or prototypes.

The tool allows researchers to create interactive tasks or scenarios for participants to complete on a digital interface, such as a website or application. Participants are usually presented with screenshots or wireframes that represent different design options or user journeys. They are then asked to perform specific tasks, such as finding information or completing a task flow, while their interactions and decision-making processes are recorded.

Chalkmark tracks participants' clicks and generates heatmaps to visualize where they focus their attention, which parts of the design are intuitive or confusing, and how easily they accomplish their goals. These heatmaps provide valuable insights into the strengths and weaknesses of different design options by highlighting which areas of the interface attract the most attention or cause confusion.

By analyzing the data collected from Chalkmark studies, UX researchers can make data-informed decisions about design improvements or iterate on existing designs. The tool's quantitative data, combined with qualitative feedback from participants, helps researchers understand users' expectations, preferences, and pain points in relation to the designs being tested.

Challenges

Challenges in the context of user research (UXR) refer to obstacles or difficulties that user researchers encounter while conducting their research. These challenges can arise at different stages of the research process and can impact the quality and validity of the results obtained.

One common challenge in UXR is recruiting participants for studies. Finding the right participants who match the target user group can be time-consuming and require extensive effort. Additionally, ensuring diversity and representing a range of perspectives is crucial for obtaining accurate insights. Another challenge is maintaining participant engagement throughout the research process. Keeping participants motivated and engaged throughout interviews, surveys, or usability tests can be challenging, particularly if the research activities are time-consuming or repetitive.

Chameleon

A chameleon, in the context of user research (UXR), refers to a flexible and adaptive approach when conducting studies and gathering insights about user behavior and preferences. Like the reptile it is named after, the chameleon method allows researchers to blend in and adapt to various research situations, environments, and user groups. This approach acknowledges the diverse nature of user research and recognizes that different situations may require different methods and techniques.

With the chameleon method, UXR practitioners are able to select and tailor research methodologies to best suit the specific goals, constraints, and contexts of a project. It involves having a comprehensive toolkit of research techniques, methodologies, and frameworks that can be applied in a versatile manner. This enables researchers to gain a deep and holistic understanding of the users, their needs, and their experiences.

Chatbot Surveys

A chatbot survey is a user-research tool used in the field of User Experience Research (UXR) to gather feedback and insights from users through the use of conversational chatbots. These surveys are typically conducted within the context of a chat-like interface, where users can interact with the chatbot by sending text messages or selecting predefined options.

The purpose of a chatbot survey is to collect qualitative and quantitative data from users in an engaging and conversational manner. By simulating a conversation, chatbots can make the survey experience more interactive and enjoyable for users, leading to higher response rates and more accurate data. Additionally, chatbots can provide instant responses or clarifications, creating a seamless and efficient survey experience.

Chatbot surveys can be used in various stages of the user research process, such as gathering feedback on a prototype, evaluating the usability of a product, exploring user needs and preferences, or collecting demographic information. They can be administered on different platforms, including websites, mobile apps, or messaging applications.

Overall, chatbot surveys provide researchers with an effective and user-friendly method to collect data from participants, enabling them to gain valuable insights into user behavior, preferences, and opinions. By leveraging the conversational nature of chatbots, researchers can create engaging and interactive survey experiences that result in more accurate and meaningful data.

Chatbot Testing

Chatbot testing is a crucial aspect of user-research (UXR) that involves evaluating the performance and usability of a chatbot system. It aims to assess the effectiveness, efficiency, and user satisfaction with the chatbot's functionalities and interactions.

The primary goal of chatbot testing in user-research is to determine whether the chatbot meets the users' requirements and expectations while providing a seamless user experience. This testing process involves various methodologies, such as functional testing, conversational testing, and usability testing.

Functional testing involves assessing the chatbot's ability to understand user inputs accurately and generate appropriate responses based on predefined functionalities. It focuses on evaluating the system's performance against expected outcomes and identifying any functional issues or bugs.

Conversational testing evaluates the chatbot's ability to engage in natural and meaningful conversations with users. This testing ensures that the chatbot understands and responds appropriately to different user queries, intents, and contexts, maintaining a coherent and

11

relevant conversation flow.

Usability testing focuses on assessing the chatbot's overall user experience, including its ease of use, intuitiveness, and user satisfaction. It involves evaluating factors such as user interface design, navigation, clarity of responses, and overall user satisfaction with the chatbot's interactions.

Churn Rate Analysis

Churn Rate Analysis in the context of user-research (UXR) refers to the examination and measurement of the rate at which users discontinue using a particular product or service over a specific period of time. It is a critical metric used to evaluate and understand user retention and loyalty, particularly in the digital space.

By analyzing churn rate, UXR professionals aim to identify the factors and patterns that contribute to user attrition. This process typically involves tracking and studying user behavior, interactions, and feedback to uncover insights into the reasons behind churn.

CleverTap

CleverTap is a user-research (UXR) tool that helps organizations gather insights and analyze user behavior to make informed decisions and improve their product or service offerings.

It provides a suite of features that allows businesses to conduct research activities such as surveys, interviews, and usability tests. With CleverTap, organizations can collect qualitative and quantitative data, track user interactions, and understand user needs and preferences.

The tool offers a range of analytics capabilities, including data visualization, segmentation, and funnel analysis. This enables businesses to extract meaningful insights from the collected data and identify patterns or trends in user behavior.

CleverTap also provides engagement and communication features that help organizations enhance user experience and drive user engagement. With features like personalized messaging, A/B testing, and push notifications, businesses can effectively communicate with their users and deliver relevant and timely information.

Furthermore, CleverTap offers integration with other tools and platforms, allowing organizations to access and leverage their data across different systems. This integration capability enables businesses to centralize their user-research efforts and streamline their workflow.

In summary, CleverTap is a comprehensive user-research (UXR) tool that empowers organizations to gather, analyze, and utilize user insights to optimize their products or services. With its wide range of research, analytics, and engagement capabilities, CleverTap assists businesses in understanding and fulfilling their users' needs effectively.

Click Heatmap Analysis

Click heatmap analysis is a user research technique used in UX research to visually analyze the areas of a web page or application where users click the most. It provides insights into user behavior and interaction patterns, helping researchers identify which elements are attracting users' attention and which are being ignored. By using click heatmap analysis, UX researchers can gain a deeper understanding of how users navigate and interact with a website or application. The analysis is based on tracking and recording users' mouse clicks, evaluating the frequency and distribution of clicks on various elements such as buttons, links, images, and forms. To conduct click heatmap analysis, researchers collect user interaction data using tools or software that track and record mouse click events. This data is then visualized using color-coded overlays that depict the intensity of clicks on different areas of the page. Areas with higher click density are represented by warmer colors, while areas with lower click density appear cooler. The insights gained from click heatmap analysis can help UX designers and developers make informed decisions about user interface elements, layout, and content positioning. For example, if certain buttons or links receive very few clicks, it may indicate a need for redesign or repositioning to increase visibility and usability. In conclusion, click heatmap analysis is a valuable method in UX research that provides visual representations of user interaction patterns on web pages or applications. By analyzing click density and distribution, researchers can optimize the design and layout to enhance user experience and achieve the desired user behavior. Overall, this technique allows for data-driven decision-making to improve the effectiveness and usability of digital products.>

Closed Card Sorting

Closed card sorting is a user research method used in the field of user experience (UX) research to understand how users categorize and organize information. In closed card sorting, participants are given a set of pre-defined categories and asked to sort different items or pieces of information into these categories.

The purpose of closed card sorting is to gain insights into how users mentally categorize and organize content, which can then be used to inform the design and organization of information on websites, applications, or other digital interfaces. By observing participants as they sort the items, researchers can identify patterns and trends in how users group and label different pieces of information.

Cognitive Load Testing

Cognitive Load Testing is a user research method commonly employed in the field of User Experience Research (UXR). It involves the evaluation of the cognitive load that users experience when interacting with a product or system.

This type of testing aims to assess the mental effort required for users to understand and learn the functionalities of a digital interface. Cognitive load refers to the total amount of mental processing power needed to complete a task. It is influenced by factors such as the complexity of the interface, the volume of information presented, and the user's prior knowledge and expertise.

Cognitive Modeling

Cognitive modeling in the context of user-research (UXR) refers to the process of creating computational representations or simulations of human cognitive processes, such as perception, attention, memory, and decision-making, to gain insights into user behavior and inform the design of user interfaces.

These models are typically based on theories and empirical evidence from cognitive psychology, and they aim to replicate the cognitive processes that underlie human interaction with technology. Cognitive modeling allows researchers to predict and explain how users perceive, process, and respond to user interfaces and tasks.

Cognitive Walkthrough

A cognitive walkthrough is a user research method used in the field of User Experience Research (UXR) to evaluate the usability of a product or system. It involves systematically analyzing and assessing the user's cognitive processes and interactions with the product, with the goal of identifying potential usability issues and improving the overall user experience. During a cognitive walkthrough, the researcher simulates the user's thought process by stepping through the product's interface and tasks, imagining themselves as the user and considering how they would approach each step. The focus is on understanding the user's mental model, expectations, and goals, and how well the product supports and guides them in achieving those. The cognitive walkthrough follows a predefined set of tasks and scenarios, allowing the researcher to examine the product from multiple perspectives. It aims to identify potential usability problems such as confusion, difficulty in understanding the interface, lack of feedback or guidance, and obstacles in achieving goals. The researcher assesses each step in terms of its complexity, discoverability, and the feedback provided to the user. This research method helps identify usability issues early in the design process, allowing for iterative improvements and avoiding costly redesigns later on. The cognitive walkthrough provides valuable insights into the user's experience, shedding light on areas that may benefit from changes or enhancements. By considering the user's cognitive processes, this method helps ensure that the product aligns with their mental model and supports their goals effectively. In conclusion, a cognitive walkthrough is a user research technique used to evaluate the usability of a product by simulating the user's cognitive processes and interactions. It helps uncover usability issues and improves the overall user experience.>

Collaboration Platform

A collaboration platform is a digital tool or software that facilitates the collaboration and communication between different individuals or teams within an organization, allowing them to work together on a common goal or project. It provides a centralized and accessible space where users can share and access information, documents, and resources, as well as communicate and interact with each other.

The main purpose of a collaboration platform is to streamline and enhance collaboration and teamwork, enabling users to work more efficiently and effectively. It promotes real-time communication and exchange of ideas, eliminating the need for lengthy email threads or physical meetings. By providing a shared workspace, it allows users to easily track the progress of projects, assign tasks, and monitor deadlines.

Furthermore, a collaboration platform often includes features such as file sharing, version control, commenting and annotation on documents, task management, and project tracking. It may also offer integration with other tools and software commonly used in the organization, such as project management systems, customer relationship management (CRM) software, or video conferencing tools.

Overall, a collaboration platform aims to improve the collaboration and coordination among team members, regardless of their location or time zones. It helps to break down silos, foster cross-functional collaboration, and promote knowledge sharing within the organization, ultimately leading to increased productivity and better outcomes.

Collaboration

Collaboration in the context of user research (UXR) refers to the process of working together with various stakeholders to gather, analyze, and interpret user data in order to inform the design and development of user-centered products or services.

Through collaboration, user researchers aim to involve stakeholders such as designers, product managers, engineers, and other relevant team members in the research process. This collective effort ensures that all perspectives are considered and enables a more comprehensive understanding of the users and their needs.

The collaboration begins with defining the research goals and objectives. This involves conducting discussions and brainstorming sessions with stakeholders to establish the focus and scope of the research. By involving the right people from the beginning, the research can be aligned with the overall product or service strategy.

During the research phase, collaboration involves sharing information about planned research activities, such as user interviews or usability testing. Stakeholders may provide input on the research questions, participant recruitment, or the evaluation of research methods. They may also participate in research activities, such as observing user interviews or analyzing qualitative data.

In the analysis and interpretation stage, collaboration includes sharing and discussing research findings with stakeholders. This enables the collective sensemaking of the data and the generation of insights that inform design decisions. Collaboration also ensures that the implications and recommendations derived from the research are understood and embraced by the entire team.

In conclusion, collaboration in user research plays a pivotal role in facilitating an inclusive and multidisciplinary approach to understanding users and guiding the design process. By involving stakeholders throughout the research journey, user researchers can leverage different perspectives and expertise to create user-centered products or services.

Color Scheme Testing

Color scheme testing in the context of user-research (UXR) refers to the evaluation process of different color combinations used in a user interface or website design. It aims to determine the impact of color choices on user experience and improve the overall usability and visual appeal of the product.

The purpose of color scheme testing is to ensure that the chosen color palette is harmonious, accessible, and suitable for the intended target audience. This process involves gathering feedback from users through various research methods, such as surveys, interviews, and usability testing, to understand their perceptions and preferences towards the color scheme.

Community

A community, in the context of user research (UXR), refers to a group of individuals with a shared interest or goal who actively engage in the process of providing feedback, insights, and support related to a particular product, service, or experience. This group can consist of various stakeholders, such as users, customers, designers, and researchers, who come together to contribute their perspectives and experiences.

By involving a community in user research, organizations can gather valuable data and insights to inform the design and development process. Community members may participate in activities such as surveys, interviews, usability testing, and co-design sessions. These engagements enable researchers to understand user needs, identify pain points, and uncover opportunities for improvement.

Comparative Usability Testing

Comparative Usability Testing is a user research method commonly used in the field of User Experience Research (UXR) to evaluate and compare the usability of different designs, prototypes, or products. Its main purpose is to identify strengths and weaknesses of each design option, and to inform decision-making in the design process.

During Comparative Usability Testing, participants are given specific tasks to perform on each design option, while the researcher observes and records their behaviors, feedback, and performance. The tests are typically conducted in a controlled lab environment or remotely using screen-sharing tools.

The collected data is then analyzed and compared across different designs, focusing on metrics such as task completion rates, time taken to complete tasks, errors made, and participant satisfaction ratings. These quantitative and qualitative findings help the researcher understand how each design option performs, and which one offers a better user experience.

By comparing designs directly, Comparative Usability Testing provides valuable insights into the usability of different options, allowing researchers and designers to make informed decisions about which design elements or features to prioritize or modify. It helps identify potential usability issues early in the design process, preventing costly and time-consuming changes in later stages.

In summary, Comparative Usability Testing is an essential method in User Experience Research that allows for direct comparison of different designs to evaluate their usability and make informed design decisions.

Compatibility Testing

Compatibility testing is a user research method conducted in the field of User Experience Research (UXR) to assess the ability of a product or system to function harmoniously and effectively across different platforms, devices, browsers, or environments. This testing is performed to ensure that users are able to access and utilize the product or system seamlessly regardless of the technology or tools they are using.

During compatibility testing, UXR professionals evaluate and validate the behavior, performance, and appearance of the product or system across various configurations. This includes testing compatibility with different operating systems, hardware devices, web browsers, screen resolutions, network conditions, and accessibility requirements. The goal is to identify and address any issues or inconsistencies that may arise due to differences in these factors.

Competitive Analysis

Competitive analysis is a research methodology used in user experience research (UXR) to evaluate and compare the features, functionality, and usability of a product with its competitors in the market. It involves studying and analyzing the strengths and weaknesses of competing products and their user experiences to gain insights and identify opportunities for improvement.

In the context of user-research, competitive analysis helps UX researchers understand how their product stacks up against the competition and identify areas of differentiation. It involves evaluating competitor products based on criteria such as user interface design, navigation, functionality, performance, and overall user experience.

Competitive Benchmarking Surveys

Competitive benchmarking surveys are a research method used in user research (UXR) to evaluate and compare the performance and user experience of a particular product or service with its competitors. These surveys involve gathering feedback and opinions from users who have used both the target product/service and its competitors, in order to gain insights into how the target product/service measures up against the competition.

The goal of competitive benchmarking surveys is to identify areas of strength and weakness in the target product/service and to understand how it can be improved to stay competitive in the market. The surveys typically involve a series of questions or tasks that users are asked to complete, such as rating the ease-of-use, satisfaction, and overall experience of the target product/service compared to its competitors.

By conducting competitive benchmarking surveys, UXR professionals can obtain valuable data and insights about the competitive landscape and understand how users perceive and interact with different products or services. This information can be used to inform design decisions, prioritize areas for improvement, and stay ahead of the competition in terms of user experience and customer satisfaction.

Competitive Benchmarking

Competitive benchmarking in the context of user research (UXR) refers to the process of comparing and evaluating a company's products, services, or user experiences with those of its direct competitors. It involves gathering data and insights on the competition's offerings to identify strengths, weaknesses, and opportunities for improvement.

The goal of competitive benchmarking in user research is to gain a comprehensive understanding of how a company's products or services measure up against its competitors in terms of user satisfaction, usability, and overall user experience. This information helps businesses identify areas for improvement, inform the development of new features or enhancements, and ultimately stay ahead in a competitive market.

Competitor Comparison Surveys

Competitor comparison surveys in the context of user research (UXR) refer to a method of gathering data and insights about a company's competitors in order to identify their strengths, weaknesses, and areas of differentiation. This type of survey allows businesses to understand how they compare to their competition from the perspective of their target audience.

The purpose of competitor comparison surveys is to gain a deeper understanding of the market landscape and to inform strategic decision-making. These surveys typically involve asking participants a series of structured questions about their experiences, perceptions, and preferences related to competing products or services. The questions are designed to uncover key attributes, features, and user experiences that participants value or find lacking in

16

comparison to the company's offering.

Compliance Testing

Compliance testing, in the context of user research (UXR), refers to the evaluation of a product or system against specific regulatory requirements, industry standards, or established guidelines. The purpose of compliance testing is to ensure that the product or system adheres to the required standards, guidelines, and regulations, providing a safe and accessible user experience.

During compliance testing, UX researchers assess various aspects of the product or system to determine its compliance with specific criteria. This can include evaluating the product's design, interface, functionality, accessibility, and privacy features. Researchers use different methods such as expert reviews, heuristic evaluations, and usability testing to gather data and insights on the product's compliance.

The findings from compliance testing are crucial in identifying potential issues, gaps, or violations in the product's compliance with the established standards. By conducting compliance testing early in the development process, researchers can provide valuable feedback to designers and developers, allowing them to address any non-compliant aspects and make necessary improvements.

Compliance testing serves as a quality assurance measure, ensuring that the product or system aligns with legal requirements and industry best practices. It helps to mitigate risks, enhance user satisfaction, and build trust with users by creating a product that meets the necessary standards for security, performance, accessibility, and privacy.

Computer-Assisted Surveys

Computer-Assisted Surveys (CAS) refer to a method of conducting research surveys with the aid of computer technology. Specifically in the context of user research (UXR), CAS involves using computer programs or applications to administer surveys and collect data from study participants.

With CAS, researchers can design, distribute, and manage surveys through various digital platforms, such as online survey tools or specialized research software. This approach offers several advantages in terms of efficiency, scalability, and data accuracy.

CAS enables researchers to easily create structured questionnaires with predefined response options, ensuring standardized data collection. Additionally, the use of skip patterns or conditional branching in CAS allows for customized survey paths based on participants' previous responses, enhancing the user experience and reducing survey completion time.

Furthermore, CAS streamlines data collection and management processes by automatically recording and organizing responses, eliminating the need for manual data entry. This not only saves time but also reduces the risk of errors associated with manual transcription.

Moreover, CAS analytics capabilities enable researchers to quickly analyze and visualize survey results, aiding in the exploration and interpretation of collected data. By integrating statistical analysis features, CAS facilitates the identification of patterns, trends, and correlations within the data, which in turn informs decision-making and enhances the overall user research process.

Concept Testing

Concept testing in the context of user research (UXR) is a method used to evaluate a product or service idea by gathering feedback from target users. It involves presenting a concept or prototype to users and asking them to provide their thoughts, perceptions, and reactions to the proposed idea.

The purpose of concept testing is to gain insights into user preferences, needs, and expectations, as well as to identify potential design flaws or areas for improvement. It allows UXR professionals to validate assumptions, identify pain points, and assess the viability of a concept before investing substantial time and resources into its development.

Concept Validation

Concept validation in the context of user research (UXR) refers to the process of assessing the viability and value of a new product or feature idea before investing significant time and resources in its development. The primary goal of concept validation is to gather feedback and insights from target users to determine if the proposed concept aligns with their needs, preferences, and expectations.

During concept validation, user researchers conduct interviews, surveys, usability tests, and other research methods to gather both qualitative and quantitative data. This data helps them understand how users perceive and interact with the concept, identify potential usability issues, and gather suggestions for improvements. The insights gathered during concept validation serve as evidence to support or refute the initial assumptions and hypotheses made during the concept's ideation stage.

By conducting concept validation early in the product development process, companies can reduce the risk of investing in ideas that may not resonate with their target audience. It also provides an opportunity to optimize the concept before moving forward, saving time and resources in the long run. Concept validation is an iterative process, and multiple rounds of testing may be necessary to refine and validate the concept further.

In conclusion, concept validation is an essential step in the user research process that helps ensure that new product or feature ideas are well-aligned with user needs and expectations. By collecting meaningful feedback early on, it enables companies to make informed decisions and increase the likelihood of developing successful products.

Conferences

A conference in the context of user-research (UXR) refers to a gathering or meeting of professionals, researchers, and stakeholders in the field of user experience to share knowledge, insights, and findings related to the study of users and their interactions with products, services, or systems.

Conferences play a crucial role in fostering collaboration, learning, and innovation within the user-research community. They provide a platform for experts to present their research, methodologies, and best practices, allowing attendees to gain new perspectives, validate their own approaches, and stay up-to-date with the latest advancements in the field. These events typically feature presentations, workshops, panel discussions, and networking opportunities, enabling participants to exchange ideas, engage in discussions, and build professional relationships.

Conjoint Analysis Surveys

Conjoint Analysis Surveys, in the context of user-research (UXR), refer to a quantitative research method used to understand how users prioritize different features or attributes of a product or service. This method aims to gain insights into users' decision-making processes by presenting them with a set of hypothetical scenarios that require trade-offs between various attributes.

In a Conjoint Analysis Survey, participants are typically presented with a series of product profiles or scenarios which vary in terms of attributes, such as price, design, brand, or functionality. Participants are then asked to rank or rate these profiles based on their preferences and opinions. By analyzing the data gathered from these surveys, UXR professionals can uncover the relative importance and impact of different attributes on user preferences and decision-making.

Conjoint Analysis

Conjoint analysis is a research technique commonly used in user research (UXR) to understand user preferences and decision-making. It is a quantitative method that helps researchers uncover the relative importance users place on different features or attributes of a product or service.

In a conjoint analysis, participants are presented with a series of hypothetical scenarios or profiles that vary in terms of different attributes. These attributes can include price, design, functionality, or any other relevant characteristic of the product or service being studied. Each profile represents a combination of these attributes, and participants are asked to rank or rate their preference for each profile.

The results of a conjoint analysis allow researchers to determine which attributes have the most impact on user preferences and to quantify the trade-offs users are willing to make. This information is valuable in guiding product development and decision-making, as it provides insights into what features or attributes should be prioritized to meet user needs and expectations.

Conjoint analysis is particularly useful in situations where there are multiple attributes that can influence user decision-making, and where understanding the relative importance of each attribute is important. By using statistical techniques to analyze the data collected, researchers can gain a deeper understanding of user preferences, predict user behavior, and make data-driven decisions to improve the user experience.

Consent

Consent in the context of user research (UXR) refers to the voluntary agreement and permission given by individuals to participate in a research study or provide their personal data for research purposes. It is the ethical responsibility of the researcher to obtain informed consent from participants before engaging them in any research activities.

Obtaining consent involves clearly explaining the purpose, goals, and potential risks and benefits of the research study to the participants. The researcher must ensure that participants understand what their involvement entails, including any data collection methods, duration of participation, and how their data will be used and shared, if applicable.

Consent also requires that participants have the freedom to choose whether they want to participate or not, without any coercion or pressure. They should be provided with sufficient time to consider their decision and ask any questions they may have before giving their consent. Researchers must respect the autonomy and rights of participants, ensuring that they are able to make an informed decision based on the information provided.

Consent is an ongoing process in user research, and participants have the right to withdraw their consent at any time without facing any negative consequences. Researchers should clearly communicate this right to participants and provide options for them to revoke their consent if they wish to do so.

Consistency Inspection

A consistency inspection in the context of user research (UXR) refers to a systematic evaluation method used to assess the consistency of a product's design elements, user interface, and overall user experience. This inspection aims to identify any inconsistencies, discrepancies, or deviations from established design guidelines or best practices, with the goal of creating a cohesive and intuitive user experience.

The process of a consistency inspection typically involves reviewing various components and aspects of a product, such as visual elements (e.g., color schemes, typography), interaction patterns (e.g., navigation menus, button placements), and content presentation (e.g., information hierarchy, formatting consistency). This review is typically conducted by experienced UX researchers or designers who possess in-depth knowledge of the product's design principles and target user demographic.

During a consistency inspection, researchers scrutinize and compare different screens, pages, or sections of the product to identify any discrepancies or inconsistencies. They may also refer to established design guidelines, industry standards, or previous research findings to determine whether the product aligns with best practices. Identified inconsistencies may include variations in terminology or labeling, inconsistencies in visual appearance, disjointed user flows, or lack of coherence in information presentation.

The insights gained from a consistency inspection help identify areas where improvements are needed to enhance the product's overall user experience and ensure visual and functional consistency across different components. By addressing these inconsistencies, product teams can create a more cohesive and intuitive interface, which in turn leads to improved user satisfaction, increased engagement, and higher usability.

Consumer Panels

A consumer panel in the context of user research (UXR) refers to a group of individuals who have been selected to provide feedback and insights on products or services. These panels are often formed to gather actionable data that can be used to improve the user experience.

The main goal of a consumer panel is to represent the target audience and collect their opinions, preferences, and behaviors regarding a specific product or service. Panel members are typically recruited based on certain criteria, such as demographics, usage habits, or specific interests, to ensure they closely resemble the intended user base.

Consumer panels can take different forms, including in-person meetings, online surveys, or one-on-one interviews. During these interactions, participants are asked to share their thoughts, experiences, and suggestions, giving the research team valuable insights into how users perceive and interact with a product or service.

By engaging with consumer panels, UXR professionals can identify pain points, uncover usability issues, and gain a deeper understanding of user needs and expectations. The feedback collected from these panels helps drive informed decision-making during the design and development process, facilitating the creation of user-centric solutions.

Overall, consumer panels play a crucial role in user research by providing valuable user perspectives, promoting user-centered design, and ensuring that products and services meet the needs of their intended audience.

Consumer Product Testing

Consumer product testing, in the context of user research (UXR), refers to the systematic evaluation of products or services by actual consumers to gather insights and feedback on their experience, preferences, and usability. This type of testing allows companies to understand how users interact with their products, identify pain points, and make informed decisions to improve the overall user experience.

During consumer product testing, participants are typically given specific tasks to perform using the product, closely observed, and their interactions and feedback are recorded. The goal is to gather qualitative and/or quantitative data that can be used to inform design decisions, uncover potential issues, or validate existing hypotheses. This testing can be conducted remotely using online platforms, in a controlled lab environment, or even in the participants' natural settings to capture real-world usage scenarios.

Content Analysis

Content Inventory

A content inventory is a systematic process of documenting and analyzing all the content elements within a website, application, or digital platform. It involves creating a comprehensive list or inventory of each piece of content, including text, images, videos, documents, and any other relevant media assets. The purpose of a content inventory is to gain a deeper understanding of the content landscape and to inform decision-making for user experience research (UXR) activities.

During a content inventory, a UX researcher reviews and catalogs each content item, noting its location, format, metadata, and any other relevant attributes. This process helps identify content gaps, inconsistencies, redundancies, and opportunities for improvement. It provides a holistic view of the content ecosystem and highlights potential issues or areas of improvement in terms of content structure, organization, and usability.

A content inventory also serves as a valuable reference for user researchers when conducting usability testing, information architecture design, or content strategy development. By understanding the existing content, researchers can identify patterns, trends, and areas of focus for their research activities. They can also evaluate the effectiveness of the content and its alignment with user needs and goals.

In summary, a content inventory is a foundational step in the user research process that helps researchers gain insights into the content landscape and make informed decisions about content strategy, usability, and information architecture.

Content Testing

User research (UXR), in the context of design and product development, refers to the systematic process of understanding users and their needs, behaviors, and motivations through various research methods and techniques. It involves gathering insights and data from target users to inform design decisions and improve the overall user experience of a product or service.

The main goal of user research is to gain a deep understanding of users' expectations, preferences, and pain points in order to design products and services that meet their needs and provide value. UXR helps identify user problems and opportunities, validate assumptions, and guide design improvements that are based on actual user feedback rather than on assumptions or personal opinions.

Through user research, designers and product teams can identify user needs, behaviors, and pain points, which can be used to inform the design and development process. This includes conducting interviews, observing users in their natural environment, and collecting quantitative and qualitative data to gain insights into user behavior and preferences.

User research also involves testing and evaluating prototypes or existing products with users to identify usability issues and gather feedback for further improvements. This iterative process helps refine and validate design decisions, ensuring that the final product meets user expectations and provides a seamless and satisfying user experience.

ContentSquare

ContentSquare is a user research tool used in the field of User Experience Research (UXR). It allows researchers to track and analyze user behavior on websites and mobile applications.

With ContentSquare, researchers can gain insights into how users navigate and interact with digital interfaces. The tool provides a visual representation of user interactions through heatmaps, clickmaps, and scrolling behavior analysis. This information helps researchers identify areas of user interest and engagement, as well as potential pain points and usability issues.

Contextual Inquiry

A contextual inquiry is a user research method used in the field of User Experience Research (UXR) to gather in-depth insights about users and their behaviors in their natural environment. It involves observing and interviewing users while they are performing specific tasks or activities to gain a better understanding of their needs, expectations, and challenges.

In a contextual inquiry, a UX researcher visits the users' physical location or interacts with them remotely to observe their interactions with a product or service. This method aims to capture the context in which users interact with the product, taking into account their environment, workflows, and other influential factors.

The researcher typically follows a structured protocol during a contextual inquiry, involving four key steps: introduction, orientation, data collection, and wrap-up. During the introduction, the researcher establishes rapport with the participant and explains the purpose and confidentiality of the study. In the orientation phase, the researcher gathers background information about the participant and their role. Data collection involves active observation and note-taking while the participant performs tasks, as well as asking questions to clarify their actions. Finally, the wrap-up includes a debrief with the participant, summarizing the key findings and addressing any outstanding questions.

The insights gathered through a contextual inquiry provide valuable information for improving the design and user experience of a product or service. By understanding users' needs, challenges, and behaviors in their natural context, UX researchers can generate meaningful recommendations for enhancing usability, functionality, and overall user satisfaction.

Continuous Improvement

Continuous improvement in the context of user research (UXR) refers to the ongoing process of enhancing the quality and effectiveness of user research practices and outcomes. It involves a systematic approach to identifying areas for improvement, implementing changes, and evaluating the impact of those changes to make iterative advancements. The goal is to continuously learn, adapt, and refine user research methodologies and processes to better meet the needs and expectations of users.

Continuous improvement in UXR is essential for several reasons. Firstly, it helps to ensure that the research methods and techniques being used are relevant and effective in gathering accurate and meaningful insights from users. By continuously evaluating and refining research practices, UXR teams can enhance the validity and reliability of their findings.

Secondly, continuous improvement enables UXR teams to stay up to date with evolving user needs and preferences. As technology and user expectations evolve, it is crucial to adapt research methodologies accordingly to capture emerging trends and insights.

Furthermore, continuous improvement fosters a culture of learning and innovation within UXR teams and organizations. By encouraging regular reflection and examination of research practices, teams can identify and capitalize on opportunities to enhance efficiency, collaboration, and overall research effectiveness.

In conclusion, continuous improvement in the context of user research involves an ongoing process of evaluating, refining, and adapting research practices to enhance the quality and relevance of user insights. By embracing continuous improvement, UXR teams can enhance their ability to inform the design and development of user-centered solutions.

Conversational User Interviews

A conversational user interview is a user-research method used in the field of user experience research (UXR). It is a guided conversation between a researcher and a participant aimed at gathering qualitative data about the participant's experiences, needs, and preferences regarding a specific product or service.

In a conversational user interview, the researcher typically starts by establishing rapport with the participant and explaining the purpose and confidentiality of the interview. The conversation then unfolds naturally, with the researcher asking open-ended and probing questions to encourage the participant to share their thoughts, feelings, and opinions.

Conversational user interviews are designed to uncover deep insights into user behavior, motivations, and pain points. They allow researchers to understand the context in which users interact with a product or service, as well as their goals and frustrations. By conducting these interviews, researchers can gather rich, qualitative data that complements quantitative metrics and provides a more comprehensive understanding of the user experience.

The data collected from conversational user interviews is often analyzed through thematic coding or content analysis, where common themes and patterns are identified. This analysis helps researchers identify user needs, pain points, and opportunities for improvement, which

22

can then inform the design and development of user-centered products and services.

Conversion Rate Optimization (CRO)

Conversion Rate Optimization (CRO) in the context of user research (UXR) is the process of analyzing and improving the effectiveness of a website or digital product in converting visitors into desired actions or goals. It involves using qualitative and quantitative research methods to understand user behaviors, preferences, and pain points, and then applying that knowledge to make data-driven design decisions and optimizations.

In order to optimize the conversion rate, UXR professionals employ a variety of research techniques. These might include conducting user interviews and surveys, analyzing website analytics and clickstream data, performing usability tests, and studying heatmaps and session recordings. By gathering insights from these research methods, UXR professionals gain a deeper understanding of users' motivations, intentions, and barriers to conversion.

Once the research has been conducted and insights have been gathered, UXR professionals use this information to develop hypotheses and experiments for improving the conversion rate. These experiments can take the form of A/B tests, multivariate tests, or sequential testing methodologies. By systematically testing variations of design elements, content, or user flows, UXR professionals can determine which changes have a positive impact on conversion rates.

Overall, Conversion Rate Optimization in the realm of user research is a continuous cycle of research, experimentation, and iteration aimed at improving the user experience and increasing the likelihood of users completing desired actions or goals on a website or digital product.

Conversion Rate

The conversion rate, in the context of user research (UXR), refers to the percentage of users who complete a desired action or goal on a website or digital platform. It is a metric used to measure the effectiveness of a user experience and the success of a website or application in achieving its objectives.

Conversion rate is typically calculated by dividing the number of successful conversions by the total number of user interactions or visits to a website. The conversion action can vary depending on the specific goals of the website or application, such as making a purchase, submitting a form, signing up for a newsletter, or downloading a file.

Cooperative Evaluation

A cooperative evaluation is a user research method used in the field of user experience research (UXR) to assess the interactive design of a product or system. It involves gathering feedback and insights from both the users and the designers or developers of the product or system.

The purpose of a cooperative evaluation is to improve the usability and user experience of a product by involving all relevant stakeholders in the evaluation process. This includes not only the end-users, but also the designers, developers, and other team members responsible for the creation and maintenance of the product or system.

In a cooperative evaluation, participants are encouraged to actively engage in the evaluation process by voicing their opinions, sharing their experiences, and providing suggestions for improvements. This collaboration between the users and the designers helps to identify usability issues, understand user needs and expectations, and generate ideas for design enhancements.

Cooperative evaluations can take various forms, such as focus groups, workshops, or collaborative design sessions. These methods often employ a combination of qualitative and quantitative research techniques, including interviews, surveys, and usability testing.

By involving all relevant stakeholders in the evaluation process, a cooperative evaluation enables a more comprehensive and holistic understanding of the usability and user experience aspects of a product or system. This can lead to improved design decisions, enhanced user satisfaction, and increased adoption and usage of the product or system.

Courses

A course, in the context of user research (UXR), refers to a structured program or set of educational materials that aim to teach individuals the theoretical and practical aspects of conducting effective user research. These courses are designed to equip students or professionals with the necessary knowledge and skills to carry out user research activities and contribute to the development of user-centered design processes.

UXR courses typically cover a range of topics, including research methodologies, data collection and analysis techniques, user testing, persona development, and usability evaluation. They may also delve into the psychological and behavioral aspects of user behavior, providing insights into how individuals interact with digital interfaces and products.

By participating in UXR courses, individuals can enhance their capabilities in understanding user needs, preferences, and behaviors. They learn how to uncover insights that inform the design and development of products and services that meet user expectations and create positive user experiences.

Whether taken in a classroom setting or online, UXR courses help individuals gain a solid foundation in user research principles and practices. These courses often involve hands-on exercises, case studies, and real-world projects to provide practical experience and ensure learners can apply their knowledge in real-world situations.

In conclusion, UXR courses play a crucial role in equipping individuals with the necessary skills and knowledge to contribute to user-centered design processes. They provide a structured educational program that covers various aspects of user research, enabling learners to become proficient in conducting effective user research activities.

Crazy Egg

Crazy Egg is a user-research (UXR) tool that provides valuable insights into how users engage with a website. It is designed to help businesses improve their website's user experience by analyzing user behavior and identifying areas for optimization.

With Crazy Egg, UXR professionals can conduct heat map analysis, track user interactions, and gather visual data on how users navigate through a website. Heat maps offer a visual representation of where users click, move their cursors, and spend the most time on a webpage. This information allows researchers to identify patterns, popular sections, and potential areas of improvement.

Critical Incident Technique (CIT)

The Critical Incident Technique (CIT) is a user-research method commonly used in the field of user experience research (UXR). It aims to gather detailed and specific information about significant events or interactions between users and a product or service.

With CIT, researchers focus on identifying critical incidents that have a significant impact on the user's experience. These incidents can be positive or negative and provide valuable insights into the strengths, weaknesses, and opportunities for improvement of the product or service being studied.

Cross-Browser Testing

Cross-Browser Testing is a crucial aspect of user-research (UXR) that involves evaluating the compatibility of a website or web application across different web browsers. It is the process of assessing how a website or application performs and displays on various web browsers such as Chrome, Firefox, Safari, Internet Explorer, and Opera, among others.

During Cross-Browser Testing, UXR professionals analyze and identify any discrepancies or inconsistencies in the appearance, layout, functionality, and user experience of the website or application across different browsers. This is important because each web browser interprets and renders HTML, CSS, and JavaScript code differently, which can lead to variations in the way a website or application is presented to the user.

Cross-Cultural Interviews

Cross-cultural interviews in the context of user research (UXR) is a method used to gather insights and understand the experiences, behaviors, and attitudes of individuals from different cultural backgrounds. It involves conducting interviews with individuals who belong to diverse cultures and communities to gain a deeper understanding of how their cultural background shapes their attitudes and usage patterns.

Through cross-cultural interviews, UXR professionals aim to uncover cultural nuances and gain insights into how people from different cultural backgrounds perceive and interact with products and services. These interviews help in identifying cultural biases, preferences, and expectations that may influence user experiences and impact design decisions.

Cross-Cultural Usability Testing

Cross-cultural usability testing, in the context of user-research (UXR), refers to the process of evaluating the usability of a product or service across different cultural backgrounds. It involves conducting user testing with individuals from diverse cultural groups to gain insights into how the product or service performs and is perceived by users from various cultural backgrounds.

The objective of cross-cultural usability testing is to identify and address any usability issues that may arise due to cultural differences, ensuring that the product or service is accessible, usable, and satisfactory to a wide range of users. It aims to uncover cultural biases, preferences, and expectations that may impact the user experience, and to make design improvements that enhance usability for all users, regardless of their cultural background.

Cross-Device Testing

Cross-device testing, in the context of user research (UXR), refers to the process of evaluating the performance and usability of a website or application across multiple devices.

As technology evolves, there is an increasing need for websites and applications to be compatible and functional on various devices such as desktops, smartphones, tablets, and smart TVs. Cross-device testing allows researchers to identify and resolve any issues or inconsistencies that may arise when users access a website or application on different devices.

Cross-Platform Testing

Cross-platform testing, in the context of user research (UXR), refers to the process of assessing the usability and functionality of a digital product or application across multiple devices, operating systems, and platforms.

As technology advances, users access digital products from a wide range of devices such as smartphones, tablets, laptops, and desktops. These devices run on different operating systems, such as iOS, Android, Windows, or macOS, and may have varying screen sizes, resolutions, and capabilities. Additionally, users may access applications through different browsers, such as Chrome, Firefox, Safari, or Edge.

Cross-platform testing allows UX researchers to evaluate the user experience and identify potential issues or inconsistencies across different platforms. It involves conducting usability tests, user surveys, and other research methods to gather data on the performance, visual design, and overall user satisfaction on each platform.

The aim of cross-platform testing is to ensure that a digital product provides a consistent and seamless experience for all users, regardless of the device or platform they use. It helps identify platform-specific quirks, design flaws, or functional limitations, enabling UX designers and developers to make necessary improvements and optimize the product for different platforms.

Overall, cross-platform testing is a crucial component of user research in order to deliver a user-centered design that meets the needs and preferences of a diverse user base across various devices, operating systems, and platforms.

Cross-Sectional Surveys

A cross-sectional survey is a research method used in user research (UXR) to collect data by asking a fixed set of questions to a representative sample of individuals at a specific point in time. It aims to gather information about the opinions, attitudes, behaviors, and preferences of a target population.

The primary purpose of a cross-sectional survey in the context of user research is to gain a broad understanding of the characteristics and needs of the user base. By administering the same set of questions to different users within the target population, UXR professionals can analyze the data to identify patterns, trends, and correlations. This information can then be used to inform the design and development of user-centered products and services.

Cultural Probes

Cultural probes are a user research technique commonly used in the field of user experience research (UXR). They are a set of tools or activities designed to gather rich, qualitative data about users' thoughts, behaviors, and experiences in relation to a particular product, service, or context.

Typically, cultural probes consist of a collection of prompts or stimuli that are given to participants to engage with over a period of time. These prompts can take various forms, such as diaries, maps, postcards, cameras, or questionnaires. The goal is to encourage participants to reflect on and document their experiences, preferences, and emotions related to the research topic, in their own unique and authentic ways.

Cultural probes are often used to gain insights into users' cultural, social, and contextual backgrounds, as well as their values, aspirations, and motivations. This approach acknowledges that individuals are influenced by their cultural and social environments, and that these influences impact their behaviors, preferences, and perceptions.

By using cultural probes in user research, UX researchers can access deep, contextualized information that may reveal unexpected insights and nuances. This qualitative data can help inform the design and development of user-centered solutions that better meet the needs and expectations of the target users.

Culture

Culture in the context of user-research (UXR) refers to the shared beliefs, values, norms, behaviors, and artifacts of a particular group of people. It encompasses the learned patterns of thinking, feeling, and acting that are passed down from generation to generation within a community.

Culture plays a significant role in shaping users' preferences, expectations, and reactions to products or services. By understanding the cultural backgrounds of users, UXR professionals can gain insights into their motivations, needs, and behaviors, leading to more effective design decisions.

Custellence

Custellence is a user research (UXR) tool that helps businesses and designers gain customer insights and improve the user experience of their products and services. It provides a structured approach to collecting, analyzing, and interpreting user feedback and data in order to inform decision-making and drive design improvements.

With Custellence, researchers can create and manage user research projects, gather and organize qualitative and quantitative data, and collaborate with team members to synthesize findings and generate actionable insights. The tool offers a range of features, including user

26

journey mapping, persona development, survey creation, data visualization, and reporting.

Customer Behavior Analysis

Customer behavior analysis refers to the process of studying and understanding the actions, preferences, and motivations of customers in order to gain insights and improve the user experience (UX) of a product or service. It involves gathering and analyzing data about customers' interactions, behaviors, and decision-making patterns through various research methods.

Customer behavior analysis in the context of user research (UXR) is crucial for designing products and services that meet the needs and expectations of the target audience. By studying how customers engage with a product or service, researchers can identify pain points, usability issues, and areas for improvement. This data-driven approach helps inform the design process and ensures that the end product is user-friendly and aligned with user preferences.

Customer Effort Score (CES) Surveys

Customer Effort Score (CES) surveys are a user-research method utilized in the field of User Experience Research (UXR) to measure and evaluate the effort customers need to exert to accomplish a specific task or goal when interacting with a product or service.

The purpose of CES surveys is to assess the overall ease or difficulty of a customer's experience, which can directly impact their satisfaction and loyalty towards a brand. These surveys typically involve asking customers a single question that measures their perceived level of effort on a scale, such as "How difficult was it to accomplish your goal?" with response options ranging from "Very Easy" to "Very Difficult".

CES surveys are commonly conducted after customer interactions, such as completing a purchase, resolving an issue, or navigating a website. The data collected from these surveys provides valuable insights to organizations, helping them identify pain points in their products or services and make data-driven decisions to improve the user experience.

By analyzing CES survey responses, UX researchers can pinpoint areas where customers are encountering challenges or frustrations, enabling them to prioritize and address those issues. Additionally, CES surveys can be used to compare different versions of a product or service, allowing organizations to measure the impact of changes made to reduce customer effort.

Customer Feedback Analysis

Customer Feedback Analysis in the context of user-research (UXR) refers to the process of systematically examining and interpreting feedback provided by customers or users in order to gain insights about a product or service. This analysis involves collecting, organizing, and analyzing feedback data to identify patterns, trends, and themes that can provide valuable information for improving user experience and meeting customer expectations.

Through customer feedback analysis, UXR professionals aim to understand user perspectives, preferences, and pain points related to a specific product or service. This process typically involves various qualitative and quantitative research methods such as surveys, interviews, usability tests, and sentiment analysis of social media data. The feedback can range from direct suggestions and complaints to indirect indicators such as usage patterns and behavioral data.

By analyzing customer feedback, UXR professionals can identify common pain points, prioritize potential improvements, and understand the impact of any changes made to the product or service. This analysis helps inform decision-making and guide product development processes, ensuring that user needs and preferences are considered and addressed. It enables organizations to make data-driven decisions and iterate on their products or services to enhance user satisfaction and achieve business goals.

Customer Feedback Surveys

A customer feedback survey is a method used in user-research (UXR) to gather information and feedback from customers about their experiences with a product or service. The goal of the survey is to obtain insights that can be used to improve the product or service to better meet customer needs and preferences.

Customer feedback surveys typically consist of a set of structured questions designed to elicit specific information from respondents. These questions can be open-ended, close-ended or a combination of both. Open-ended questions allow respondents to provide detailed feedback in their own words, while close-ended questions provide predefined response options for respondents to choose from.

The survey is usually administered online or in-person, and can be conducted through various mediums such as web-based forms, email, phone interviews, or face-to-face interviews. The survey questions should be carefully crafted to obtain the most relevant and actionable feedback from customers.

Customer feedback surveys play a crucial role in the user-research (UXR) process as they help in understanding customer needs, preferences, and pain points. The insights obtained from these surveys can be used to identify areas of improvement in the product or service, prioritize feature enhancements, and validate design decisions.

By regularly conducting customer feedback surveys, organizations can continuously gather data and feedback from customers, enabling them to make informed decisions and drive product improvements that align with customer expectations and goals.

Customer Interviews

Customer interviews are a qualitative user research method used by UX researchers to gain insights, perspectives, and feedback directly from the target users of a product or service. This method involves conducting one-on-one conversations with customers to understand their experiences, needs, desires, and pain points related to the product or service being investigated.

During a customer interview, the researcher asks open-ended questions, probes deeper into the responses, and actively listens to the user's thoughts and opinions. The goal is to uncover valuable information that can inform design decisions, uncover usability issues, validate assumptions, and identify areas for improvement.

Customer Journey Mapping

Customer journey mapping is a user research method used in the field of user experience research (UXR). It involves visually representing the various touchpoints and interactions that a customer or user goes through when engaging with a product, service, or brand. This mapping technique helps researchers gain insights into the customer's overall experience, emotions, expectations, and pain points at different stages of their journey.

The purpose of customer journey mapping is to create a clear and structured understanding of the customer's interactions and experiences throughout their journey. By capturing important moments, thoughts, and emotions, researchers can identify key opportunities for improvement and deliver a more personalized and seamless experience for customers. This method also helps organizations understand how customers move across different channels or platforms and how these interactions influence their overall perception and satisfaction.

When conducting customer journey mapping, researchers typically engage in various qualitative research techniques such as interviews, observations, and ethnographic studies. These methods allow researchers to gather rich data about the customer's goals, motivations, and behaviors at each touchpoint. The collected data is then visualized in a map or diagram, which often includes stages or phases of the customer journey, customer actions, emotions, pain points, and potential opportunities for improvement.

Overall, customer journey mapping is a valuable tool in user research and UX design as it enables organizations to better understand the customer experience, identify pain points, and make data-driven improvements to enhance customer satisfaction and loyalty.

Customer Journey

A customer journey is a key concept in user research (UXR) that refers to the complete series of steps or touchpoints that a user goes through when interacting with a product, service, or brand.

It encompasses the entire user experience from the initial awareness and discovery phase, through the process of consideration and evaluation, to the final decision and post-purchase experience. The customer journey takes into account both the online and offline interactions and can involve various channels and devices.

Customer Retention Analysis

Customer retention analysis, in the context of user-research (UXR), refers to the process of assessing and understanding the factors that influence the likelihood of customers to continue using a product or service. It involves analyzing various aspects of the customer experience, such as user satisfaction, engagement, and loyalty, to identify patterns and trends that can help improve customer retention.

This analysis typically involves gathering qualitative and quantitative data through methods such as surveys, interviews, and user behavior tracking. By examining customer feedback, usage patterns, and behavioral data, UX researchers can gain insights into the reasons behind customer churn and identify opportunities for enhancing the product or service to increase customer loyalty.

Customer Satisfaction Surveys

A Customer Satisfaction Survey is a research method used in User Experience Research (UXR) to assess the satisfaction level of customers or users with a product, service, or experience. It involves gathering feedback from customers through a structured questionnaire or interview to measure their level of satisfaction.

The purpose of conducting Customer Satisfaction Surveys in UXR is to obtain valuable insights and understand the needs, expectations, and preferences of customers. By collecting quantitative and qualitative data, researchers can identify areas of improvement, identify strengths and weaknesses, and make informed decisions to enhance the user experience.

Customer Segmentation

Customer segmentation in the context of user research (UXR) refers to the process of categorizing customers into distinct groups based on common characteristics, behaviors, and needs. This approach allows businesses to better understand and cater to the diverse needs of their customer base.

By segmenting customers, user researchers can gain deeper insights into their preferences, motivations, and pain points. This understanding helps businesses develop more targeted and effective strategies for product design, customer experience, and marketing campaigns. Customer segmentation also enables businesses to identify specific user groups that may be more valuable or have untapped potential.

Customer Support Ticket Analysis

A customer support ticket analysis refers to the process of examining and interpreting customer support tickets or service requests to uncover insights and patterns that can inform improvements in the user experience (UX) of a product or service. This analysis is typically conducted by user researchers (UXRs) who aim to understand customer needs, pain points, and preferences in order to enhance the overall customer experience and satisfaction.

During a customer support ticket analysis, UXR professionals review various aspects of the tickets, such as the types of issues reported, the urgency or impact of those issues, and the ways in which they were resolved. They may also categorize or tag the tickets based on common themes or patterns. By consolidating and analyzing this information, UXR professionals can identify recurring problems, spot trends in customer feedback, and gain insights into areas of improvement for the product or service.

Customer Surveys

Customer Surveys in the context of user-research (UXR) are formal methods used to gather data and feedback from customers or users of a product or service. The goal of conducting customer surveys is to gain insights into customers' preferences, needs, and experiences in order to inform decision-making and improve the overall user experience.

Customer surveys often involve the use of structured questionnaires that can be administered online, by phone, or in person. These questionnaires typically consist of a series of predetermined questions, which can be closed-ended (e.g., multiple choice, rating scales) or open-ended (e.g., text-based responses), depending on the goals of the research. The questions may cover a range of topics, such as product usability, satisfaction, demographics, and behavior patterns.

By collecting responses from a representative sample of customers, organizations can analyze the data to identify trends, patterns, and areas for improvement. The insights gleaned from customer surveys can help inform product design, marketing strategies, customer support initiatives, and other business decisions. Additionally, customer surveys can serve as a mechanism for capturing feedback on specific features or identifying pain points that may require attention.

To ensure the validity and reliability of the data collected, customer surveys should be designed and administered using rigorous research methodologies. This includes carefully selecting the target audience, using unbiased questioning techniques, and implementing proper data collection and analysis procedures. It is also important to consider the ethical implications of customer surveys, such as ensuring respondents' privacy and obtaining informed consent.

Customer.Io

Customer.io is a user engagement platform that allows businesses to send targeted and personalized messages to their customers. It enables companies to automate and optimize their communication strategies for different user segments.

Using Customer.io, User Experience Researchers (UXRs) can gain valuable insights into user behavior and preferences. They can analyze the effectiveness of different messaging strategies and optimize communication to enhance the overall user experience. The platform provides UXR teams with the ability to track user actions, measure engagement metrics, and segment users based on their behavior or attributes.

The data collected through Customer.io can be used to create user personas and understand their needs and pain points at a deeper level. UXR teams can leverage this information to conduct targeted research studies, surveys, or interviews, which can then help inform product improvements and feature enhancements.

Furthermore, by utilizing Customer.io, UXR teams can conduct A/B testing to identify the most effective messaging variations for different user segments. This allows for data-driven decision-making and the refinement of communication strategies to drive better user engagement and retention.

In conclusion, Customer.io is a powerful tool in the arsenal of UXR professionals, providing them with the means to understand user behavior, optimize communication, and create a more tailored and engaging user experience.

Dashboard

A dashboard in the context of user research (UXR) refers to a graphical user interface that provides an overview of key information and metrics in a condensed and visually appealing manner. It is a central hub where UXR professionals can access and analyze data related to user behavior, preferences, and experiences.

Typically, a UXR dashboard includes various visualizations such as charts, graphs, and tables that summarize and present data collected from user research studies. These visual representations help UXR professionals quickly understand trends, patterns, and insights without having to delve into the raw data. Additionally, a well-designed dashboard enables easy navigation and interaction, allowing users to filter, sort, and explore the data in a flexible and user-friendly way.

Dashboards

Dashboards in the context of user research (UXR) refer to visual representations of data and insights that provide a comprehensive overview of key performance indicators (KPIs) and other relevant metrics. These dashboards are used to monitor and track the user experience of a product or service.

UXR dashboards typically include various interactive charts, graphs, and tables that showcase important data points, such as user satisfaction scores, task completion rates, conversion rates, and user behavior metrics. These visualizations help UXR professionals to analyze and interpret the data in a clear and concise manner.

Data Analysis

Data analysis in the context of user research (UXR) refers to the process of examining and interpreting collected data to gain insights and make informed decisions. It involves systematically organizing, cleaning, and transforming large amounts of raw data into a structured format that can be analyzed and interpreted to understand user behavior and preferences. Through data analysis, researchers can identify patterns, trends, and correlations that provide valuable information to guide product development and design decisions.

During the data analysis stage, researchers employ various techniques and methods to uncover meaningful insights. This may include quantitative analysis, which involves using statistical tools to measure and analyze numerical data, such as survey responses or website analytics. Qualitative analysis, on the other hand, involves interpreting and categorizing non-numerical data, such as interview transcripts or observation notes, to identify themes and patterns. Additionally, researchers may use exploratory analysis techniques to discover hidden patterns or anomalies in the data.

Data Privacy And Security Compliance Testing

Data Privacy and Security Compliance Testing refers to the evaluation process conducted to assess whether an organization's data handling practices and security measures comply with relevant privacy regulations and industry standards. This testing aims to ensure that the organization's systems, processes, and policies adequately protect the privacy and security of user data.

During the testing phase, user-researchers focus on assessing various aspects related to data privacy and security compliance. This includes examining how the organization collects, stores, and manages user data, ensuring that it adheres to privacy laws and regulations, such as the General Data Protection Regulation (GDPR) or the Health Insurance Portability and Accountability Act (HIPAA).

Furthermore, user-researchers evaluate the organization's data security measures by assessing the effectiveness of encryption techniques, access controls, data breach response plans, and vulnerability management procedures. This testing helps identify potential vulnerabilities and weaknesses in the organization's infrastructure, which can then be addressed and strengthened to enhance data protection.

Overall, data privacy and security compliance testing plays a crucial role in ensuring that organizations handle user data ethically, transparently, and securely. By conducting thorough assessments and making necessary improvements, organizations demonstrate their commitment to safeguarding user privacy and instilling user trust. This not only protects individuals' sensitive information but also mitigates legal and reputational risks for the organization.

Data Repository

A data repository, in the context of user-research (UXR), refers to a centralized and organized collection of data that is used for analysis and reference by user researchers. It serves as a central hub where various types of data related to user research are stored, managed, and accessed.

The data stored in a repository typically includes qualitative and quantitative information gathered during user research activities such as interviews, surveys, usability testing, and observation studies. This can include raw data, synthesized findings, personas, journey maps, usability metrics, and other relevant artifacts.

The purpose of a data repository is to provide a secure and easily accessible location for user researchers and other stakeholders to store, retrieve, and share research data. It allows for better organization, searchability, and collaboration, enhancing the efficiency and effectiveness of user research efforts.

Furthermore, a data repository enables researchers to maintain a consistent and standardized approach to data management, ensuring data integrity, accuracy, and reliability. It facilitates data analysis and synthesis by providing a centralized location where researchers can aggregate, organize, and compare findings from different studies.

Additionally, a data repository promotes knowledge sharing and reusability, as it allows researchers to easily locate and reuse previously collected data. This can help reduce duplicative research efforts and facilitate longitudinal studies or benchmarking analyses.

Data Synthesis

Data synthesis in the context of user research (UXR) refers to the process of analyzing and interpreting collected data in order to derive meaningful insights and make informed decisions. It involves organizing, categorizing, and combining different sources of data to identify patterns, trends, and correlations.

Data synthesis is a crucial component of user research as it helps researchers make sense of the vast amount of information gathered from various research methods such as interviews, surveys, observations, and usability testing. It allows them to identify common themes, user needs, and pain points, which can then guide the design and development of user-centered products and services.

Data Validation

Data Validation is a process in user research (UXR) that involves ensuring the accuracy, consistency, and reliability of the data collected. It is a crucial step that enables researchers to identify and eliminate any errors or inconsistencies in the data, ensuring that the results obtained are valid and trustworthy. Data validation includes various techniques and methods to assess the quality of the data, such as checking for missing or incomplete information, validating the data against predefined rules or criteria, and verifying the consistency of the data across different sources or methods of data collection.

By conducting data validation, UXR professionals can ensure that the data collected during user research is of high quality and can be used confidently to inform decision-making processes. This helps to mitigate the risk of drawing incorrect conclusions or making flawed design recommendations based on unreliable data. Additionally, data validation helps to maintain the integrity and credibility of research findings, which is essential for building trust with stakeholders and ensuring the validity of research outcomes. It also contributes to improving the overall rigor and robustness of the research process, leading to more accurate and meaningful insights.

Data Visualization

Data Visualization is the graphical representation of data to provide a clear and concise understanding of complex information. In the context of user-research (UXR), data visualization is used to present research findings and insights in a visually appealing way, making it easier for stakeholders and design teams to comprehend and analyze the data.

By using various types of charts, graphs, and interactive visuals, data visualization allows UXR professionals to communicate research findings effectively. Visual representations of data can reveal patterns, relationships, and trends that might be difficult to identify in raw data. This enhances the ability to highlight user behavior, preferences, and needs, guiding the development of user-centered designs.

Decibel

A decibel (dB) is a unit of measurement used in user research (UXR) to quantify the intensity or level of sound or audio stimuli. It is commonly used to assess the loudness or volume of sounds, such as user interface feedback or audio prompts, in various user research studies.

The decibel scale is logarithmic, which means that each increment of 10 dB represents a tenfold increase or decrease in the sound intensity. This scale allows us to compare and describe different levels of sound in a more meaningful and precise way than using linear measurements alone.

In the context of UXR, decibels are often used to measure the perceived loudness of audio stimuli and its impact on the user experience. By carefully controlling and measuring the decibel levels of sound, researchers can evaluate the effectiveness and usability of different audio cues or prompts within a product or user interface.

Decibel measurements in user research can help determine optimal sound levels that provide clear and concise feedback without being too loud or distracting to users. By understanding the decibel levels that contribute to a positive user experience, researchers can make informed decisions when designing or modifying product audio features.

Overall, decibels play a crucial role in user research by providing a standardized and quantifiable way to assess sound levels and their impact on user experience. By utilizing decibel measurements, researchers can gain valuable insights into the auditory aspects of their products and improve the overall usability and satisfaction for users.

Desirability Studies

Desirability studies in the context of user-research (UXR) aim to evaluate users' attitudes and preferences towards a product or service. These studies provide insights into the users' emotional responses and overall satisfaction, helping designers and researchers understand how to improve the desirability and appeal of their designs.

By conducting desirability studies, researchers can determine what aspects of a product or service resonate positively with users and what aspects may need improvement. The studies often involve collecting qualitative data through interviews, observations, or surveys to gain a deeper understanding of users' perceptions and desires.

Desirability Testing

Desirability testing is a method used in user research (UXR) to evaluate the appeal, attractiveness, and emotional responses of users towards a product or design. It aims to understand the subjective experience and overall desirability of the product from the perspective of the target users. During desirability testing, participants are presented with the product or design and are asked to provide their opinions, thoughts, and feelings about various aspects such as aesthetics, usability, and overall satisfaction. The focus is on the emotional and affective responses rather than objective measurements. The goal of desirability testing is to gather qualitative data that can help uncover user needs, preferences, and expectations. By understanding what aspects of the product are appealing and desirable to users, designers and researchers can identify areas for improvement and make informed design decisions. Desirability testing is typically conducted using various methods such as interviews, surveys, or observational studies. Participants may be asked to rate or rank different design elements, describe their emotional reactions, or provide feedback on specific aspects of the product. It can be performed at different stages of the design process, allowing iterative refinements based on user feedback. Overall, desirability testing provides valuable insights into how users perceive and emotionally connect with a product or design. By understanding the subjective experiences and desires of users, designers can create more appealing and user-centric solutions that meet the needs and expectations of their target audience.>

Diary Studies

A diary study is a method of user research used in UX (User Experience) research to gather detailed, longitudinal data about participants' experiences, behaviors, and attitudes over a specific period of time.

In a diary study, participants are assigned the task of documenting their thoughts, actions, and experiences related to a specific product or service in a diary or journal. They are typically asked to record their experiences on a regular basis, such as daily or weekly, for an extended period of time, which can range from a few days to several weeks or months.

Diary Surveys

Diary surveys, in the context of user-research (UXR), refer to a qualitative research method where participants maintain a written record or diary of their experiences, thoughts, and feelings over a specific period of time.

These diary surveys are used as a means to gather rich and detailed insights into participants' behaviors, attitudes, and interactions with a particular product, service, or experience. Participants are typically asked to document their experiences on a regular basis, providing a continuous stream of information over the designated period.

Discrete Choice Analysis

Discrete choice analysis is a statistical method used in user research (UXR) to understand and predict user preferences and choices among a set of alternatives. It aims to uncover the factors that influence user decision-making and the trade-offs they make when selecting one option over another.

In discrete choice analysis, participants are presented with a series of scenarios or choice sets, each consisting of several alternatives. They are asked to choose one option from each set, based on their personal preferences or priorities. By analyzing the patterns of choices made by participants, researchers can extract valuable insights about user preferences, product features, and the impact of different factors on decision-making.

Key elements of discrete choice analysis in user research include attribute selection and design, choice set configuration, and the estimation of choice models. Attributes refer to the characteristics or features of the alternatives being evaluated, which may include price, design, functionality, or any other relevant factor. These attributes and their levels are carefully chosen to represent real-world options and capture the factors that drive user decision-making.

Choice set configuration involves the creation of different choice sets, considering the number of alternatives, the number of attributes, and the levels included in each set. This ensures that participants are presented with a diverse set of options to choose from, and allows for the estimation of the relative importance of different attributes.

The estimation of choice models involves analyzing the collected data to identify the underlying factors that influence user choices. This often includes the use of statistical techniques such as multinomial logit or conditional logit models, which help quantify the impact of different attributes on decision-making.

Distributed Surveys

Distributed surveys, in the context of user research (UXR), refer to the collection of data from a large and diverse group of participants using online survey tools and platforms. They are a popular method for gathering quantitative data and feedback from a wide range of users, which can provide valuable insights for UX designers and researchers.

These surveys are typically designed to be completed independently by participants at their own convenience, allowing for a flexible and scalable data collection process. Various online tools and platforms offer features such as question branching, skip logic, and randomization to enhance the survey experience and ensure accurate responses.

Distributed surveys can be an integral part of user research studies, as they allow researchers to gather feedback on specific aspects of a product or service, measure user satisfaction, identify pain points, and gather demographic information. The collected data can be analyzed quantitatively, enabling researchers to identify patterns, trends, and statistical correlations.

However, it is important for researchers to carefully design and structure their distributed surveys to ensure that they capture the necessary information effectively. Clear and concise questions, logical flow, and appropriate response options are key elements to consider when creating these surveys.

In conclusion, distributed surveys offer a valuable method for gathering quantitative data and feedback from a diverse group of participants in user research studies. By utilizing online survey tools, researchers can collect and analyze large amounts of data to inform and improve the user experience of products and services.

Documentation

Documentation in the context of user research (UXR) refers to the process of recording, organizing, and presenting information gathered during the research phase of a user-centered design project. It involves creating clear and comprehensive records of the methods, findings, and insights discovered during user research activities.

Documentation plays a vital role in user research as it enables a UXR team to effectively communicate and share their findings with various stakeholders, including designers, developers, and product managers. It helps ensure that valuable insights and user needs are properly understood and integrated into the design and development process.

Dovetail

Dovetail is a user research software that aids in capturing, analyzing, and synthesizing insights gathered from user research activities. It provides a centralized platform for researchers to store and organize their raw research data, such as interview transcripts, observations, and surveys. Through its intuitive interface, Dovetail assists researchers in uncovering patterns, themes, and trends within the collected data.

The software allows researchers to create and manage codes, which are labels applied to specific sections of the data. These codes help researchers identify and categorize recurring themes or topics that emerge from the research. By applying codes to different sections of the data, researchers can easily navigate and filter through the information based on specific criteria.

The software also offers collaboration features, enabling multiple researchers to work together efficiently. They can share their findings, provide feedback, and collaborate on analyzing the research data. Dovetail supports seamless integration with popular research tools such as Google Drive, Zoom, and Slack, allowing researchers to import data from various sources and collaborate using their preferred tools.

Furthermore, Dovetail provides powerful visualization capabilities, including charts, graphs, and heatmaps, which help researchers present their findings in a compelling and easily understandable format. These visualizations allow stakeholders to grasp key insights and make informed decisions based on user research.

Drift

Drift in the context of user research (UXR) refers to a phenomenon where users of a product or service gradually deviate from its intended use or desired behavior. It is important for user researchers to identify and understand drift as it impacts the effectiveness and success of the product or service. Drift can occur for various reasons, such as changing user needs, evolving market trends, or design flaws. By studying and addressing drift, user researchers aim to enhance user experience and ensure that the product or service aligns with users' expectations and goals. In user research, drift is typically identified through various methods, including user interviews, observations, surveys, and behavioral analysis. These research techniques help uncover patterns of behavior and identify instances of drift. By capturing data and insights related to drift, user researchers can inform design decisions, validate assumptions, and guide improvements to the product or service. In practice, user researchers collaborate with designers, product managers, and developers to address drift. They analyze user feedback and behavior to uncover drift-causing factors and determine how to mitigate them. This can involve making adjustments to the product's features, improving usability, or enhancing the overall user journey. By actively monitoring and addressing drift, user researchers contribute to the ongoing optimization and evolution of the product or service, ensuring its continued success in meeting user needs and expectations.

Dscout

Dscout is a user research platform that enables user researchers (UXR) to gather data about user experiences and behaviors. The platform allows researchers to create and customize studies or "missions," which participants complete using their smartphones. These missions can range from in-the-moment capture of experiences through photos, videos, or diaries, to real-time surveys and interviews.

Dscout provides a variety of tools and features that help researchers engage with participants and document their insights effectively. Researchers can design interactive surveys, ask open-ended questions, or prompt participants to complete specific tasks. The platform also offers video streaming and transcription services to facilitate the analysis of user-generated content.

With Dscout, researchers can recruit and manage participants easily, access their data in real-time, and collaborate with their team members to analyze and interpret the findings. The platform offers various data visualization options, allowing researchers to present their findings clearly and concisely to stakeholders.

In summary, Dscout is a comprehensive user research platform that empowers UXRs to conduct studies, capture user experiences, and gain valuable insights through the use of mobile missions. Its features and tools facilitate participant engagement, data collection, and analysis, ultimately aiding in the creation of user-centered designs and enhancing the overall user experience.

Dyad Interviews

Dyad interviews are a qualitative research method used in user experience research (UXR) to gather insights and data from two individuals simultaneously. In this method, a researcher conducts a structured interview with two participants, often referred to as dyads or pairs, who interact with each other while answering the interview questions.

This approach provides a unique perspective as participants have the opportunity to discuss and debate their thoughts, opinions, and experiences in real-time during the interview. Dyad interviews are particularly useful when studying social dynamics, decision-making processes, or when exploring shared experiences and interactions between users.

Ecological Momentary Assessment (EMA)

Ecological Momentary Assessment (EMA) is a research method commonly used in user-research (UXR) to understand and measure individuals' experiences, behaviors, and emotions in real-time and naturalistic settings. It involves the collection of data from participants' subjective reports at various points in their daily lives, allowing for a comprehensive understanding of their lived experiences.

EMA typically utilizes mobile devices or wearable technology to administer brief surveys or prompts to participants at random or predetermined intervals throughout the day. These surveys aim to capture information about participants' current activities, moods, social interactions, and environmental factors. By capturing data in the moment as it happens, EMA minimizes recall bias and provides more accurate and reliable information about users' experiences.

EMA is particularly valuable for capturing fleeting or subtle experiences that may not be accurately recalled in retrospective self-reports. This method enables researchers to gather rich and detailed data about users' real-time experiences, which can be used to inform the design of user-centered products and services.

Furthermore, EMA allows researchers to examine how various factors, such as time of day, location, or social context, influence users' experiences and behaviors. By considering the situational and contextual factors, researchers can gain a deeper understanding of the complex relationship between user experiences, behaviors, and the environment, leading to more informed design decisions.

Email Surveys

Email surveys are a method of gathering user feedback and data for user-research (UXR) in a formal and structured manner. This approach involves sending out survey questionnaires via email to a targeted group of users or customers, with the aim of collecting specific insights and opinions. The process typically starts by designing a questionnaire with a series of questions relating to the research objectives. The questions can vary in format, including multiple-choice, open-ended, or rating-scale questions. The survey should be concise and easy for participants to understand. Once the questionnaire is finalized, it is distributed to the targeted group via email. The email should provide a clear introduction to the purpose of the survey and outline the expected time commitment. Participants are encouraged to respond honestly and thoughtfully, while respecting their time and effort. To ensure a higher response rate, it is important to personalize the emails and tailor them to the recipients' characteristics or previous interactions. Additionally, acknowledging and thanking participants for their time and valuable insights can help create a positive impression and motivate future participation. Once the survey responses are received, the collected data needs to be carefully analyzed and interpreted. It is crucial to pay attention to potential biases and limitations inherent in the survey methodology. The insights gained from email surveys can provide valuable input for improving products, services, or user experiences. In conclusion, email surveys are a structured and formal approach to gathering user feedback and data for user-research (UXR). By sending out questionnaires via email to a targeted group, valuable insights can be gained to inform decision-making and enhance user experiences.>

Emotion Recognition Testing

Emotion Recognition Testing, in the context of user-research (UXR), refers to the process of evaluating and understanding users' emotional responses and expressions while interacting with a product or system. This testing technique aims to uncover users' emotional experiences, allowing designers and researchers to gain valuable insights into how the user interface and overall user experience impact users' feelings and behaviors.

During Emotion Recognition Testing, participants are typically exposed to different stimuli, such as specific tasks or scenarios, while their emotional responses are measured and analyzed. This may involve various methods, including self-reporting, facial expression analysis, physiological measurements, or a combination of these approaches. By assessing users' emotions, researchers can gain a deeper understanding of how users perceive and engage with a product or system, helping them identify areas of improvement and optimize the user experience.

Emotional Response Testing

Emotional response testing, in the context of user research (UXR), refers to a method used to collect and analyze data on users' emotional reactions and experiences while interacting with a product, service, or interface. The goal of emotional response testing is to understand how users feel, both consciously and unconsciously, as they engage with a product or interface.

During emotional response testing, participants are typically observed and recorded as they interact with the product or interface while also providing verbal feedback on their emotional experiences. This method can involve various techniques, such as facial expression analysis, self-reporting of emotional states, and physiological measurements like heart rate monitoring or galvanic skin response.

The collected data from emotional response testing is then analyzed to identify patterns, trends, and insights related to users' emotional experiences. This information can guide the design and development process by ensuring that the product or interface is optimized for positive emotional responses, which can lead to increased usability, customer satisfaction, and overall user experience.

Error Analysis

Error analysis in the context of user research (UXR) refers to the systematic process of identifying, categorizing, and analyzing errors or issues that users encounter when interacting with a product or service. This analytical approach helps UXR professionals understand the difficulties users face and find opportunities for improvement. In error analysis, a range of techniques and tools may be employed to gather users' feedback and data, including observation, surveys, interviews, and usability testing. These methods help identify common patterns and trends in user errors, enabling researchers to pinpoint the root causes and assess their impact on the overall user experience. Once errors are identified, they are typically categorized based on their severity and frequency, allowing researchers to prioritize and address the most significant issues first. Categorization may also help identify recurring themes or specific usability problems that can be targeted for specific improvements or feature enhancements. The analysis phase involves delving deeper into the errors to understand the underlying reasons behind their occurrence. Researchers may investigate factors such as confusing interface design, lack of clear instructions, or inefficient workflows that contribute to user errors. By identifying these factors, researchers can propose actionable recommendations for design modifications or process changes to minimize errors and enhance user experience. Error analysis plays a crucial role in UXR as it provides valuable insights into the pain points users encounter while using a product or service. By understanding and addressing these errors, organizations can improve user satisfaction, increase user adoption, and ultimately achieve their business goals. In conclusion, error analysis is a methodical process that allows researchers to identify, categorize, and analyze the errors users face when interacting with a product or service. By uncovering and understanding these errors, UXR professionals can make informed design decisions to enhance the overall user experience.>

Error Message Testing

Error Message Testing in the context of user research (UXR) refers to the evaluation and analysis of error messages displayed to users while interacting with a digital product or service. It involves assessing the effectiveness of these messages in conveying informative and meaningful content to users when they encounter errors or unexpected situations during their journey. The primary objective of error message testing is to determine the clarity, accuracy, and usability of the error messages. This process helps identify any potential issues or areas for improvement in the design, wording, and overall user experience of these messages. By conducting error message testing, UXR professionals can gain insights into how users perceive and understand the errors they encounter, enabling the development of more user-friendly error messages. During testing, researchers typically present users with scenarios that require them to perform specific tasks or actions. They carefully observe and document users' responses to error messages, including their comprehension level, emotional reactions, and ability to resolve the errors. This information is then analyzed to validate if the error messages effectively guide users towards resolving the issue or provide appropriate instructions to overcome the error. The findings from error message testing can help UX designers and developers enhance the error messaging system to prevent confusion, frustration, and potential abandonment of the product or service. By communicating error conditions clearly and providing actionable insights, error messages can contribute to a positive user experience and facilitate users in accomplishing their goals effectively.

Ethics Review

Ethics Review in the context of user-research (UXR) refers to the systematic examination and evaluation of the ethical considerations and implications associated with conducting research that involves human participants.

It involves a thorough analysis of the potential risks and benefits of the research project, and the steps taken to ensure the protection of the rights, privacy, and well-being of the participants. The aim is to ensure that the research is conducted in an ethical and responsible manner.

Ethics

Ethics in user research (UXR) refers to a set of principles and guidelines that govern the ethical conduct of research activities involving human participants to ensure their welfare and rights are protected. It encompasses the responsibility of the researcher to act in an ethical manner when conducting studies, collecting data, and analyzing and reporting findings.

At its core, ethics in UXR involves respect for individuals and their autonomy, honesty and transparency in research practices, minimization of harm, and the pursuit of benefiting society through the knowledge gained. Researchers must uphold ethical standards by obtaining informed consent from participants, maintaining confidentiality and anonymity, and providing a safe and inclusive research environment.

Ethnio

Ethnio is a user-research tool widely used in the field of User Experience Research (UXR). It provides researchers with the ability to recruit participants for studies, collect qualitative feedback, and analyze user behavior, all within a single platform.

With Ethnio, researchers can create customizable screeners to filter and recruit participants based on specific criteria. This helps ensure that the study includes individuals who match the target user persona, leading to more accurate insights. The tool also offers various recruitment options, such as inviting participants through email, pop-up intercepts on websites, or social media channels.

Once participants are recruited, Ethnio enables researchers to conduct remote or in-person interviews, usability tests, and surveys. It provides a seamless user experience for both the researcher and the participant, offering features like screen sharing, video recording, and live chat. Researchers can easily moderate sessions, ask follow-up questions, and capture real-time feedback.

Additionally, Ethnio allows researchers to analyze and organize the collected data efficiently. It provides features for coding responses, tagging important insights, and generating visualizations. Researchers can easily identify patterns, trends, and user preferences through the tool's intuitive interface.

In summary, Ethnio simplifies the process of user-research by providing researchers with a comprehensive platform for participant recruitment, data collection, and analysis. It streamlines the workflow and enhances the research experience, ultimately leading to more informed design decisions and improved user experiences.

Ethnographic Interviews

Ethnographic interviews are a qualitative research method commonly used in user research (UXR) to gain in-depth insights into users' behaviors, needs, and experiences. In this approach, the researcher engages in a one-on-one conversation with participants, allowing them to share their thoughts, feelings, and motivations openly and in their own words.

The goal of ethnographic interviews is to uncover deep-seated patterns of behavior and understand the context in which these behaviors occur. The researcher typically spends a significant amount of time observing participants in their natural environment before conducting the interview. This contextual understanding helps to provide richer and more accurate insights into the users' mindset and behaviors.

Ethnography

Ethnography is a qualitative research method used in user-research (UXR) to understand the cultural, social, and behavioral aspects of a group of users or a community. It involves immersing the researcher in the natural environment of the users, observing their behaviors, and engaging in conversations to gain deep insights into their thoughts, experiences, and needs.

The goal of ethnography in UXR is to uncover the underlying motivations, values, and beliefs of users within their cultural context. By spending time with users in their everyday lives, researchers can observe how they interact with products or services, analyze their decision-making processes, and identify any pain points or areas for improvement.

Experience Prototyping

Experience prototyping is a user research method used in the field of UX design to gather feedback and insights on the design of a product or service. It involves creating tangible prototypes that simulate the user experience to help designers understand how users interact with the product or service in real-life situations.

This method aims to bridge the gap between concept and reality by providing users with a hands-on experience of the proposed design. Experience prototypes can take various forms, such as physical models, interactive mock-ups, or even virtual simulations. They are carefully crafted to mimic the key aspects of the intended user experience, allowing participants to engage with the design and provide valuable feedback.

Experience Sampling Method (ESM)

The Experience Sampling Method (ESM) is a research technique commonly used in user research (UXR) to gather real-time and in-the-moment feedback from participants. It involves periodically interrupting participants in their natural environment and asking them to report on their current experiences, thoughts, and behaviors.

During an ESM study, participants are equipped with mobile devices or other tools that can prompt them to provide feedback at random or predetermined intervals throughout the day. These prompts typically consist of a series of questions or statements related to the study's objectives, such as user satisfaction, task performance, or emotional states. Participants then respond to these prompts using a rating scale, open-ended responses, or other structured formats.

By collecting data at multiple time points and in real-world contexts, the ESM allows researchers to capture participants' experiences as they naturally occur. This method helps overcome biases associated with retrospective recall and provides richer insights into users' motivations, behaviors, and preferences.

The ESM has various applications in user research, including evaluating the usability of digital products or services, assessing user experience over time, and identifying pain points or opportunities for improvement. Its strengths lie in capturing real-time data, reducing memory biases, and uncovering valuable insights that might not be accessible through other research methods. However, it also presents challenges, such as participant burden, sample representativeness, and potential privacy concerns.

Expert Review Surveys

Expert Review Surveys are a user-research method used in the field of User Experience Research (UXR) to gather insights and feedback from experts in a specific domain or industry. This method involves asking a group of experts to evaluate a product, system, or design based on their knowledge and expertise.

During an Expert Review Survey, the experts are typically provided with a set of predetermined criteria or guidelines to assess the product or design. They examine various aspects such as usability, functionality, visual design, and overall user experience. The experts then provide feedback and recommendations based on their observations and expertise.

Expert Review

Exploratory Testing

Exploratory testing is a user-research technique that involves dynamically and informally exploring a software application or website to find any potential issues or areas for improvement from a user experience (UX) perspective. It is a technique where the tester explores the system with limited or no initial knowledge of the application's functionality or design specifications.

The primary goal of exploratory testing in the context of user-research is to discover usability issues, potential bottlenecks, and areas that might hinder or enhance the overall user experience. It focuses on understanding how users interact with the application and aims to identify any unexpected behavior, confusing interfaces, or other barriers to usability.

Eye Tracking Testing

Eye tracking testing is a user research method used in the field of user experience research (UXR) to analyze and understand how users visually interact with a website, application, or digital interface. This technique involves measuring and capturing the movements of a user's eyes as they navigate and engage with different elements on the screen. During an eye tracking test, participants wear special eye-tracking devices or cameras that detect and record their eye movements. These devices use infrared light to track the position and movement of the eyes, allowing researchers to gather precise data on which areas of the screen the participant is focusing on, how long they spend looking at specific elements, and the sequence in which they view different parts of the interface. The primary goal of eye tracking testing is to gain insights into users' visual attention and behavior, and to identify any usability issues or areas for improvement within the interface being tested. By analyzing eye tracking data, researchers can determine which elements on the screen are most visually engaging or distracting, whether users are able to find and focus on important information efficiently, and how users naturally navigate through the interface. Eye tracking testing can provide valuable data for user experience design decisions, such as optimizing the placement of important elements, improving the visibility of certain features, or identifying areas of visual clutter that may confuse or distract users. In conclusion, eye tracking testing is a user research method that measures and analyzes participants' eye movements to gain insights into users' visual attention and behavior when interacting with digital interfaces. This technique helps identify usability issues and inform improvements in user experience design.>

Eye Tracking

Eye tracking is a user research method used in the field of UX research to understand and analyze how users visually interact with digital interfaces or physical stimuli. It involves tracking and recording the movements and focus of the user's eyes using specialized equipment.

Eye tracking provides valuable insights into users' attention patterns, gaze fixation, and overall visual behavior. By capturing and analyzing this data, UX researchers can gain a deeper understanding of users' cognitive processes, decision-making, and emotional responses while interacting with a product or interface.

Eyetracking Analytics

Eyetracking analytics refers to the process of collecting and analyzing data on how users visually interact with digital interfaces, such as websites, applications, or advertisements. This method involves the use of specialized eye-tracking technology to monitor and record the movements and behaviors of a user's eyes as they navigate and engage with visual content.

By capturing precise and accurate information about where users focus their attention and how their gaze moves across a screen, eyetracking analytics provides valuable insights for user-research (UXR) professionals. These insights help to understand user behavior, preferences, and cognitive processes, which can be used to improve the design, layout, and overall user experience of digital products.

Eyetracking Heatmaps

Eyetracking heatmaps are a user research methodology used in the field of user experience research (UXR) to analyze and visualize the eye movements and attention patterns of users while interacting with a digital interface. The technique involves using specialized eyetracking devices to record the gaze data of participants, which is then processed and translated into visual heatmaps. Eyetracking heatmaps provide valuable insights into user behaviors and cognitive processes when navigating through a website, application, or any other digital interface. By identifying areas of visual interest, attention, and fixation, researchers can gain a better understanding of how users engage with different elements and content within the interface. These heatmaps are generated by aggregating and overlaying the gaze data of multiple participants onto the visual representation of the interface. The result is a heat gradient map, where warmer colors (such as red and orange) indicate higher user attention and cooler colors (such as blue and green) represent areas with less visual focus. By analyzing eyetracking heatmaps, UX researchers can evaluate the effectiveness and efficiency of the interface design. They can identify areas that capture user attention and determine whether important content or functionalities are being overlooked. Insights from eyetracking heatmaps can be used to inform design decisions, optimize information hierarchy, improve user flow, and enhance overall user experience. In conclusion, eyetracking heatmaps are a valuable tool in user research, providing visual representations of users' eye movements and attention patterns while interacting with a digital interface. They offer insights that help researchers understand user behaviors, optimize design choices, and ultimately improve the user experience.>

Eyetracking Studies

Eyetracking studies in the context of user research (UXR) refer to the collection and analysis of data related to the movement and focus of a user's eyes while interacting with a particular interface or stimulus. This observational research technique uses specialized hardware and software to track and record the precise point of gaze, commonly referred to as the gaze point, as well as the sequence and duration of fixations (instances when the gaze lingers on a specific point) and saccades (rapid eye movements between fixations).

By conducting eyetracking studies, researchers can gain valuable insights into users' visual attention patterns and behavior, providing a deeper understanding of how users interpret and interact with interfaces or content. These studies can reveal information such as which elements of an interface attract the most attention, how users navigate through a website or app, which parts of a visual design are most engaging, and potential usability issues that may affect users' experience.

Face-To-Face Surveys

Face-to-Face Surveys in the context of user research (UXR) refer to a method of gathering data and insights by directly interacting with participants in person. This approach involves a researcher asking a series of structured questions to individuals or small groups, with the aim of collecting qualitative or quantitative information regarding their experiences, preferences, or behaviors.

During a Face-to-Face Survey, a researcher typically uses a predefined questionnaire or interview guide to ensure consistency across participants. The survey may cover various aspects of user experience, such as usability, satisfaction, or perceptions of a product or service. The questions may be open-ended, allowing participants to provide detailed, narrative responses, or closed-ended, providing predetermined response options for participants to choose from.

>

Feedbackify

Feedbackify is a user-research tool used in the field of User Experience Research (UXR). It is designed to collect feedback and insights from users to improve the overall user experience of a product or service.

Feedbackify allows researchers to gather feedback in various formats, such as surveys, polls, and questionnaires, to understand the needs, preferences, and opinions of users. It provides a platform for users to share their thoughts, ideas, and suggestions, which can be valuable for identifying areas of improvement and making informed design decisions.

Field Studies

A field study in the context of user research (UXR) is a research method that involves observing and gathering data about users in their natural environment or real-life context. Unlike laboratory-based studies, field studies offer insights into how users interact with a product or service in their everyday lives, allowing researchers to observe and understand user behavior, needs, and challenges in a real-world setting.

During a field study, researchers typically visit users' homes, workplaces, or other relevant locations to observe and interview them while they engage with a product or service. This method helps uncover the context in which users interact with the product, factors influencing their behavior, and the impact of the product on their daily routines and tasks.

The goal of a field study is to gain a deeper understanding of users, their needs, goals, and frustrations in order to inform the design and development of user-centered products and services. By directly observing users, researchers can capture rich qualitative data that reveals insights and patterns that may not be apparent through other research methods.

Field studies often involve a combination of ethnographic research techniques, such as observation, interviews, and note-taking. The data collected during field studies can be used to identify design opportunities, evaluate prototypes, and prioritize features and improvements based on the real-world experiences and needs of users.

Field Surveys

A field survey is a qualitative research method used in user research (UXR) to gather data and insights about users' behaviors, needs, and preferences in their natural environments or real-world contexts.

During a field survey, researchers directly observe users as they interact with a product, service, or environment. This method allows for rich and contextual data collection, providing a deeper understanding of how users engage with a given system. It also offers valuable insights into users' emotions, motivations, pain points, and decision-making processes.

Field surveys typically involve researchers visiting users' physical locations, such as their homes, workplaces, or public spaces, to observe and record user behavior and interactions. These visits may include interviews or informal conversations to gain additional insights and user feedback.

The data collected during a field survey can be used to identify user needs, uncover usability issues, and inform the design and development of products and services. By observing users in their natural environments, researchers can better understand the context and constraints in which users operate, leading to more user-centered and effective design solutions.

Overall, field surveys play a crucial role in user research, allowing for direct observation and contextual understanding of users' behaviors and experiences. This method helps researchers generate actionable insights that can inform the design and improvement of user-centered products and services.

Field Testing

Field testing is a user-research method commonly employed in the field of User Experience Research (UXR). It involves observing and collecting data on user behavior and interactions with a product or service in a real-world setting, outside of a controlled lab environment.

During field testing, researchers closely observe users as they interact with a product or service to gain insights into how it is used in its intended context. This method allows researchers to gather firsthand information about user experiences, preferences, challenges, and needs.

Findings Report

A findings report in the context of user research (UXR) is a concise and structured document that presents the outcomes and insights derived from the research process. It serves as a summary and analysis of the data collected during the study, offering an overview of the key findings and recommendations for the design or improvement of a product or service.

The findings report aims to communicate the research findings to stakeholders, designers, and decision-makers in a clear and accessible manner. It typically includes a brief introduction to the research objectives and methodology, followed by a systematic presentation of the key findings, insights, and related user quotes or anecdotes.

The report should provide a comprehensive understanding of the user's needs, preferences, and behaviors, ultimately informing the design decisions and driving UX improvements. It may include charts, tables, or visual representations of the data to enhance the readability and impact of the findings.

Moreover, the findings report often incorporates a section with actionable recommendations that bridge the gap between the research insights and the practical implementation. These recommendations may suggest specific design changes, feature enhancements, or further research directions to address the identified gaps or opportunities.

In conclusion, a findings report in the realm of user research is a concise and informative document that presents the outcomes of the research process, including key findings, insights, user quotes, and actionable recommendations. Its purpose is to inform and guide the design process, ensuring the creation of user-centered products or services.

Findings

Findings refer to the results and insights obtained from user research activities in the field of user experience research (UXR). This term encompasses the analysis and interpretation of data collected during research studies conducted to understand the needs, preferences, and behaviors of users. Findings are derived from various research methods, including interviews, surveys, observations, and usability testing, among others. In a UXR context, findings are the factual descriptions of observed user behavior, opinions, preferences, and pain points, supported by data and evidence. These insights help inform the design and development of products or services that align with user needs and expectations. Findings are typically presented in a clear and concise manner, allowing stakeholders to understand the research outcomes and make informed decisions based on the identified patterns and themes. The analysis of findings might involve identifying common user problems, usability issues, or areas for improvement. Additionally, findings often include recommendations for design enhancements or changes to better meet user requirements. The presentation of findings can take several formats, such as verbal or written reports, presentations, or data visualizations. The goal is to effectively communicate the research results to key stakeholders, including designers, developers, product managers, and other decision-makers. Overall, findings play a crucial role in the user-centered design process, as they provide valuable insights into user behavior and preferences. By utilizing these insights, organizations can create products and services that not only meet user needs but also enhance the overall user experience.>

Flowcharts

A flowchart in the context of user research (UXR) is a visual representation of the steps involved in a process or the sequence of events that occur in a user's interaction with a product or service. It is a useful tool for understanding and mapping out the user's journey, identifying pain points, and optimizing the overall user experience.

Flowcharts consist of various symbols and arrows that represent different actions, decisions, or steps within a process. The symbols and arrows are connected in a logical order to depict the flow of the user's actions and interactions. This visual representation helps researchers and designers analyze and communicate complex processes or interactions in a clear and structured manner.

Form Field Testing

Form Field Testing is a user research method primarily used in the field of user experience research (UXR). It involves evaluating and assessing the usability and effectiveness of form fields in web interfaces or applications. In this method, a group of participants are asked to complete tasks that involve interacting with form fields. These tasks can range from simple actions like entering their name or email address to more complex actions like submitting a form or selecting multiple options from a dropdown menu. The main focus of form field testing is to understand how users interact with the form fields, identify any usability issues or errors, and gather feedback on the overall user experience. This method helps to uncover any problems or confusion that users may face while providing input in the form fields. During the testing process, researchers observe and take note of how participants interact with the form fields, including the time taken to complete a task, the accuracy of the input provided, and any difficulties encountered. The insights gained from form field testing can be used to improve the design and functionality of form fields, making them more user-friendly, intuitive, and efficient. By addressing any issues identified through this method, organizations can enhance the overall user experience, increasing user satisfaction and reducing barriers to completing tasks. In conclusion, form field testing is a valuable user research method that helps identify and address usability issues in form fields, ultimately improving the overall user experience.>

Formative Assessment Surveys

A formative assessment survey in the context of user-research (UXR) is a tool used to gather feedback and insights from users during the early stages of a design or development process. This type of survey aims to assess the usability, functionality, and overall user experience of a product, service, or website.

The main purpose of a formative assessment survey is to identify areas of improvement and gather user preferences and opinions in order to inform the iterative design process. The survey typically consists of a set of questions that are designed to prompt users to provide specific feedback on different aspects of the product or service, such as its layout, navigation, visuals, and functionality.

The survey questions are carefully crafted to ensure that the feedback provided by the users is meaningful and actionable. The responses collected through the formative assessment survey can help designers and researchers identify pain points, uncover usability issues, and gain insights into user preferences and behaviors.

Formative assessment surveys are often conducted through online platforms or tools that allow for easy data collection and analysis. The findings from these surveys can be used to guide the design decisions and inform the next steps in the development process.

Formative Usability Testing

Formative Usability Testing is a research method commonly used in the field of User Experience Research (UXR) to evaluate the usability of a product or service during its design and development phase.

During formative usability testing, users are observed while they interact with the product or service, and their feedback is collected. This feedback is then used to identify usability issues and make iterative improvements to the design, aiming to enhance the overall user experience. The primary goal of formative usability testing is to inform and guide the design process, allowing for early detection and resolution of potential usability problems before the product is finalized.

Front

User research, also known as UXR or UX research, is a systematic process of gathering and analyzing information about end-users and their behaviors, needs, and motivations to improve the user experience of a product or service. It involves using various research methods and techniques to gain valuable insights that can inform the design and development of user-friendly experiences.

UX researchers employ a combination of qualitative and quantitative research methods to understand the thoughts, feelings, and behaviors of users. These methods may include interviews, surveys, usability testing, field studies, and analytics data analysis, among others. By directly observing and engaging with users, UXR aims to uncover patterns, identify pain points, and discover opportunities for enhancement.

The findings from user research are used to inform design decisions, validate assumptions, and uncover potential usability issues. UXR helps to ensure that products and services align with user expectations and needs, leading to improved user satisfaction, engagement, and loyalty.

Through user research, organizations can gain a deeper understanding of their target audience, identify new market opportunities, and gain a competitive advantage. By placing users at the center of the design process, UXR helps organizations create user-centric and intuitive experiences that meet user needs and drive business success.

FullStory

FullStory is a user-research tool that provides comprehensive insights into user experiences on websites and apps. It allows User Experience Researchers (UXRs) to gather detailed data about user interactions, behavior, and issues to improve the overall user experience.

With FullStory, UXR professionals can record and replay individual user sessions, capturing every mouse movement, click, scroll, and form interaction. This enables a deep understanding of how users engage with a website or app, identifying pain points and areas for improvement.

Functional Testing

Functional testing, in the context of user-research (UXR), refers to the evaluation of a product or system's functionality to ensure it meets the intended user needs and requirements. It involves conducting tests on the product or system to verify that all features and functionalities are working as expected and in alignment with user expectations.

During functional testing, the focus is on assessing the product's ability to perform the tasks it was designed for, without considering its aesthetic aspects or visual design elements. The primary goal is to identify any functional defects, bugs, or usability issues that may hinder the user's interaction with the product.

Gainsight

Gainsight is a user-research (UXR) tool that facilitates the collection and analysis of feedback from users to enhance the user experience of a product or service. It provides a platform for conducting surveys, interviews, and usability tests to gain insights into the needs, preferences, and challenges faced by users.

With Gainsight, researchers can design and distribute surveys to gather quantitative data on user satisfaction, usability, and overall experience. The tool also enables the recruitment of participants for interviews and usability tests, allowing researchers to obtain qualitative feedback and observe user interactions with the product or service.

Gainsight offers various features to streamline the research process, including customizable survey templates, automated data collection, and data analysis tools. Researchers can generate reports and visualizations to present findings and identify patterns or trends in user feedback.

Furthermore, Gainsight allows researchers to segment and analyze user data based on demographics, usage patterns, or other variables, supporting in-depth persona development and user journey mapping. By integrating with other research tools and platforms, Gainsight facilitates seamless data sharing and collaboration among researchers and stakeholders.

Overall, Gainsight serves as a comprehensive user-research platform that empowers researchers to systematically collect, analyze, and interpret feedback from users. It helps organizations make informed decisions, prioritize design improvements, and enhance the overall user experience of their products or services.

Gamestorming

Gamestorming is a user research technique commonly used in the field of User Experience Research (UXR). It involves the use of interactive, collaborative activities and games to gather insights and stimulate creativity from participants in order to uncover user needs and preferences.

Through gamestorming, researchers aim to create an engaging and inclusive environment that encourages participants to express their thoughts, ideas, and feedback. This technique is especially effective in breaking down barriers and fostering collaboration among participants, leading to more open and honest discussions.

Gaming Interviews

Gaming interviews refer to a user research method used by UX researchers to gather valuable insights and feedback from gamers. These interviews are conducted to understand the user experience, preferences, and behaviors of gamers in order to improve the design and overall gaming experience.

During gaming interviews, researchers engage with participants who are avid gamers and have experience playing various types of games. The interviews can be conducted in person, over the phone, or through video conferencing tools.

The purpose of gaming interviews is to gain a deeper understanding of gamers' motivations, goals, and expectations. Researchers aim to uncover the specific elements of a game that players enjoy or find frustrating. They ask open-ended questions to encourage participants to provide detailed responses and share their experiences, opinions, and emotions related to gaming.

Gaming interviews can cover a range of topics such as game mechanics, user interface, visual design, audio, storyline, multiplayer experiences, and overall satisfaction. Researchers use these insights to identify areas of improvement and inform the iterative design process. They may also test prototypes and gather feedback to validate design decisions.

Through gaming interviews, researchers gain valuable insights into the needs and preferences of gamers, helping them create more engaging, immersive, and enjoyable gaming experiences.

Globalization Testing

Globalization Testing is a user-research method that aims to evaluate the usability and effectiveness of a product or service in various international markets and cultural contexts. It involves identifying and addressing potential issues that may arise when the product or service is used by users from different countries, with diverse languages, cultural backgrounds, and technological infrastructures.

This type of testing focuses on ensuring that the user experience (UX) remains consistent across different languages, while also taking into account the unique needs and preferences of each target market. It involves testing different aspects of the product or service, such as functionality, content, design, and localization to identify any issues that may hinder its adoption or cause confusion among users from different cultural backgrounds.

Goals

Goals in the context of user research (UXR) refer to the desired outcomes or objectives that UXR professionals aim to achieve through their research activities. These goals help guide the research process by providing a clear direction and purpose.

In UXR, goals are typically set at the beginning of a research project and help define the scope and focus of the research. They can encompass a wide range of areas, such as understanding user needs and preferences, evaluating the usability of a product or interface, identifying pain points or friction in the user experience, or informing design decisions.

Group Interviews

A group interview in the context of user-research (UXR) is a qualitative research method that involves conducting interviews with a small group of individuals simultaneously, usually between three to eight participants. The purpose of a group interview in UXR is to gather insights and understanding about user experiences, behaviors, and attitudes related to a specific product, service, or design.

During a group interview, a moderator facilitates a discussion and encourages participants to share their thoughts, opinions, and experiences openly. The moderator may use open-ended questions, prompts, or activities to stimulate conversations and observe group dynamics. This research method allows for capturing a wide range of perspectives, ideas, and interactions within a limited time frame.

Guerilla Usability Testing

Guerilla usability testing is a method used in user research (UXR) to quickly and informally gather feedback on the usability of a product or design. It involves recruiting participants in an ad-hoc manner, often in public spaces, and conducting brief usability tests with them.

During guerilla usability testing, researchers typically approach potential participants in public places such as cafes, parks, or libraries, depending on the target user group. These participants are often unfamiliar with the research study and may not have any prior experience with the product being tested.

The tests themselves are usually brief and focused, aiming to assess specific aspects of usability, such as ease of navigation, clarity of instructions, or efficiency of completing certain tasks. The researcher may use scenarios or tasks to guide the participants, while taking note of any issues or difficulties encountered during the test.

Guerilla usability testing has several advantages as a research method. It is low-cost and can be rapidly conducted, allowing for quick insights and feedback. The informality of the approach often results in more genuine user reactions and feedback, as participants are not influenced by the artificial environment of a traditional lab setting.

However, it is important to note that guerilla usability testing also has limitations. The sample size of participants is often small, which may limit the generalizability of the findings. Additionally, the ad-hoc nature of recruitment may result in a biased sample, as certain demographics or user groups may be overrepresented or underrepresented.

Guidelines

User research (UXR) is a systematic and empirical approach to understanding users, their needs, behaviors, and preferences in order to inform and improve the design of products, services, and experiences. It involves employing various methods to collect and analyze data, such as surveys, interviews, observations, and usability tests.

The goal of user research is to gain deep insights into users and their interactions with a product or service throughout its lifecycle. By understanding users' motivations, expectations, and pain points, UX researchers can identify opportunities for improvement and enhance user satisfaction, engagement, and overall experience.

Heap

Heap is a data structure used in user research (UXR) to organize and analyze large sets of quantitative and qualitative data. In the context of UXR, a heap refers to a structured arrangement of user data that allows researchers to efficiently store, sort, and retrieve information. It is particularly helpful when dealing with a significant amount of data collected from user interactions, surveys, interviews, or other research methods. Heaps offer a way to manage and process data in a systematic manner to uncover insights and patterns. By storing data in a heap, researchers can easily access specific information or group data points based on certain criteria. This enables them to identify trends, common themes, or outliers in the data, leading to meaningful and actionable findings. Moreover, heaps provide flexibility in organizing different types of data, whether it be numeric values, categorical variables, textual responses, or timestamps. This makes it easier to extract relevant information based on specific research questions or objectives. In summary, a heap is a vital tool in UX research that facilitates the efficient storage, organization, and analysis of large datasets. Its ability to uncover patterns and insights from diverse data sources helps researchers make informed decisions that can drive product improvement and enhance the overall user experience.

Heap is a data structure used in user research (UXR) to efficiently store, sort, and retrieve large sets of quantitative and qualitative data. It allows researchers to analyze user interactions, surveys, interviews, and other research data in a structured and systematic manner.

Heatmap Analysis

A heatmap analysis is a visual representation of data collected during user research (UXR). It is used to identify patterns and trends in user behavior, specifically relating to their interactions with a website or software interface.

The heatmap is created by overlaying color-coded areas onto a webpage or screen recording, with each color representing the frequency or intensity of user activity in that particular area. The warmer colors, such as red and orange, indicate higher levels of user engagement or interaction, while cooler colors like blue and green suggest less engagement.

Heatmap Surveys

Heatmap surveys are a user research method used in the field of user experience research (UXR) to visualize and understand user behavior on a website or application. This method provides valuable insights into how users interact with digital interfaces by capturing and analyzing their activity patterns and preferences.

A heatmap survey involves collecting data on user interactions, such as mouse movements, clicks, and scrolling behavior, and representing this data in a visual format. The resulting heatmap provides researchers with a visual representation of the areas of the website or application that receive the highest and lowest levels of user engagement.

The purpose of conducting a heatmap survey is to identify user behavior patterns, improve website or application design, and optimize user experience. By analyzing the heatmap, researchers can gain insights into which sections of the interface are most engaging, which elements attract the most attention, and which areas may be overlooked by users. This information can help inform design decisions, prioritize content placement, and guide user flow improvements.

Heatmap surveys are typically conducted by using specialized software or tools that capture and analyze user interaction data, and generate heatmaps based on the collected data. Researchers can customize the heatmaps based on different parameters, such as click density, scroll depth, or time spent on each section of the interface, to gain specific insights into user behavior.

In conclusion, heatmap surveys are an effective user research method used in UXR to visualize and understand user behavior on digital interfaces. They help identify user behavior patterns, improve design, and enhance user experience by analyzing and interpreting heatmaps generated from user interaction data.

Heatmaps

Heatmaps are a visual representation of data that shows the distribution and intensity of user interactions on a webpage or screen. In the context of user research (UXR), heatmaps are used to analyze and understand how users engage with digital interfaces. They provide insights into user behavior and preferences, helping researchers and designers make data-driven decisions to optimize the user experience. Heatmaps are created by aggregating and displaying data points collected during user testing or through other data collection methods. These data points can include mouse movements, clicks, scrolling, and other interactions. The intensity of user activity is typically represented by color gradients, with warmer colors (such as red or orange)

49

indicating higher activity and cooler colors (like blue or green) indicating lower activity. By visually representing user interactions, heatmaps help identify patterns and trends that may not be immediately apparent from raw data. They allow researchers to understand which areas of a webpage are most engaging or neglected, where users encounter difficulties or confusion, and where they tend to focus their attention. This information can inform decisions about layout, content placement, call-to-action positioning, and other design elements. Heatmaps are particularly useful for identifying areas of a webpage that are underperforming or require improvement. For example, if a specific call-to-action button is not receiving much attention, it may need to be repositioned or redesigned to attract more user interaction. Heatmaps can also help validate design decisions by providing evidence-based insights into user behavior. Overall, heatmaps are a valuable tool in user research, providing visual representations of user behavior and enabling researchers to make informed decisions to enhance the user experience.>

Helio

Helio is a user-research software commonly used by UX researchers to collect, organize, and analyze data in order to gain insights into user behavior and preferences. It provides a platform for conducting various research methods such as surveys, interviews, and usability testing, allowing researchers to gather both quantitative and qualitative data. The software offers features that streamline the research process, including participant recruitment, data collection, and data analysis.

With Helio, researchers can create and distribute surveys to collect quantitative data on user preferences, opinions, and behavior. The software also allows for the creation of discussion guides and interview scripts to guide qualitative research. Additionally, Helio facilitates remote usability testing, enabling researchers to observe and collect feedback on user interactions with a product or interface.

The collected data is automatically organized and presented in a visually accessible manner, allowing researchers to easily identify patterns and trends. Helio also provides various analytical tools, such as data filters, segmentation, and statistical analysis, to aid in the interpretation and synthesis of research findings. The software enables researchers to generate reports and share insights with stakeholders, facilitating data-driven decision-making in product design and development.

Overall, Helio is a comprehensive user-research software that supports the entire research process, from planning and data collection to analysis and reporting. Its user-friendly interface and powerful features make it a valuable tool for UX researchers in understanding user needs and improving the design and usability of products and interfaces.

Hellonext

Hellonext is a user-research (UXR) platform that facilitates the process of collecting and analyzing user feedback for the improvement of digital products or services. It acts as a centralized hub for designers, researchers, and product managers to efficiently manage and prioritize user feedback.

With Hellonext, teams can easily collect user feedback through various channels, such as websites, mobile apps, or email, and categorize them based on different criteria like feature requests, bug reports, or general feedback. The platform allows users to upvote or comment on feedback, enabling teams to understand the popular demand and prioritize accordingly.

Hellonext provides features for analyzing feedback data, such as sentiment analysis, to gauge user satisfaction or frustration levels. This helps teams identify pain points and areas of improvement. In addition, the platform allows users to collaborate and discuss feedback internally, aiding in the decision-making process and fostering transparency within the team.

Furthermore, Hellonext offers integration capabilities with popular project management tools, allowing seamless transfer of feedback items to the team's existing workflow. This ensures that user feedback is not lost, and the relevant stakeholders can take appropriate action in a timely manner.

In summary, Hellonext is a user-research platform that streamlines the process of collecting, organizing, and analyzing user feedback, enabling teams to gain valuable insight into user perception and enhance the overall user experience of digital products or services.

Heuristic Evaluation

Heuristic Evaluation is a method used in user research (UXR) to assess the usability of a user interface by evaluating it against a set of predefined heuristics or principles. It involves a usability expert or evaluator inspecting the interface and identifying any usability issues that may hinder the user experience.

The process of heuristic evaluation typically involves the following steps:

1. Selecting a set of heuristics: The evaluator selects a set of heuristics or principles that are considered best practices in user interface design. These heuristics are often based on established usability guidelines and previous research findings.

2. Independently evaluating the interface: The evaluator examines the user interface and assesses its compliance with each heuristic. They look for any violations or deviations from the established principles that could potentially affect the usability of the system.

3. Identifying usability issues: During the evaluation, the evaluator identifies specific usability issues and documents them. These issues can range from minor design flaws to major usability problems that may hinder the user's ability to accomplish their tasks efficiently.

4. Providing recommendations: Based on the identified usability issues, the evaluator provides recommendations for improving the user interface. These recommendations are typically prioritized based on their severity and potential impact on the user experience.

Heuristic evaluation is a cost-effective method as it requires fewer resources compared to other user research techniques such as usability testing. It provides valuable insights into the usability of a user interface early in the design process, allowing designers to make informed decisions and improve the overall user experience.

Heuristic Walkthrough

A heuristic walkthrough is a user research method in the field of user experience (UX) that aims to identify potential usability issues or areas of improvement in a product or interface. It involves a group of evaluators who collectively examine and evaluate a system's user interface based on a set of predefined heuristics or principles. During a heuristic walkthrough, evaluators simulate user tasks and scenarios in order to assess the overall usability of a product. They analyze the interface design, interaction patterns, and overall user experience based on a set of heuristic guidelines. These heuristics are typically derived from well-established usability principles such as visibility of system status, consistency and standards, error prevention, recognition rather than recall, flexibility and efficiency of use, aesthetic and minimalist design, and help and documentation. The evaluators independently review the interface and its functionality, noting any potential usability issues or violations of the predefined heuristics. They provide feedback on areas that are unclear, confusing, inconsistent, or difficult to navigate. The findings and recommendations from the heuristic walkthrough can then be used to inform design decisions and improve the overall user experience. By conducting a heuristic walkthrough, UX researchers can quickly identify and prioritize usability issues without the need for extensive user testing. It provides valuable insights into potential areas of improvement and helps ensure that a product or interface aligns with established usability principles. Ultimately, the goal of a heuristic walkthrough is to create a more user-friendly and intuitive experience for the target audience.

A heuristic walkthrough is a user research method that helps identify potential usability issues or areas of improvement in a product's interface.

It involves a group of evaluators who examine the interface design and interaction patterns based on predefined usability principles.

Hotjar

Hotjar is a user research tool used in the field of user experience research (UXR). It allows researchers to gain valuable insights into user behavior and preferences by capturing and analyzing various data points on a website or app.

Hotjar's main feature is its ability to record and visually display user interactions, such as mouse movements, clicks, and scrolling behavior, through heatmaps. These heatmaps provide researchers with an overview of how users navigate and interact with different elements on a webpage, allowing them to identify potential usability issues or areas of improvement.

In addition to heatmaps, Hotjar also offers other powerful research tools. One of these tools is session recordings, which allows researchers to watch real-time recordings of user sessions on a website. This allows them to observe how users navigate through the site, where they encounter difficulties, and how they interact with specific elements or features.

Another useful feature is the ability to create and analyze surveys or polls. Hotjar offers a flexible survey builder that researchers can use to gather feedback directly from users. This helps to uncover user sentiments, preferences, and pain points, allowing researchers to gain a deeper understanding of their target audience.

Overall, Hotjar provides valuable insights for UX researchers, enabling them to make data-driven decisions and improve the overall user experience of a website or app. Its powerful combination of heatmaps, session recordings, and surveys makes it a versatile and essential tool in the field of user research.

Hypothesis

Hypothesis in the context of user research (UXR) refers to a statement or proposition that is derived from observations, data, or existing theories, and is used to guide the research process. It is a tentative explanation or prediction about a specific aspect of user behavior, preferences, or interaction with a product or service. The purpose of a hypothesis in UXR is to provide a starting point for investigation and to act as a framework for designing research studies and collecting relevant data. It helps researchers focus their efforts and define clear objectives for their research. A well-formulated hypothesis consists of two components: the independent variable and the dependent variable. The independent variable is the element that is manipulated or measured by the researcher, while the dependent variable is the outcome or behavior that is expected to be influenced by the independent variable. When conducting user research, a hypothesis can be used to test assumptions, validate design decisions, or explore new areas of investigation. By clearly stating the expected relationship between variables, researchers can design experiments or surveys that gather meaningful data to either support or refute the hypothesis. In conclusion, a hypothesis in the context of user research is a proposed explanation or prediction that guides the research process. It helps researchers define objectives, design experiments, and collect data to validate or challenge their assumptions about user behavior or interaction with a product or service.>

Image And Multimedia Testing

Image and multimedia testing, in the context of user-research (UXR), refers to the process of evaluating the visual and interactive aspects of images and multimedia elements within a user interface. This type of testing is aimed at assessing the effectiveness, usability, and overall user experience of these visual components.

During image and multimedia testing, researchers typically focus on various factors, including the clarity and quality of images, the relevance and comprehension of visual content, the responsiveness of interactive elements, and the overall aesthetic appeal. This involves conducting usability tests, gathering user feedback, and analyzing user behavior to identify any issues or areas for improvement within the images and multimedia elements.

Additionally, image and multimedia testing often involves evaluating the accessibility and inclusiveness of these visual components. Researchers consider factors such as color contrast, alternative text for images, captioning for videos, and other features that ensure that users with disabilities are able to perceive and engage with the content effectively.

The insights gained from image and multimedia testing help inform design decisions and guide iterative improvements to enhance the user experience. By understanding how users interact with and perceive visual elements, designers can create more engaging and user-friendly interfaces that effectively communicate information and meet the needs of the target audience.

In-Home Interviews

In-home interviews in the context of user research (UXR) refer to a research method where the researcher conducts interviews with participants in their own homes or familiar environments. This approach aims to gather insights and understand the user's needs, behaviors, and preferences by observing them in their natural settings.

By conducting interviews in participants' homes, researchers are able to gain a deeper understanding of the user's context, the way they interact with their environment, and the factors that may influence their decision-making processes. This method allows for a more comprehensive exploration of users' experiences and can uncover insights that might not be captured in a controlled lab environment.

In-Home Usage Testing (IHUT)

In-Home Usage Testing (IHUT) is a user-research technique commonly used in the field of User Experience Research (UXR).

This method involves gathering data by allowing participants to use a product or service in their own homes, under normal conditions. The goal is to understand how users interact with the product in their natural environment, providing valuable insights into their needs, preferences, and behaviors.

To conduct an IHUT, researchers typically recruit a diverse group of participants who are willing to test the product and provide feedback. These participants are given the product to use for a specific period of time, during which they are asked to document their experiences, thoughts, and observations. Researchers may also conduct interviews or follow-up sessions to gather additional insights from the participants.

Advantages of IHUT include a more realistic and authentic user experience compared to lab-based testing. It allows researchers to observe how a product fits into the users' daily routines and how it solves their problems. An IHUT also provides an opportunity to identify potential issues or areas of improvement that may not have been apparent in controlled laboratory settings.

However, it is important to note that IHUT has its limitations as well. Participants may not accurately document their experiences, or their opinions may be influenced by biases or external factors. Researchers also rely heavily on participants' self-reports and may not have complete control over the testing environment.

In conclusion, In-Home Usage Testing is a valuable user-research technique that provides insights into users' real-world experiences with products or services. It offers a more authentic and comprehensive understanding of user needs and behaviors, but researchers must be mindful of its limitations in order to draw accurate conclusions.

In-Depth Interviews

In user research, in-depth interviews refer to a qualitative research method aimed at gathering detailed and comprehensive insights from individuals. These interviews typically involve one-on-one sessions between the researcher and the participant, where the researcher asks open-ended questions to explore the participant's thoughts, experiences, opinions, and motivations related to a particular topic or area of interest.

The objective of conducting in-depth interviews in user research is to gain a deep understanding of users' needs, behaviors, and preferences. Unlike quantitative research methods, such as surveys, in-depth interviews allow for more dynamic and flexible interactions, enabling the researcher to delve into the participant's responses and probe further into specific areas of interest. By engaging in a conversation-like format, researchers can uncover rich insights that may not be captured through other research techniques.

Inclusive Design/User Testing

Inclusive Design is an approach to design that aims to create products and experiences that can be accessed, understood, and used by a wide range of people, including those with disabilities, older adults, and those from diverse cultural and linguistic backgrounds. Inclusive design goes beyond accessibility requirements to consider the diverse needs, abilities, and preferences of users.

User testing is a research method commonly used in user experience research (UXR) to evaluate the usability of a product or experience. It involves observing and gathering feedback from actual users as they interact with the product to identify usability issues, understand user behaviors and preferences, and validate design decisions.

Individual Interviews

An individual interview is a user research method in the context of user experience research (UXR) where a researcher engages in a one-on-one conversation with a participant to gather insights and feedback about a product or service.

The goal of an individual interview is to obtain an in-depth understanding of the participant's thoughts, behaviors, and experiences related to the product or service being studied. The researcher typically prepares a set of open-ended questions to guide the conversation, but also allows for flexibility to explore unexpected or interesting topics that arise during the interview.

Influencers

In the context of user research (UXR), influencers can be defined as individuals who have a significant impact on the opinions, behavior, and choices of others within a specific target audience.

These influencers often have a large following on social media platforms, such as Instagram, YouTube, or TikTok, and are able to leverage their authority and credibility to shape the opinions and preferences of their followers. They are seen as trusted sources of information and recommendations, which makes them valuable assets for companies and brands looking to promote their products or services.

Information Architecture Testing

Information Architecture Testing in the context of user-research (UXR) refers to the evaluation process of assessing the effectiveness, efficiency, and overall user experience of an information architecture (IA). It involves conducting user tests and gathering insightful feedback to ensure that the IA of a digital product or website is well-organized, intuitively structured, and easily navigable for the users.

The primary goal of information architecture testing is to identify potential usability issues and friction points within the IA, allowing UX designers and researchers to make informed decisions and improvements for enhancing the user experience. Through careful observation, data collection, and analysis, information architecture testing provides valuable insights into user's understanding, findability, and ability to accomplish tasks within the digital environment.

During an information architecture test, participants are typically given specific tasks to perform, such as finding particular content or completing specific actions (e.g., making a purchase). Their interactions, navigation patterns, and overall ease of use are closely observed and recorded. The data collected from these tests can include metrics such as task completion rates, time taken to complete tasks, and error rates.

Information architecture testing helps to identify potential navigation issues, confusing labels, missing information, or any other barriers that may hinder users from finding content or performing desired actions. It also aids in evaluating the effectiveness of the IA's labeling, grouping, and overall structure, ensuring that it aligns with the mental models of the target users.

By incorporating information architecture testing within the user-research process, UX designers and researchers can gain valuable insights into the strengths and weaknesses of the IA, making data-driven decisions to optimize the overall user experience.

Insights Repository

An insights repository, in the context of user research (UXR), refers to a centralized and organized collection of valuable findings and learnings derived from user research activities. It serves as a knowledge base that allows user researchers, design teams, and stakeholders to access and reference insights gained from past research studies.

The main purpose of an insights repository is to facilitate the storage, sharing, and retrieval of user research insights, ensuring that the knowledge gained from user research activities is easily accessible and reusable. This helps in avoiding duplication of efforts and enables teams to make data-driven decisions based on past research findings.

Insights

Insights in the context of user research (UXR) refer to the valuable and actionable understandings gained from observing and analyzing user behavior, needs, and preferences. These insights provide a deep understanding of users' motivations, pain points, and desires, allowing UX designers and researchers to make informed decisions and improve the user experience. User research aims to uncover insights by conducting various qualitative and quantitative research techniques, such as interviews, surveys, usability testing, and analytics analysis. Through these methods, designers gather data that uncovers patterns, trends, and underlying themes in user behavior and perception. Insights are derived from thorough analysis and synthesis of the collected data. Researchers identify common patterns, pain points, and motivations of the users. These insights provide the groundwork for designing user-centered solutions and experiences. By identifying and understanding users' needs and expectations, insights guide the decision-making process throughout the design and development lifecycle. They inform design choices, enable designers to prioritize features, and help optimize usability. Insights emerge from multi-faceted research, involving different user segments and contexts. They provide a holistic view of the users and uncover opportunities for innovation and improvement. Insights are often shared among cross-functional teams to align stakeholders and communicate user needs effectively. Through continuous user research and insights, UX designers can iterate and refine their designs, improving the overall user experience and increasing user satisfaction. In summary, insights in user research refer to the valuable understandings obtained through the analysis of user behavior and needs. They guide design decisions, inform strategies, and ultimately help create user-centered experiences, leading to improved user satisfaction.>

Inspectlet

Inspectlet is a user-research tool commonly used in the field of User Experience Research (UXR). It offers website heatmaps, session recordings, and analytics to gain insights into user behavior and interactions on a website or web application.

With Inspectlet, researchers can analyze how users navigate through a website, where they click, scroll, and hover their mouse. Heatmaps display this data visually, helping researchers identify popular areas of interest, areas of confusion, or potential user frustrations. This information assists in optimizing the website's design and layout for better user experience.

Instant Messaging Surveys

An Instant Messaging Survey is a user research method that involves conducting surveys through instant messaging platforms or applications. This method allows researchers to gather feedback, opinions, and data from participants in a more immediate and interactive manner, using chat-based conversations as the communication medium.

Unlike traditional survey methods that typically rely on static, one-way questionnaires or forms, instant messaging surveys provide a more conversational and dynamic experience for participants. Through the use of instant messaging platforms, such as WhatsApp, Slack, or Facebook Messenger, researchers can engage with participants in real-time, asking questions, providing clarifications, and guiding the conversation as needed.

Instant messaging surveys offer several advantages in user research. Firstly, they enable researchers to capture rich qualitative data by engaging in back-and-forth conversations with participants, allowing for deeper insights and more nuanced responses. Secondly, conducting surveys through instant messaging platforms can be more convenient for participants, as they can respond at their own pace and in their preferred environment. This can result in higher response rates and more accurate data compared to traditional survey methods.

However, instant messaging surveys also have limitations. The conversational nature of this method may lead to longer response times or incomplete responses from participants. Additionally, researchers need to take into account potential biases introduced by the chat-based format, such as the lack of non-verbal cues or the influence of social desirability. Nevertheless, instant messaging surveys provide a valuable tool for user researchers to gather qualitative data and gain a deeper understanding of user experiences and opinions.

Interactive Prototyping

Interactive prototyping is a user-research (UXR) method that involves creating a visual representation of a product's design and functionality to gather feedback and test its usability. It is an iterative process that allows designers to collaborate with users and stakeholders effectively.

The purpose of interactive prototyping is to provide a tangible and interactive experience of the product, allowing users to interact with it and provide feedback on its design, features, and overall user experience. By creating a prototype, designers can validate their design choices, uncover potential usability issues, and make informed decisions during the product development process.

Intercept Surveys

Intercept surveys are a type of user-research method used in the field of user experience research (UXR). They involve capturing feedback from users in real-time as they interact with a product or service. This type of survey is typically conducted on-site or within the context of the user's immediate interaction with the product.

Intercept surveys aim to gather insights and understand users' thoughts, feelings, and reactions while they are engaging with a specific product or service. Researchers often use this method to gain immediate feedback on a particular feature, design element, or overall user experience. Intercept surveys can be conducted using various mediums such as paper-based questionnaires, digital surveys displayed on mobile devices, or through online forms.

Intercom

Intercom is a user research tool that enables UX researchers to gather and analyze qualitative data from their target audience through in-app messaging and real-time conversations. It serves as a platform for conducting user interviews, surveys, and feedback sessions, allowing researchers to gain a deeper understanding of their users' needs, behaviors, and preferences.

With Intercom, researchers can reach out to specific segments of their user base and engage in personalized conversations, making it easier to gather rich insights. It allows for seamless communication between researchers and participants, reducing the potential for miscommunication and enabling researchers to ask follow-up questions or clarify any uncertainties in real-time.

Internationalization Testing

Internationalization testing in the context of user research (UXR) refers to a process of evaluating the functionality, usability, and overall user experience of a product or service in relation to its ability to cater to a diverse range of cultural, linguistic, and regional differences. The goal of internationalization testing is to ensure that the product or service can be used effectively and with minimal barriers by users from different countries and cultural backgrounds.

During internationalization testing, UXR professionals examine various aspects of the product or service, such as language support, localization, date and time formats, currency symbols, and cultural sensitivities. This testing process involves simulating real-world scenarios and user interactions to identify potential issues or challenges that may arise due to differences in language, culture, or context.

Interviews

Interviews are a crucial method used in user research (UXR) to gather qualitative data by conducting face-to-face conversations with individuals. It involves a structured or semi-structured interaction between a researcher and a participant, aimed at understanding the users' needs, behaviors, and preferences. The primary objective of conducting interviews in UXR is to gain in-depth insights and detailed information about the user's experiences, motivations, and thought processes.

During the interview, the researcher asks open-ended and sometimes targeted questions, actively listening and observing the participant's responses. By engaging in the interview process, researchers can explore the user's attitudes, beliefs, and emotions concerning a particular product, service, or experience. These conversations are an opportunity to recognize patterns, uncover pain points, and discover areas of improvement.

Interviews can be conducted in various formats, such as one-on-one, group, or contextual inquiries, depending on the research objectives and constraints. They can be structured, following a predetermined set of questions, or semi-structured, allowing for flexibility and adaptability based on the participant's responses. In either case, the interviewer plays a crucial role in establishing rapport and creating a comfortable environment for participants to share their perspectives openly and honestly.

By conducting interviews in UXR, researchers can gather rich qualitative data that goes beyond what can be obtained through quantitative methods alone. These insights inform the design process, facilitate empathy, and help create user-centered solutions that meet the needs and expectations of the target audience.

Intro.Js

Intro.js is a user-research tool commonly used by User Experience Researchers (UXRs) to better understand user behavior and interactions with a website or application. It is a JavaScript library that provides a simple and intuitive way to guide users through various features or aspects of a website, resulting in a more engaging and informative user experience.

With Intro.js, UXR professionals can create interactive tours or step-by-step walkthroughs that highlight specific elements or functionalities within the user interface. These tours can be customized to cater to different user segments or user tasks, ensuring that the research objectives are met effectively.

KPIs

KPIs, or Key Performance Indicators, refer to specific metrics that are used to measure the success of a user research (UXR) initiative. They provide insights into the effectiveness and impact of the research activities in meeting the desired goals and objectives. KPIs play a crucial role in evaluating the performance of the user research team and help in making informed decisions for improving the user experience.

In the context of user research, KPIs can include various quantitative and qualitative measures. Some common KPIs used in UXR may include the number of participants involved in the research, the completion rates of research activities, the time taken to achieve research objectives, the level of user satisfaction, and the improvement in UX metrics such as user engagement, task success rate, or conversion rates.

Kano Model Surveys

Kano Model Surveys are a user-research method used in UX research to understand customer preferences and satisfaction levels regarding specific product features. The Kano Model is a theory developed by Dr. Noriaki Kano in the 1980s, which classifies customer preferences into five categories: Must-Be, One-Dimensional, Attractive, Indifferent, and Reverse.

Must-Be attributes are basic features that customers expect to be present in a product and are taken for granted. If these attributes are not met, customers will be extremely dissatisfied. One-Dimensional attributes are the desirable features that directly impact customer satisfaction. The more these features are present and improved, the more satisfied customers become. Attractive attributes are unexpected features that surprise and delight users, exceeding their expectations. These attributes can differentiate a product from its competitors. On the other hand, Indifferent attributes do not significantly affect customer satisfaction, as their presence or absence does not impact the overall experience. Finally, Reverse attributes are features that customers do not want or find annoying, and their presence can lead to dissatisfaction.

Kissmetrics

Kissmetrics is a user research tool commonly used in the field of User Experience Research (UXR). It provides extensive insights into user behavior and helps businesses optimize their websites, products, and services based on data-driven decisions.

With Kissmetrics, UXR professionals can track and analyze user interactions, such as clicks, conversions, and journey paths, throughout the website or app. The tool offers features like cohort analysis, funnel visualization, and A/B testing, allowing researchers to dive deep into the user experience and understand how different elements impact user behavior.

Knowledge Sharing

Knowledge sharing in the context of user research (UXR) can be defined as the process of transferring and exchanging information, insights, and expertise among individuals or teams within an organization, with the aim of improving the collective understanding of users and their needs.

This involves the dissemination of user research findings, methods, and best practices to relevant stakeholders, such as designers, developers, product managers, and other interested parties. The goal of knowledge sharing in UXR is to foster collaboration, encourage informed decision-making, and ultimately enhance the overall user experience of a product or service.

Laddering Technique

The laddering technique is a qualitative research method commonly used in user research (UXR) to gain a deeper understanding of users' attitudes, beliefs, and motivations. It aims to uncover the underlying reasoning behind users' preferences and decision-making processes. In this technique, the researcher asks participants a series of open-ended questions to elicit their thoughts and feelings. The questions are designed to probe beyond surface-level responses and delve into the underlying values and meaning attributed to certain behaviors or choices. The laddering technique is rooted in the theory of cognitive mapping, where respondents construct mental maps of their thoughts and associations. The process involves systematically exploring the connections between three key elements: attributes, consequences, and values. Attributes represent the specific features or characteristics of a product or experience, consequences refer to the outcomes or impacts of those attributes, and values relate to the personal importance or significance attached to those consequences. By continuously probing deeper with each question, the laddering technique helps uncover the hierarchical relationship between these elements. Each subsequent question builds upon the previous answer, progressively climbing the ladder to extract more detailed and nuanced information. The laddering technique is valuable in user research as it provides insights into users' underlying motivations and enables the identification of unmet needs or opportunities for improvement. Understanding the hierarchy of attributes, consequences, and values helps inform the design and development of user-centered products and experiences. Overall, the laddering technique is a powerful tool in user research that helps researchers uncover users' underlying thoughts, beliefs, and motivations by systematically exploring the connections between attributes, consequences, and values.>

Leadership

Leadership, in the context of user research (UXR), can be defined as the ability to guide and influence a team or organization towards achieving user-centered goals and objectives. It involves effectively managing a group of researchers and collaborating with stakeholders to ensure that user insights are integrated into the decision-making process.

A successful UX leader possesses several key qualities, including strong communication skills, empathy, adaptability, and a deep understanding of both the user's needs and the business goals. They are responsible for fostering a culture of empathy and continuous learning within the research team, encouraging collaboration and open communication among team members.

Leadership in UXR involves leading by example, demonstrating a commitment to user-centered design principles, and advocating for the value of research in informing strategic decisions. UX leaders also play a critical role in mentoring and developing the skills of the researchers, providing guidance, and ensuring that the team has the necessary resources to conduct effective research.

Furthermore, leadership in user research encompasses the ability to navigate complex organizational structures and influence stakeholders at various levels. This includes presenting research findings in a compelling manner, translating insights into actionable recommendations, and driving change by advocating for the user's perspective.

In conclusion, leadership in the field of user research is about effectively guiding and influencing a team or organization towards creating user-centered experiences. It requires a combination of strong communication, empathy, and strategic thinking skills to integrate user insights into decision-making processes and drive meaningful change.

Load Testing

Load testing is a method used in user-research (UXR) to evaluate the performance and stability of a website or application under normal and peak usage conditions. It involves simulating real-time user interactions to measure the system's response time, reliability, and resource usage.

During load testing, the website or application is subjected to a high volume of concurrent user requests, simulating the expected load it will experience in the production environment. This allows researchers to identify any bottlenecks or performance issues that may arise when multiple users access the system simultaneously.

Localization Testing

Localization testing is the process of evaluating a user interface or software application to ensure that it is culturally and linguistically adapted for a specific target audience in different geographical regions. This type of testing focuses on verifying that the application functions properly and displays content correctly in different languages, using appropriate regional settings and formatting conventions.

During localization testing, user researchers assess several aspects of the application's localized version. This includes validating the accuracy and consistency of translations, checking for any truncation or text overflow issues, and ensuring that the text is aligned correctly within the interface. They also examine the application's compatibility with various character sets, fonts, and input mechanisms specific to the target regions.

LogRocket

LogRocket is a user research tool that helps UX researchers gain insights into user behavior on websites and applications. It captures and records user interactions such as clicks, scrolls, and form submissions, as well as any errors or exceptions that occur during the user session.

With LogRocket, UX researchers can playback user sessions to better understand how users interact with their product. They can pinpoint areas of friction or confusion in the user interface and use this information to make data-driven decisions for improving the user experience.

Longitudinal Surveys

A longitudinal survey is a research method used in the field of user research (UXR) to collect data from the same group of participants over a period of time. It aims to observe and understand changes in user behavior, preferences, and attitudes by collecting data at multiple intervals.

In a longitudinal survey, participants are selected based on specific criteria and are asked to complete the survey at different points in time, such as weekly, monthly, or yearly. The surveys are designed to capture longitudinal data, which allows researchers to analyze trends or patterns that emerge over time.

The main advantage of using longitudinal surveys in user research is the ability to track changes and developments in user experiences and perceptions. By collecting data from the same group of participants over time, researchers can gain deeper insights into the long-term impact of design changes, product updates, or UX interventions.

Additionally, longitudinal surveys enable researchers to assess the stability or consistency of user behaviors and preferences. By comparing data collected at different time points, researchers can identify whether certain trends are temporary or long-lasting.

However, longitudinal surveys also have some limitations. They require a longer time commitment from both the participants and the researchers, making them more resource-intensive. There is also a risk of attrition, as participants may drop out or lose interest over time.

Lookback

Lookback in the context of user research (UXR) refers to the process of reviewing and analyzing recorded sessions of user interactions with a product or service.

During a user research study, researchers typically conduct interviews, observe users performing tasks, or conduct usability tests. Lookback allows researchers to revisit and analyze these recorded sessions to gain valuable insights into user behavior, preferences, and pain points.

Loop11

Loop11 is a user research tool used by UX researchers to gather quantitative and qualitative data about user interactions with a digital product or website. It is a web-based platform that enables researchers to create and run remote usability tests, surveys, and other research studies.

With Loop11, researchers can create tasks and scenarios for participants to complete, track their interactions with the product, and collect their feedback and opinions. The tool provides various features to design and customize the research studies, such as branching logic, participant tracking, and survey integration. Loop11 also offers features to recruit participants, either by providing a testing panel or by integrating with external participant recruitment platforms.

During a research study, Loop11 records and logs the participants' actions, including mouse movements, clicks, and time spent on each task. The platform also captures participants' feedback through open-ended questions or structured surveys. Researchers can then analyze the collected data using various visualizations and statistical analysis tools provided by Loop11.

Overall, Loop11 aids UX researchers in understanding user behavior, identifying pain points, and evaluating the effectiveness of design solutions. The tool is designed to be user-friendly, allowing researchers to conduct remote studies easily and efficiently. It provides researchers with valuable insights into user experiences, helping them make data-driven decisions to improve the usability and user satisfaction of a digital product or website.

Machine Learning Model Validation

Machine Learning Model Validation in the context of user research (UXR) refers to the process of evaluating the performance and accuracy of a machine learning model that has been developed for a specific user experience purpose.

This validation process involves several steps. First, the model is trained using a labeled dataset, where the desired user experience outcomes are clearly defined. The model then undergoes testing using a separate dataset to assess its ability to accurately predict these outcomes based on new, unseen data.

The validation process also includes assessing the model's generalizability - how well it performs on different datasets and in real-world scenarios beyond the training and testing data. Additionally, the model's sensitivity to different input variations and potential biases is explored to ensure fair and reliable results for diverse user groups. Various metrics, such as accuracy, precision, recall, and F1 score, are computed to provide a comprehensive evaluation of the model's performance.

By conducting rigorous machine learning model validation in user research, researchers and practitioners can ensure that the developed model aligns with the desired user experience goals, performs reliably across different datasets and scenarios, and does not introduce any unintended biases or unfairness. This validation process helps to build trust in the model's predictions and enables data-driven decision-making to enhance the user experience in various domains such as recommendation systems, personalization, and user interface design.

Market Advertising Testing

Market advertising testing is a user research technique that aims to evaluate the effectiveness and impact of advertising campaigns in the target market. It involves collecting feedback and data from users to assess how well the advertisements resonate with the target audience and whether they effectively convey the intended message.

During market advertising testing, participants are typically exposed to various advertisements, which can include print, TV, radio, online, or any other form of media, depending on the campaign. Participants are then asked to provide their opinions and impressions about the ads, as well as their likelihood to engage with or respond to them.

Market Affiliate Marketing Analysis

Affiliate marketing is a market analysis technique that involves promoting products or services through third-party affiliates who earn a commission for each sale they generate.

In the context of user-research (UXR), market affiliate marketing analysis refers to the process of studying and understanding the effectiveness and impact of affiliate marketing strategies on user behavior and preferences. It involves evaluating how users engage with affiliate marketing content and determining its influence on their decision-making process.

Market Ambient Advertising Analysis

A market ambient advertising analysis in the context of user-research (UXR) refers to the examination and evaluation of ambient advertising strategies within a specific market or industry. Ambient advertising, also known as experiential marketing or guerilla advertising, involves promoting products or services in unconventional and unexpected ways in the environment where the target audience resides. It utilizes elements of surprise, creativity, and immersion to engage and captivate consumers.

In a market ambient advertising analysis, user-researchers study the impact and effectiveness of these unconventional marketing techniques on the target audience. This research aims to uncover insights into how ambient advertising influences consumer behavior, perception, and purchasing decisions. It involves conducting interviews, surveys, observations, and usability testing to gather qualitative and quantitative data.

Market Basket Analysis

Market Basket Analysis, in the context of user research (UXR), refers to the method of analyzing and identifying relationships between products or items that users tend to purchase together. It is based on the concept that if certain items are frequently bought together, they may share some association or dependence.

This analysis technique is used to uncover patterns and insights in users' purchasing behavior, providing valuable information for businesses in various sectors, including e-commerce and retail. By understanding these associations, businesses can optimize their marketing, sales, and user experience strategies to increase customer satisfaction, cross-selling opportunities, and overall revenue.

Market Benchmarking

Market benchmarking is a user-research practice used in the field of UX research to evaluate and compare a product or service against its competitors within a specific market. This technique allows researchers to understand how well a product or service is performing in relation to its competitors, identify areas for improvement, and gather insights that can guide the design and development process.

The process of market benchmarking involves collecting data on various metrics such as usability, user satisfaction, user engagement, and other relevant indicators. This data is then compared to data from competitors to determine how the product or service measures up. By analyzing this data, researchers can identify strengths and weaknesses, identify areas where the product or service is outperforming or underperforming the competition, and uncover opportunities for improvement.

Market Broadcast Advertising Analysis

Market broadcast advertising analysis refers to the process of systematically evaluating and interpreting the impact and effectiveness of advertisements that are broadcasted in various media channels such as television, radio, and online platforms. This analysis is often conducted as part of user research (UXR) to gain insights into the users' perception, preferences, and behavior towards these advertisements.

Through market broadcast advertising analysis, UX researchers aim to understand how users engage with the advertisements, whether they find them informative, persuasive, or entertaining. The analysis involves collecting and analyzing data related to key metrics such as reach, frequency, recall, recognition, attention, and emotional response. These metrics help in assessing the effectiveness of the advertisements in capturing and retaining users' attention, delivering the intended message, and driving desired user actions.

Market Buzz Marketing Analysis

Market Buzz Marketing Analysis refers to the process of conducting user research to evaluate the impact and effectiveness of marketing strategies on generating buzz and word-of-mouth in the market. It involves gathering insights and feedback from users to understand their perceptions, attitudes, and behaviors in relation to a brand or product.

User-research (UXR) plays a crucial role in Market Buzz Marketing Analysis as it focuses on understanding the experience and preferences of users. Through various methods such as surveys, interviews, and usability testing, UXR professionals collect and analyze data to determine the reach and influence of marketing campaigns in creating buzz.

Market Cause Marketing Analysis

Cause marketing is a marketing strategy that involves a partnership between a for-profit company and a non-profit organization or cause. This strategy aims to promote the company's products or services while also raising awareness and support for the chosen cause.

The concept of cause marketing emerged in the 1980s and has gained significant popularity and traction since then. Companies are increasingly recognizing the importance of social responsibility and the positive impact it can have on their brand image and consumer loyalty. By aligning themselves with a cause, companies can demonstrate their commitment to making a difference and engage their customers in supporting that cause.

Market Channel Analysis

Market Channel Analysis in the context of user research (UXR) refers to the systematic examination and evaluation of the different channels or platforms used by a company to reach and interact with its target market or customers. It involves understanding and analyzing the various channels through which a company communicates, sells, promotes, and delivers its products or services to its customers.

The goal of market channel analysis is to gain insights into how users or customers interact with different channels and how these channels contribute to their overall experience with the company's products or services. This analysis helps in identifying the strengths and weaknesses of each channel, understanding the preferences and behaviors of customers within each channel, and determining the most effective strategies to improve the overall user experience and increase customer satisfaction.

Market Competitive Analysis

A market competitive analysis, in the context of user research (UXR), is a systematic examination and evaluation of the competitive landscape in a specific market or industry. It involves gathering and analyzing information about competitors, their products or services, and their strategies to gain a better understanding of how they are positioning themselves in the market.

During a market competitive analysis, a UXR professional may conduct thorough research to identify and review competitors' websites, user interfaces, and overall user experiences. This research may also involve studying competitors' marketing materials, customer reviews, and social media presence.

The goal of a market competitive analysis is to gain insights into competitors' strengths, weaknesses, opportunities, and threats. By understanding how competitors are meeting user needs and preferences, a UXR professional can identify areas where their own product or service can differentiate and improve upon the competition.

Through a market competitive analysis, a UXR professional can also identify potential opportunities for collaboration or strategic partnerships, as well as determine potential threats that may impact the success of their own product or service in the market.

Overall, a market competitive analysis in UXR provides valuable insights for decision-making, product development, and strategic planning, helping businesses improve their user experience and gain a competitive advantage in the market.

Market Competitor Analysis

Market Competitor Analysis in the context of user research (UXR) refers to the process of identifying and evaluating the strengths and weaknesses of competing products, services, or companies within a specific market. This analysis aims to gather insights into the competitive landscape to inform the design and development of a product or service that meets the needs and preferences of users while addressing the gaps and opportunities in the market.

During a market competitor analysis, a UXR professional assesses the features, functionality, and user experience of competing products or services through various research methods such as usability testing, expert reviews, and comparative analysis. The analysis involves examining the target market, understanding user preferences, and benchmarking against key competitors to identify areas of differentiation or improvement. By understanding how competitors are meeting user needs, UXR practitioners can identify potential gaps or pain points in the market that can be addressed through innovative design or enhanced user experience.

Market Content Marketing Analysis

Market content marketing analysis is a user research technique used to evaluate the effectiveness of content marketing strategies within a specific market or industry. As part of the user research process, it involves collecting and analyzing data to gain insights into how potential users and customers interact with content produced by a company or organization.

By conducting market content marketing analysis, user researchers aim to understand the preferences, needs, and behaviors of target audiences in relation to the content they consume. This includes examining the types of content that resonate most with users, the channels through which they discover and engage with content, and the impact of content on their decision-making process. The analysis also explores how users perceive and interpret the messaging, tone, and value proposition conveyed through the content.

Market Demand Analysis

Market demand analysis is a user-research approach used in the field of User Experience Research (UXR) to gather and analyze data on the attractiveness and viability of a product or service in the market. It involves conducting research to understand the needs, preferences, and behaviors of target users, as well as their willingness to pay for the product or service.

During a market demand analysis, UXR professionals employ various methods to collect both qualitative and quantitative data. Qualitative methods, such as interviews and focus groups, help uncover deep insights into users' desires, pain points, and motivations. On the other hand, quantitative methods involve surveys and analytics to collect measurable data on user preferences, market trends, and competitive landscapes.

Once the data is collected, market demand analysis involves analyzing and synthesizing the findings to identify patterns, trends, and opportunities. This analysis helps inform product strategy, design decisions, and marketing efforts to align them with customer needs and expectations. By understanding the market demand, organizations can make informed decisions about resource allocation, prioritize features, and identify opportunities to differentiate their product or service.

In conclusion, market demand analysis is a crucial component of user-research in the field of UX. It helps gather insights into user preferences and behaviors, allowing organizations to create products and services that better meet customer needs and expectations. By employing various research methods, analyzing data, and identifying market trends, organizations can stay competitive and deliver valuable products to the market.

Market Digital Marketing Analysis

Market Digital Marketing Analysis is a user-research technique focused on analyzing and evaluating digital marketing efforts in order to gain insights that can inform strategic decision-making and improve the user experience. This analysis involves examining various marketing channels, such as social media, search engine advertising, email marketing, and content marketing, to assess their effectiveness and impact on user behavior and engagement.

The primary goal of Market Digital Marketing Analysis is to provide data-driven insights into the effectiveness of marketing strategies and tactics, as well as to identify areas for improvement and optimization. It involves gathering and analyzing data from multiple sources, including web analytics tools, social media platforms, email marketing software, and customer feedback. By examining key metrics such as reach, engagement, conversion rates, and ROI, this analysis helps to assess the overall performance of digital marketing efforts and identify trends and patterns that can drive decision-making and improve user experience.

Market Direct Mail Marketing Analysis

In user research (UXR), market direct mail marketing analysis refers to the process of gathering, analyzing, and interpreting data related to direct mail marketing campaigns in order to gain insights and inform decision-making.

During market direct mail marketing analysis, UXR professionals collect and examine various metrics and indicators, such as response rates, conversion rates, customer segmentation, and return on investment (ROI), to evaluate the effectiveness and success of direct mail campaigns. This analysis often involves comparing different campaigns, target segments, or creative elements to identify trends, patterns, and areas for optimization.

Market Direct Marketing Analysis

A market direct marketing analysis, in the context of user research (UXR), refers to the systematic process of gathering and evaluating data to understand the effectiveness and impact of direct marketing strategies on target markets. It involves collecting and analyzing information about user behaviors, preferences, and attitudes towards direct marketing efforts.

The ultimate goal of a market direct marketing analysis is to provide insights that can inform the development and improvement of direct marketing campaigns. This analysis helps organizations understand how their target audience responds to various marketing tactics such as email campaigns, social media advertising, and direct mail. By studying user behavior and preferences, UXR professionals can identify gaps or areas for improvement in their marketing strategies.

Market Distribution Analysis

Market Distribution Analysis is a user-research method used in the field of user experience (UX) research. It involves analyzing the distribution channels and strategies used by companies to distribute their products or services to the target market.

The goal of Market Distribution Analysis is to understand how companies reach their customers and the effectiveness of their distribution strategies. This research method helps UX researchers gain insights into the user journey and identify any pain points or areas for improvement in the distribution process.

Market Dynamics Analysis

Market Dynamics Analysis in the context of user research (UXR) refers to the systematic examination and interpretation of the factors and conditions that influence the behavior, needs, and preferences of a target market. It involves the study of various aspects such as economic, social, cultural, technological, and competitive factors, as well as consumer trends and behaviors.

The purpose of conducting market dynamics analysis in user research is to gain a deep understanding of the external factors that impact user experiences and behaviors. It helps researchers identify opportunities, challenges, and potential risks in relation to a product or service. By comprehensively examining the market dynamics, UXR professionals can make informed decisions and develop strategies that align with the needs and expectations of the target audience.

Market E-Commerce Marketing Analysis

E-commerce marketing analysis refers to the process of analyzing various marketing strategies and techniques used in the e-commerce industry. This analysis aims to understand the effectiveness of these strategies in attracting and retaining customers and driving sales. It involves examining data from different marketing channels, such as social media, search engine optimization (SEO), email marketing, and paid advertising, to gain insights into the performance of these channels and make data-driven decisions.

User research (UXR) plays a crucial role in e-commerce marketing analysis. It focuses on understanding the needs, preferences, and behaviors of the target audience to improve the user experience and optimize marketing efforts. Through user research, insights can be gathered through methods like surveys, interviews, usability testing, and analytics data analysis.

Market Email Marketing Analysis

Email marketing analysis in the context of user research (UXR) refers to the process of conducting research and analysis on email marketing campaigns to understand user behaviors, preferences, and responses towards the content and design of the emails. This analysis helps to optimize the effectiveness of email marketing by identifying strengths, weaknesses, and opportunities for improvement. During the user research phase, data is gathered from various sources such as email open rates, click-through rates, conversion rates, and user feedback. This data is then analyzed to gain insights into the audience's engagement with the emails, the impact of the email content on user actions, and any barriers or pain points that may be hindering the desired outcomes. Through email marketing analysis, user researchers aim to uncover patterns and trends in user behavior, identify successful email strategies, and pinpoint areas for refinement. This analysis can involve the evaluation of subject lines, email templates, personalization techniques, and call-to-action placement, among other factors. By understanding user preferences and behaviors through email marketing analysis, companies can tailor their email campaigns to better meet user needs, improve user engagement, and achieve their marketing goals. Ultimately, this analysis helps to drive the optimization of email marketing initiatives and enhance the overall user experience with the brand's communication efforts.

Market Entry Analysis

A market entry analysis in the context of user research (UXR) refers to the process of assessing the feasibility and potential success of entering a new market or introducing a new product or service into an existing market. This analysis involves conducting thorough research and gathering insights to understand the target market, user needs, competitive landscape, and potential barriers to entry. To effectively conduct a market entry analysis, user researchers utilize various qualitative and quantitative research methods. These methods may include surveys, interviews, usability testing, focus groups, market research, and competitive analysis. The primary objective of a market entry analysis is to provide valuable insights that inform decision-making and minimize risks associated with entering a new market. By understanding the target market's needs, preferences, and behaviors, organizations can tailor their offerings to effectively meet user demands and gain a competitive advantage. Through user research, market entry analysis can yield valuable information regarding market potential, target audience segmentation, market size, market trends, user pain points, and opportunities for differentiation. This information enables businesses to develop customer-centric strategies, refine their offerings, establish pricing strategies, identify potential partnerships, and develop effective marketing campaigns to successfully enter or expand into a new market. Overall, a market entry analysis conducted through user research is an essential step in mitigating risks, understanding user needs, and maximizing the chances of success when entering a new market or introducing a new product or service.>

Market Event Marketing Analysis

Market event marketing analysis refers to the process of evaluating the effectiveness and impact of marketing events in a specific market or industry. It involves gathering and analyzing data related to various marketing events such as trade shows, conferences, product launches, and promotional campaigns. The goal of this analysis is to understand the overall impact of these events on the target audience, as well as to identify any areas for improvement and optimization.

During the user research (UXR) process, market event marketing analysis can provide valuable insights into how users perceive and engage with different marketing events. By conducting user interviews, surveys, and observations, researchers can collect qualitative and quantitative data to evaluate the effectiveness of marketing events in achieving their objectives. This analysis can help identify user preferences, satisfaction levels, and areas of improvement for future events.

Market Exit Analysis

Market Exit Analysis is a user-research method that focuses on understanding why users leave a particular market or stop using a product or service. It aims to identify the factors that contribute to market exit and gather insights to inform decision-making and improve user experience.

During Market Exit Analysis, user researchers employ various techniques to gather data and insights from users who have exited the market. These may include conducting surveys, interviews, and usability testing with these users to understand their motivations, reasons, and experiences that led to their decision to no longer use the product or service.

The primary objective of Market Exit Analysis is to uncover the pain points, frustrations, and shortcomings that users encountered, leading to their exit. By understanding these aspects, businesses can identify areas for improvement and make informed decisions to address these issues, enhance their product or service, and retain users.

Through Market Exit Analysis, businesses can gain valuable insights into user behavior, preferences, and perceptions that may have contributed to market exit. These insights can help inform product development, marketing strategies, and overall business decisions to attract and retain more users in the market.

Market Experiential Marketing Analysis

Experiential marketing, in the context of user-research (UXR), refers to a marketing approach that focuses on creating immersive and memorable experiences for customers. This form of marketing aims to engage users on a personal level, encouraging them to actively interact with a brand and its products or services.

The goal of experiential marketing is to establish a deeper and more meaningful connection between the user and the brand. By providing users with unique and engaging experiences, companies aim to foster positive emotions, brand loyalty, and word-of-mouth marketing. Through user-research, experiential marketing allows companies to gain insights on users' behaviors, preferences, and attitudes towards the brand and its offerings.

Market Feasibility Analysis

A Market Feasibility Analysis, in the context of user-research (UXR), refers to the systematic assessment of a potential market for a product or service to determine its viability. This analysis involves gathering and analyzing data about the target audience, competitors, market trends, and customer needs and preferences.

During the market feasibility analysis, UXR professionals conduct various research methods, such as surveys, interviews, and observation, to gain insights into the potential users' behaviors, attitudes, and expectations related to the product or service. They aim to understand the problems and pain points that users face and assess whether the proposed solution aligns with their needs.

Furthermore, the analysis includes examining the competitive landscape to identify key competitors, their offerings, and the market share they hold. This helps in understanding the market dynamics, identifying gaps or opportunities, and determining the differentiation strategies needed to succeed.

By conducting a market feasibility analysis, UXR professionals can validate the demand and potential success of a product or service. The findings from this analysis assist in making informed decisions about product development, positioning, pricing, and marketing strategies. Ultimately, the goal is to ensure that the product or service meets the needs and expectations of the target market, leading to a higher likelihood of market acceptance and success.

Market Forecasting

The market forecasting in the context of user research (UXR) refers to the process of predicting the future performance and trends of a specific market based on data-driven analysis and research. It involves using various qualitative and quantitative research methods to gather relevant and accurate information about market conditions, customer preferences, industry trends, and competitor analysis.

Market forecasting in UXR requires the collection and analysis of both primary and secondary research data. Primary research involves directly interacting with users, customers, and industry experts through interviews, surveys, and usability testing. This helps in understanding user needs, preferences, and behaviors, which play a critical role in determining market forecasts. Secondary research involves gathering data from existing sources like market reports, industry publications, and historical data, to validate and supplement primary research findings.

The market forecasting process in UXR typically includes analyzing market size, market segmentation, potential market growth, competitive landscape, and other relevant factors. This analysis helps in identifying market opportunities, potential customer segments, and assessing the feasibility of new product or service offerings. Additionally, it helps businesses in making informed decisions related to pricing strategies, go-to-market plans, and resource allocation.

By leveraging market forecasting in UXR, businesses can anticipate market trends, identify target audience preferences, and align their product development and marketing strategies accordingly. This helps in optimizing user experience, increasing customer satisfaction, and driving business growth and profitability.

Market Gap Analysis

A market gap analysis in the context of user research (UXR) refers to the process of identifying and evaluating the opportunities and shortcomings in the market that can be addressed through the development of user-centered solutions. It involves analyzing the gap between the existing products or services in the market and the needs, preferences, and pain points of the target users.

During a market gap analysis, UXR professionals aim to understand the current state of the market, the competitive landscape, and the expectations of users. They gather data through various research methods such as interviews, surveys, and usability testing to gain insights into customer expectations, identify unmet needs, and uncover areas where existing solutions fail to satisfy users.

The analysis of the market gap helps inform the design and development of new products or services that can fill the identified gaps and meet the unmet needs of users. It helps companies gain a competitive advantage by creating innovative solutions that better align with user expectations, resulting in improved user satisfaction, higher adoption rates, and increased market share.

This process is crucial for UXR professionals as it ensures that the solutions they design are user-centered and address real-world problems, resulting in a more successful and impactful product or service in the market.

Market Growth Analysis

Market Growth Analysis is a method used in user research (UXR) to examine and understand the growth potential of a particular market segment or industry. It involves collecting and analyzing various data points and market trends to determine the past, current, and future performance of the market. This analysis helps businesses gain insights into the opportunities and challenges they may face when entering or expanding in a specific market.

During Market Growth Analysis, UX researchers gather and assess quantitative and qualitative data related to market size, customer preferences, industry trends, and competitor analysis. They use techniques such as surveys, interviews, and data analysis to gather information and identify market opportunities. By understanding market growth potential, businesses can make informed decisions regarding product development, marketing strategies, and expansion plans.

Market Guerrilla Marketing Analysis

Market guerrilla marketing analysis is a research process in UX design that involves studying and evaluating the effectiveness of guerrilla marketing strategies in the target market. Guerrilla marketing refers to the unconventional and low-cost promotional activities used by businesses to create a buzz and generate brand awareness.

The analysis aims to gain insights into the impact of guerrilla marketing techniques on user perceptions, attitudes, and behavior. It involves comprehensive data collection and analysis of various marketing campaigns, including their objectives, execution methods, target audience, and outcomes.

During the market guerrilla marketing analysis, UX researchers conduct user interviews, surveys, and observational studies to understand how users perceive and respond to these unconventional marketing tactics. They explore factors such as the level of engagement, emotional response, brand recall, and overall brand perception.

By analyzing the data collected, UX researchers can identify patterns and trends in user behavior and determine the effectiveness of guerrilla marketing strategies. This analysis helps businesses make informed decisions about the incorporation of guerrilla marketing techniques into their overall marketing strategy.

In conclusion, market guerrilla marketing analysis in UX research involves evaluating the impact of unconventional marketing tactics on user perceptions and behavior. Through data collection and analysis, researchers gain insights into the effectiveness of these strategies and inform decision-making for future marketing efforts.

Market Influencer Marketing Analysis

Market influencer marketing analysis in the context of user-research (UXR) refers to the examination and assessment of the impact and effectiveness of influencer marketing campaigns in the market. This analysis involves studying the behaviors, attitudes, and opinions of users towards influencer marketing initiatives and their perception of the influencers themselves.

Through user-research methods such as surveys, interviews, and observation, UXR professionals gather data and insights on how users engage with influencer content, whether it influences their purchasing decisions, and how it affects their overall perception of brands. The goal is to understand the level of trust, authenticity, and credibility that users attribute to influencer endorsements and collaborations.

Market Landscape Analysis

A market landscape analysis is a research method used in user research (UXR) to gain a comprehensive understanding of the competitive landscape and market trends within a specific industry or market segment.

During a market landscape analysis, the user researcher collects and analyzes data and information from various sources, such as market reports, industry publications, competitor websites, and user feedback. The purpose of this analysis is to identify key players in the market, understand their offerings, and uncover potential gaps or opportunities for the product or service being researched.

Market Maturity Analysis

Market maturity analysis in the context of user research (UXR) refers to the process of evaluating the current stage of a market in terms of its growth and development. It involves assessing the level of competition, the size of the target audience, and the level of adoption of products or services within the market.

Through market maturity analysis, UXR professionals aim to gain a comprehensive understanding of the market dynamics and trends that may impact user behavior and preferences. This helps them in designing user-centered strategies and experiences that are aligned with the market's maturity stage.

Market Needs Analysis

A market needs analysis, in the context of user research (UXR), refers to the process of identifying and evaluating the needs, wants, and preferences of a target market or user base. It involves conducting research and collecting data to understand the underlying challenges and requirements of the users so that the product or service can be designed or improved accordingly.

Through market needs analysis, UXR professionals aim to gain insights into user behaviors, expectations, pain points, and motivations. They utilize various research methods such as surveys, interviews, usability testing, and analytics to gather relevant data and observations. By analyzing this information, UXR teams can identify patterns, trends, and gaps in the market, enabling them to make informed decisions regarding product development, user experience design, and marketing strategies.

Market Opportunity Analysis

A market opportunity analysis, in the context of user research (UXR), refers to the process of assessing and evaluating potential opportunities for a business or organization to enter or expand into a specific market segment. It involves gathering and analyzing data and insights about the target market, competition, customer needs, and market trends to identify areas of potential growth and profitability.

The purpose of conducting a market opportunity analysis in user research is to enable businesses to make informed decisions and develop targeted strategies that align with user needs and preferences. It helps UXR professionals understand the market landscape, identify gaps or unmet needs, and evaluate the potential demand for a product or service.

During the market opportunity analysis, UXR professionals gather data through various research methods, such as surveys, interviews, and observation. They analyze customer behavior, preferences, and pain points to uncover opportunities that can lead to competitive advantages and attract target customers.

By conducting a thorough market opportunity analysis, businesses can identify the right market segments to target, define their value proposition, and create products or services that meet the specific needs of their target audience. It also helps in identifying potential barriers, challenges, or risks associated with entering a new market, allowing businesses to develop appropriate strategies to mitigate them.

Market Outdoor Advertising Analysis

Market outdoor advertising analysis refers to the process of gathering and analyzing data related to outdoor advertising campaigns or strategies. It involves research methods used to understand the effectiveness, reach, and impact of outdoor advertisements on target audiences.

As a part of user research (UXR), market outdoor advertising analysis aims to provide insights into how outdoor advertising influences user behavior, attitudes, and perceptions. It helps in evaluating the success of advertising campaigns, identifying the most effective channels, and informing decisions on message placement, design, and targeting.

Market PESTEL Analysis

PESTEL analysis is a framework used in user research (UXR) to analyze and understand the external factors that may have an impact on a market or industry. It helps UXR professionals to assess the political, economic, sociocultural, technological, environmental, and legal aspects that can shape the market dynamics and influence user perceptions and behaviors.

Political factors refer to the government policies, regulations, and stability that can affect the market. It includes factors such as taxation policies, trade regulations, and political stability, which can impact user preferences and experiences.

Economic factors focus on the economic conditions that can influence the market. This includes factors like inflation rates, employment levels, and consumer spending patterns, which can affect user purchasing power and willingness to pay.

Sociocultural factors consider the cultural, social, and demographic trends that can impact the market. This includes factors such as social norms, cultural attitudes, and population demographics, which can influence user behavior, preferences, and expectations.

Technological factors analyze the technological advancements and innovations that can shape the market. It includes factors like digitalization, automation, and disruptive technologies, which can impact user experiences and create new opportunities or challenges.

Environmental factors examine the environmental and ecological aspects that can affect the market. This includes factors such as climate change, sustainability, and environmental regulations, which can influence user attitudes towards eco-friendly products or services.

Legal factors consider the legal and regulatory frameworks that can impact the market. This includes factors like intellectual property rights, consumer protection laws, and industry-specific regulations, which can shape user trust and affect market competitiveness.

Market Pay-Per-Click (PPC) Advertising Analysis

Market Pay-Per-Click (PPC) Advertising Analysis in the context of user-research (UXR) refers to the process of thoroughly examining the effectiveness and impact of Pay-Per-Click advertising campaigns in the market.

PPC advertising involves placing ads on search engine results pages (SERPs) or websites, where advertisers pay a fee each time their ad is clicked. UXR focuses on evaluating the user experience and understanding user behavior to improve the overall effectiveness of marketing strategies.

Market Penetration Analysis

Market penetration analysis is a method utilized in user research (UXR) to assess the market share or penetration of a product or service within a specific target audience or market segment. It involves gathering data and insights from users and potential customers to understand the existing usage and adoption rates of a particular product or service within the target market.

Through market penetration analysis, UXR professionals aim to determine how well a product or service is gaining traction and acceptance among its intended users. By conducting surveys, interviews, and observations, researchers gather valuable information about users' awareness, familiarity, frequency of use, and satisfaction with the product or service being evaluated.

Market Positioning Analysis

Market positioning analysis is a research technique used in user experience research (UXR) to determine how a product or service is perceived by its target audience compared to its competitors. It involves gathering data and insights from users to understand their perceptions, preferences, and needs related to a particular product or service.

Through market positioning analysis, UXR professionals aim to identify the unique value proposition and differentiating factors of a product or service in order to effectively position it in the market. This analysis helps businesses understand their target audience's perception of their product or service, as well as the strengths and weaknesses of competitors' offerings.

During the research process, UXR professionals employ various methods such as surveys, interviews, and usability testing to gather relevant information from users. These insights are then analyzed to identify patterns, trends, and common themes that shape the market perception of the product or service.

In addition, market positioning analysis may involve conducting a competitive analysis to gain a comprehensive understanding of the competitive landscape. By examining competitor products or services, UXR professionals can determine how their own offering compares and how it can be positioned to stand out in the market.

Overall, market positioning analysis in user research helps businesses make informed decisions about product development, marketing strategies, and brand positioning. By understanding how their target audience perceives their product or service, businesses can create a competitive advantage and effectively communicate their value to customers.

Market Price Analysis

Market Price Analysis refers to the process of gathering, analyzing, and interpreting data related to the pricing of products or services in a specific market. It involves studying the various factors that influence pricing decisions, such as supply and demand dynamics, competitor prices, customer preferences, and market trends. The goal of market price analysis is to gain insights into the pricing strategies of businesses and to understand how prices impact consumer behavior and market competitiveness.

In the context of user research (UXR), market price analysis focuses on understanding how price influences user behavior, preferences, and decision-making processes. By conducting market price analysis, UXR professionals can uncover valuable insights into how users perceive the value of a product or service based on its price. This helps businesses optimize their pricing strategies to better meet user expectations and achieve their revenue goals.

Market Pricing Strategy Testing

Market pricing strategy testing refers to the research process of evaluating and analyzing the effectiveness of different pricing strategies in a market context. It aims to determine the most optimal pricing strategy that maximizes profitability, market share, and customer satisfaction.

This type of user research (UXR) involves gathering feedback, conducting experiments, and performing quantitative and qualitative analysis to assess the impact of various pricing strategies on user behavior and decision-making. The insights gained from market pricing strategy testing help businesses understand how users perceive and respond to different pricing models, such as cost-based pricing, value-based pricing, competitive pricing, or penetration pricing.

Market Print Advertising Analysis

The market print advertising analysis, in the context of user research (UXR), is the process of evaluating and understanding the effectiveness and impact of print advertisements in the market. This analysis aims to gather insights and data to inform decision-making regarding the design, content, placement, and targeting of print advertisements.

Through the market print advertising analysis, researchers can assess various elements of print advertisements, such as their visual appeal, messaging clarity, call-to-action effectiveness, and overall brand communication. By conducting interviews, surveys, and usability tests, UXR professionals can gather feedback from users to gain an understanding of their perceptions, preferences, and behaviors towards print advertisements.

Market Promotions Testing

The term "Market Promotions Testing" in the context of user research (UXR) refers to the process of evaluating and analyzing different marketing promotions or strategies to determine their effectiveness in engaging and converting target users or customers. This type of testing is commonly conducted to gather insights and data that can be used to optimize marketing campaigns, attract potential customers, and drive desired actions.

Market promotions testing often involves designing experiments or A/B tests to compare multiple variations of a promotional message, offer, or design element. These variations can include different headlines, visuals, calls-to-action, or pricing strategies. By presenting these variations to different segments of users or customers and analyzing their responses, UXR professionals can identify which promotion or strategy performs better in terms of generating interest, increasing click-through rates, conversions, or other desired metrics.

Market Public Relations (PR) Analysis

Market Public Relations (PR) analysis in the context of user research (UXR) refers to the examination and evaluation of the communication efforts and strategies used by a company or brand to promote their products or services to the general public and key stakeholders. This analysis focuses on understanding how the company's PR activities impact the target audience's perception, knowledge, and preferences.

Through market PR analysis, UXR professionals gather data and insights on various aspects of a company's public relations initiatives. This includes examining press releases, media coverage, social media campaigns, events, sponsorships, and other communication channels utilized by the company. The goal is to understand how these activities affect the overall brand reputation, consumer sentiment, and market positioning.

By conducting market PR analysis, UXR professionals can uncover valuable insights about the effectiveness of the company's PR strategies. They can identify areas of improvement, determine if the messaging is aligned with the target audience's values and preferences, and assess the impact of PR efforts on brand perception. This analysis provides crucial information for optimizing PR campaigns, refining messaging strategies, and enhancing the overall brand communication approach.

Ultimately, market PR analysis enables UXR professionals to understand how a company's PR activities influence the target audience's perception and behavior. It helps to identify key opportunities, mitigate potential risks, and align the company's communication efforts with the needs and expectations of the target market.

Market Retail Marketing Analysis

A Market Retail Marketing Analysis, in the context of user-research (UXR), refers to the process of evaluating and studying the marketing strategies and tactics employed by retail businesses in a particular market. This analysis aims to understand how these strategies and tactics impact the user experience and behavior of customers.

Through market retail marketing analysis, user researchers can gather valuable insights about the effectiveness of various marketing initiatives, such as advertising campaigns, promotions, product displays, and pricing strategies, among others. By studying their impact on user behavior, researchers can identify areas where improvements can be made to enhance the customer experience and drive sales.

Market Risk Analysis

Market risk analysis refers to the process of evaluating and understanding the potential risks and uncertainties associated with a specific market or industry. In the context of user research (UXR), market risk analysis involves gathering and analyzing data related to user preferences, behaviors, and market trends in order to identify potential risks and opportunities for a product or service.

The goal of market risk analysis in UXR is to inform the design and development process by providing insights into user needs and expectations, as well as the competitive landscape. This analysis helps UX researchers and designers make informed decisions about the features, functionality, and overall user experience of a product or service. During market risk analysis, UX researchers may collect and analyze various types of data, including demographic information, user feedback and opinions, market trends, and competitor analysis. By examining this data, researchers can identify potential risks such as changing user preferences, emerging market trends, or competitive threats that may impact the success of a product or service. By understanding and addressing market risks through research, UX designers can develop strategies to mitigate potential challenges and maximize opportunities. This analysis helps to ensure that the final product or service meets user expectations, aligns with market trends, and is positioned for success in the competitive landscape.

Market SWOT Analysis

A market SWOT analysis is a strategic planning tool used in user research (UXR) to evaluate the strengths, weaknesses, opportunities, and threats of a specific market or industry. It enables UXR professionals to have a comprehensive understanding of the market dynamics, competitor landscape, and potential opportunities for their product or service.

The analysis begins by identifying the strengths of the market, which include its unique selling points, competitive advantages, and favorable conditions. These factors help to highlight the positive aspects that can be capitalized on to drive success. On the other hand, weaknesses refer to the internal factors that hinder the market's growth or competitiveness. UXR professionals assess the market's weaknesses to identify areas that require improvement or attention.

Opportunities are external factors that indicate potential avenues for growth, innovation, or expansion within the market. UXR professionals study these opportunities to develop strategies that align with market trends and leverage untapped potential. Lastly, threats refer to external factors that can pose challenges or risks to the market's growth. These threats could include emerging competitors, changing customer preferences, or economic factors.

By conducting a market SWOT analysis, UXR professionals can gain insights into the overall market landscape, identify any gaps or areas of improvement, and make informed decisions on product positioning, user experience design, and market entry strategies. It serves as a valuable framework to guide user research activities and align them with the broader goals and objectives of the organization.

Market Sales Channel Testing

Market sales channel testing, in the context of user research (UXR), refers to the process of evaluating and analyzing different sales channels to understand their effectiveness in reaching and converting customers. It involves testing various methods and platforms through which a company distributes and sells its products or services to gain insights into their impact on user experience and sales performance.

During market sales channel testing, UXR professionals gather data and feedback from users to identify the strengths and weaknesses of each sales channel. This may involve conducting interviews, surveys, or usability tests to understand user preferences, behaviors, and expectations. By comparing different sales channels, researchers can determine which ones are most effective in driving conversions, generating revenue, and delivering a positive user experience.

>

Market Saturation Analysis

Market saturation analysis in the context of user research (UXR) refers to the assessment of the level of market saturation for a particular product or service. It involves understanding the extent to which the market is already saturated with similar offerings and how this impacts the potential success and adoption of the product or service being studied.

During market saturation analysis, the UXR team gathers data on the competitive landscape, existing market share, and consumer preferences to determine the level of saturation. This analysis helps in identifying potential opportunities and challenges for the product or service. By understanding the level of saturation, the team can make informed decisions regarding product differentiation, positioning, and marketing strategies.

Market Scanning

A market scanning in the context of user research (UXR) refers to the process of gathering relevant information about a particular market or industry in order to better understand user needs, behaviors, and preferences. It involves systematically collecting and analyzing data from various sources to identify market trends, opportunities, and potential challenges.

Market scanning in UXR typically starts with defining the scope of the research and identifying the target audience. Researchers then conduct a comprehensive review of available market reports, industry publications, and online resources to gain insights into the market landscape, competition, and customer segmentation. This may involve analyzing market size, growth rates, market share, customer demographics, and market trends.

Additionally, market scanning in UXR often involves gathering qualitative data through interviews, focus groups, or surveys with potential users or existing customers. This helps to understand their needs, pain points, preferences, and motivations. Researchers may also

74

analyze user-generated content such as online reviews, social media discussions, and customer support interactions to uncover valuable insights.

The information obtained through market scanning is then used to inform the design and development of products or services that meet the identified user needs and align with market trends. It allows UXR teams to make data-driven decisions, identify opportunities for innovation, and adapt their strategies to ensure a competitive edge in the market.

Market Search Engine Marketing (SEM) Analysis

Semantic search engine marketing (SEM) analysis is a user research technique used to assess the effectiveness of a website or online advertising campaign in targeting the desired market audience. It involves analyzing the data collected from search engine marketing campaigns to gain insights into user behavior, preferences, and needs.

The SEM analysis begins by collecting data from various search engines and online advertising platforms. This data includes the number of impressions, clicks, click-through rates, bounce rates, and conversions. The data is then analyzed to identify trends, patterns, and insights about user behavior and preferences.

By examining the SEM data, user researchers can understand the effectiveness of different keywords, ad copies, landing pages, and targeting strategies in attracting and engaging the target audience. This analysis helps in optimizing the online advertising campaigns by identifying successful tactics and refining the underperforming ones. It also provides valuable insights into user preferences, which can be used to enhance the overall user experience and tailor the website or campaign to better meet the needs of the audience.

In conclusion, SEM analysis in the context of user research is a valuable technique for understanding user behavior and preferences in online advertising campaigns. By analyzing the data collected from search engines and online platforms, user researchers can gain insights to optimize campaigns and improve the overall user experience.

Market Search Engine Optimization (SEO) Analysis

Market Search Engine Optimization (SEO) Analysis is a process of evaluating and assessing the performance and visibility of a website in search engine results pages (SERPs) for specific keywords or phrases related to the market or industry it operates in. This analysis aims to identify opportunities and areas of improvement in order to enhance the website's visibility, increase organic traffic, and ultimately improve its search engine rankings.

During a Market SEO Analysis, various factors are considered, including keyword relevance, website structure and architecture, on-page and off-page optimization, content quality and relevance, backlink profile, and user experience. By analyzing these factors, marketers can identify the strengths and weaknesses of their website's SEO strategy and make informed decisions to optimize it.

The analysis begins with keyword research to identify the most relevant and high-performing keywords in the market. Marketers then examine the website's content, both on the page and off the page, to optimize it for these keywords. Additionally, they assess the website's technical infrastructure, such as its URL structure, sitemap, and internal linking, to ensure it is easily crawlable by search engines.

Furthermore, the analysis may involve evaluating the website's backlink profile, checking the quality and relevance of incoming links, and identifying opportunities to build authoritative and relevant links. Lastly, marketers assess the overall user experience of the website, including its loading speed, mobile-friendliness, and user interface, which are important factors considered by search engines for ranking purposes.

Market Segmentation Analysis

Market segmentation analysis is a research technique conducted in the field of user research (UXR) to divide a target market into distinct subsets or segments based on specific characteristics or behaviors. It involves gathering and analyzing data about the target market to identify patterns and trends, which can then be used to understand and target different groups of users effectively.

Through market segmentation analysis, UXR practitioners aim to gain insights into the diverse needs, preferences, and behaviors of different user segments within a target market. This allows them to tailor their products, services, or experiences to meet the specific requirements of each segment. By understanding the unique characteristics of each segment, UXR professionals can design user-centric solutions, create targeted marketing strategies, and optimize user experiences.

Market Sensing

Market sensing is a user-research practice in the field of user experience research (UXR) that involves gathering information and insights about the market conditions, trends, and preferences in order to understand the needs and expectations of users.

The goal of market sensing is to gain a deep understanding of the market dynamics, such as user demographics, behaviors, and motivations. This research helps UX researchers and designers make informed decisions and develop user-centric solutions that meet the needs of the target market.

>

Market Share Analysis

Market share analysis is a user-research method that examines the distribution and relative strength of a company or product in a specific market. It involves gathering data and analyzing the market share of various competitors or products to understand how well a particular company or product is performing compared to others in the market.

The purpose of conducting market share analysis is to identify market trends, evaluate competition, and assess the success of a company or product in a particular industry. By understanding the market share, companies can make informed decisions regarding their marketing strategies, product development, and overall business growth.

Market Simulation

A market simulation is a research methodology used in user research (UXR) to study the behavior and preferences of users in a controlled environment that mimics real-life market conditions. This approach allows researchers to observe and analyze how users interact with products, services, or designs, providing valuable insights for product development and marketing strategies.

In a market simulation, participants are typically given specific tasks or scenarios to complete, such as purchasing a product or comparing different options. The simulation aims to replicate real market dynamics, including factors such as pricing, competition, and limited resources, to create a realistic context for users to make decisions and provide feedback.

The objectives of conducting market simulations in user research include understanding user preferences, identifying potential usability issues, testing different product or service variations, and evaluating the effectiveness of marketing strategies. By observing user behavior, researchers can gather quantitative and qualitative data to inform design decisions and optimize user experiences.

Market simulations can take various forms, including in-person or online studies, prototypes, or interactive virtual environments. The choice of simulation method depends on the research goals, target audience, budget, and resources available. Regardless of the format, market simulations provide a valuable opportunity to iterate and refine designs, validate assumptions, and gain deep insights into user needs and expectations.

Market Size Estimation

Market size estimation is a research method used by user researchers (UXRs) to determine the potential size of a market. It involves collecting and analyzing data to understand the total value of a specific market segment or industry.

UXRs conduct market size estimations to gain insights into the potential demand for a product or service, identify market opportunities, and make informed decisions about product development, marketing strategies, and investment plans.

Market Social Media Marketing Analysis

A marketing social media marketing analysis is a user-research method that aims to understand how social media platforms are used in marketing campaigns. It involves the systematic collection and analysis of data from social media platforms to gain insights into user behaviors, preferences, and trends in relation to marketing efforts.

During a marketing social media marketing analysis, UXR professionals examine various aspects of social media marketing, such as target audience engagement, content effectiveness, campaign performance, and social media trends. They may use a combination of qualitative and quantitative research methods to gather data, including surveys, interviews, observation, and analytics tools.

The analysis helps businesses and marketers better understand their target audience's needs, preferences, and behaviors on social media. By understanding how users engage with marketing content on social media, companies can optimize their marketing strategies and improve their campaigns' effectiveness.

The findings of the analysis can inform decision-making processes, such as campaign planning, content creation, platform selection, and budget allocation. Additionally, marketers can use the insights to measure the success of their social media marketing efforts, identify areas for improvement, and make data-driven decisions to drive business growth.

Market Sponsorship Marketing Analysis

Market sponsorship marketing analysis refers to the process of conducting research and analysis to evaluate the effectiveness and impact of sponsorship marketing strategies within a specific market. It involves gathering data and insights related to sponsorship initiatives and the market in which they operate, with the goal of understanding how these initiatives are perceived by consumers and how they contribute to the overall marketing objectives of the sponsoring brand.

Market sponsorship marketing analysis entails various UXR techniques and methodologies, such as surveys, interviews, and focus groups, to gather qualitative and quantitative data from target audiences and stakeholders. This research helps uncover consumer attitudes, preferences, and behaviors towards sponsorship marketing, as well as the effectiveness of specific sponsorship campaigns and activations. By analyzing this data, researchers can identify potential gaps, challenges, and opportunities in sponsorship marketing strategies, and recommend insights and recommendations for optimizing future sponsorship initiatives.

Market Strategy Testing

Market strategy testing, in the context of user research (UXR), refers to the process of evaluating and validating marketing strategies or approaches with the target audience or consumer base.

It involves gathering feedback, insights, and data from users to assess the effectiveness, viability, and potential impact of specific marketing strategies or campaigns. This helps businesses understand how their target audience perceives and responds to different marketing messages, channels, and tactics.

Market strategy testing is essential in user research because it enables businesses to refine their marketing efforts based on real user feedback. By directly involving users in the evaluation process, organizations can gain valuable insights regarding user preferences, motivations, and needs. This, in turn, helps them tailor their marketing strategies to be more relevant, engaging, and impactful.

Market strategy testing often involves various research methods such as surveys, interviews, focus groups, or usability testing. These methods allow businesses to gauge user perceptions, attitudes, and behaviors towards different marketing strategies and messaging. The collected data can then be analyzed to identify patterns, trends, and key insights to inform decision-making and optimize marketing campaigns.

Overall, market strategy testing in user research plays a crucial role in ensuring that businesses understand their target audience's preferences and align their marketing efforts accordingly. By leveraging user insights, organizations can effectively position their products or services, enhance user experiences, and drive successful marketing campaigns.

Market Supply Analysis

Market supply analysis is a research method employed in the field of user research (UXR) to understand the availability, quantity, and distribution of products or services in a specific market. It involves examining the various factors that impact the supply side of a market, such as production capabilities, price levels, resource availability, and competition.

Through market supply analysis, UXR professionals aim to gain insights into how different suppliers operate within a market and how their offerings meet or fail to meet customer needs. This analysis involves collecting and analyzing data on supply chain networks, production capacities, pricing strategies, and product/service specifications.

Market Targeting Analysis

Market targeting analysis in the context of user-research (UXR) refers to the process of identifying and evaluating specific groups of users or customers who would benefit most from a product or service. It involves examining user demographics, behavior, preferences, and needs, in order to understand the target market better and tailor the user experience accordingly.

The goal of market targeting analysis is to narrow down the focus of user research efforts and ensure that the product or service meets the specific requirements and expectations of the target market. By identifying the target audience, researchers can create more relevant and user-centered designs, features, and functionalities.

Market Telemarketing Analysis

Market Telemarketing Analysis refers to the process of gathering and analyzing data related to telemarketing campaigns and their impact on the market. It involves conducting research and collecting information about the effectiveness of telemarketing strategies and their influence on consumer behavior, market trends, and sales performance.

During the Market Telemarketing Analysis, user-research (UXR) plays a crucial role in understanding the experiences, perspectives, and behaviors of individuals who have been targeted by telemarketing efforts. UXR helps identify the effectiveness of different marketing techniques, the level of customer satisfaction, and the potential for improvement in telemarketing strategies.

Market Trade Show Marketing Analysis

Market Trade Show Marketing Analysis is a user research process that focuses on studying the effectiveness of marketing strategies and tactics used during trade shows. It involves evaluating the impact of various marketing activities conducted before, during, and after a trade show event.

During Market Trade Show Marketing Analysis, user researchers gather qualitative and quantitative data to understand the success of different marketing efforts, such as booth designs, promotional materials, presentations, and attendee engagement. They conduct interviews, surveys, and observations to gain insights into the target audience's perceptions, preferences, and behaviors. By analyzing this data, researchers can identify strengths and weaknesses in the marketing approach and make data-driven recommendations to optimize future trade show marketing efforts.

Market Trend Analysis

Market trend analysis in the context of user research (UXR) is the process of examining and analyzing patterns and changes in the market to gain insights into user behavior, preferences, and expectations. It involves collecting and interpreting data on market trends, such as consumer behavior, market size, competitor analysis, and industry shifts, in order to inform and improve the design and development of products or services for a specific target audience.

Market trend analysis helps UXR professionals understand the current state of the market and identify emerging trends that may impact user experiences. By studying market trends, UXR professionals can gain a deeper understanding of user needs and desires, as well as identify potential opportunities for innovation and competitive advantage. This analysis provides valuable input for the creation of user personas, user journeys, and other design tools that guide the development of user-centered products or services.

Market Trend Forecasting

Market trend forecasting is a strategic process used in the field of user research (UXR) to predict and analyze future changes or developments in the market. It involves gathering and analyzing data from various sources to identify patterns, trends, and shifts in consumer behaviors, preferences, and market conditions.

The goal of market trend forecasting in the context of user research is to gain insights and understanding of the potential impact on user experience and inform decision-making processes. By anticipating future market conditions, UXR professionals can proactively adapt and optimize products, services, and solutions to meet the evolving needs and expectations of users.

Market Viral Marketing Analysis

Market Viral Marketing Analysis is a research method used in User Experience Research (UXR) to analyze the impact and effectiveness of viral marketing campaigns in the market. Viral marketing refers to marketing strategies that aim to spread rapidly through online sharing and word-of-mouth, engaging users to actively share and promote a product, service, or brand to others.

The analysis involves evaluating the reach, engagement, visibility, and impact of viral marketing campaigns through various channels such as social media, email, blogs, and video platforms. UXR professionals conduct research to understand the motivations and behaviors of users who engage with viral marketing content, as well as the reactions and responses of the target audience.

Through market viral marketing analysis, researchers can identify the elements that make a campaign successful, including the content, message, timing, and target audience. This analysis helps businesses to refine their marketing strategies, optimize their campaign content, and effectively leverage viral marketing to enhance brand awareness, increase user engagement, and drive business growth.

By studying the data and insights gained from market viral marketing analysis, UXR professionals can provide valuable recommendations to businesses on how to create and implement effective viral marketing campaigns. They can also help in identifying potential challenges, risks, and opportunities associated with viral marketing, empowering businesses to make informed decisions and allocate resources strategically.

Maze

Mental Model Diagrams

Mental Model Diagrams in the context of user-research (UXR) refer to visual representations that depict the underlying cognitive processes, beliefs, and expectations of individuals interacting with a product or system. These diagrams aim to capture the users' mental models, which are their internal representations and understandings of the product or system, its functionality, and how it should be used.

By using Mental Model Diagrams, UXR practitioners can gain insights into users' thought processes, motivations, and behaviors when interacting with a product. These diagrams help uncover patterns, gaps, and areas for improvement in the user experience. They provide a visual structure to illustrate the mental connections, associations, and hierarchies that users have constructed to make sense of the product or system.

Mentorship

Mentorship in the context of user research (UXR) is a professional relationship in which an experienced researcher, known as the mentor, provides guidance, support, and knowledge to a less experienced researcher, known as the mentee. The mentor serves as a trusted advisor and role model, helping the mentee develop their skills, knowledge, and understanding of user research practices.

This relationship is characterized by open and transparent communication, mutual respect, and a commitment to the growth and development of the mentee. The mentor provides guidance and feedback on various aspects of user research, including study design, data collection methods, analysis techniques, and reporting. They share their own experiences and lessons learned, helping the mentee avoid common pitfalls and navigate challenges effectively.

Mentorship in user research is not just about imparting technical knowledge. It also includes providing emotional support and encouragement to the mentee, helping them gain confidence in their abilities and overcome imposter syndrome. The mentor acts as a sounding board for the mentee's ideas and provides constructive criticism to help them refine their research skills.

The ultimate goal of mentorship in user research is to foster the mentee's professional growth and success. This may involve providing opportunities for the mentee to collaborate on projects, connect with other professionals in the field, and gain exposure to different research methodologies and domains.

Methods

Methods in the context of user research (UXR) refer to the systematic techniques or approaches that are used to gather data and insights about users' needs, preferences, and behaviors. These methods enable researchers to understand users, their context of use, and their interaction with a product or system. In UXR, methods can be broadly categorized into qualitative and quantitative methods. Qualitative methods focus on gathering in-depth, subjective data through techniques such as interviews, observations, and usability testing. These methods help researchers uncover users' motivations, attitudes, and pain points, providing rich and contextual insights. Qualitative methods are particularly useful for exploring new ideas, uncovering underlying issues, and generating design recommendations. On the other hand, quantitative methods involve gathering data in a more structured and numerical manner. Surveys, questionnaires, and analytics are common quantitative methods used in UXR. These methods provide statistical data and numerical analysis, allowing researchers to understand patterns, trends, and measure the impact of design changes. Quantitative methods are helpful for evaluating the usability of a product, measuring user satisfaction, and making data-driven decisions. In addition to qualitative and quantitative methods, UXR also encompasses mixed-methods approaches. Mixed-methods involve the combination of both qualitative and quantitative techniques to gain a more holistic understanding of users. By triangulating findings from different methods, researchers can validate and corroborate their insights. Overall, the choice of methods in UXR depends on the research objectives, the stage of the design process, and the available resources. The selection of appropriate methods should align with the research goals and provide meaningful insights to inform design decisions.>

Metrics

Metrics in the context of user-research (UXR) refer to quantifiable measures that are used to assess and evaluate various aspects of user experience. These measures help UXR professionals to collect and analyze data in order to gain insights, make informed decisions, and track the progress of design improvements.

There are several types of metrics commonly utilized in UXR, including:

1. *Usability Metrics:* These metrics focus on evaluating the usability of a product or system. They often involve measures such as task completion time, error rate, and user satisfaction ratings. Usability metrics provide insights into how efficient, effective, and satisfying a user's experience is when interacting with a product or system.

2 . *Engagement Metrics:* These metrics aim to gauge the level of user engagement and involvement with a product or system. They can include measures such as time spent on a website or app, frequency of visits, and number of interactions. Engagement metrics help UXR professionals understand how users are interacting with a product and identify opportunities for improving engagement.

3. *Conversion Metrics:* These metrics are focused on measuring the effectiveness of a product or system in converting users' actions or behaviors into desired outcomes. Conversion metrics can include measures such as click-through rates, sign-up rates, or purchase rates. By analyzing conversion metrics, UXR professionals can identify areas of improvement to optimize the user experience and drive desired user actions.

In conclusion, metrics play a crucial role in user-research (UXR) by providing quantifiable measures to evaluate and understand various aspects of user experience. Usability, engagement, and conversion metrics are commonly used to gain insights, track progress, and inform decision-making in designing user-centered products or systems.

Microinteractions Surveys

A microinteraction is a small, focused user interface element that is designed to communicate and engage with users during their interaction with a product or system. These interactions are often subtle and occur in response to specific user actions, such as clicking a button or hovering over an element. Microinteractions serve to provide feedback, guide users through a process, or provide information or confirmation about an action.

In the context of user research (UXR), surveys can be used to gather feedback and insights from users regarding their experience with microinteractions. Surveys are a common method in UXR that involve asking a series of questions to a sample of users in order to collect quantitative or qualitative data about their preferences, opinions, or behaviors. By specifically focusing the survey questions on microinteractions, researchers can gain valuable insights into how users perceive and interact with these small interface elements.

Mixpanel

Mixpanel is a user-analytics tool that is commonly used in user-research (UXR). It provides insights and data on how users interact with a product, allowing researchers to analyze and understand user behavior.

As a UXR tool, Mixpanel offers various features that help researchers track and measure user actions within a product or website. It utilizes event tracking, where researchers can define specific events or actions they want to monitor. These events could include anything from clicking a button to completing a purchase. By tracking these events, researchers can gain valuable insights into how users navigate through a product and identify any pain points or areas for improvement.

Mobile App Surveys

A mobile app survey in the context of user-research (UXR) refers to a method of collecting data and feedback from mobile app users in order to gain insights on their experiences, preferences, and satisfaction levels with the app. It is a structured questionnaire or set of questions designed to gather specific information about the app's usability, functionality, design, and overall user experience.

This type of survey can be conducted through various means, such as in-app pop-ups, push notifications, email invitations, or social media advertisements. It typically involves a combination of multiple-choice questions, rating scales, and open-ended questions to capture both quantitative and qualitative data.

The primary goals of mobile app surveys in user-research are to understand user behavior and attitudes, identify pain points or areas for improvement, measure user satisfaction, and inform decision-making for app enhancements or updates. The collected data can provide valuable insights for UX designers, product managers, and developers to optimize the app's performance, usability, and user engagement.

Mobile app surveys are an effective tool for user-research as they allow for direct feedback from the target audience, enabling app owners to align their product roadmap with user needs and expectations. By leveraging these surveys, organizations can enhance the user experience, increase user retention, and gain a competitive edge in the mobile app market.

Mobile App Testing

Mobile app testing is the process of evaluating the functionality, usability, and performance of a mobile application to ensure its effectiveness and user satisfaction. It involves conducting a series of tests and evaluations to identify any bugs, errors, or usability issues that may impact the overall user experience.

During mobile app testing, user-research (UXR) plays a vital role in gathering valuable insights and feedback from target users. UXR focuses on understanding user behaviors, preferences, and needs in relation to the app's interface and features. It involves observing and interviewing users, analyzing user interactions and responses, and collecting data to inform design decisions and improvements.

Moderated Remote Usability Testing

Moderated remote usability testing is a user research method used in the field of user experience research (UXR) to evaluate the usability of a digital product or service. In this method, participants are remotely located and interact with the product or service under observation while being guided and moderated by a researcher.

The process involves the researcher and the participant connecting remotely using a variety of communication tools such as video conferencing software, screen sharing, or remote collaboration platforms. The researcher provides instructions and tasks to the participant, who then performs them on the product or service being tested. The researcher closely observes and takes notes, asking follow-up questions and probing for more detailed feedback as needed.

Moderated remote usability testing allows for a more comprehensive understanding of user interactions and experiences with a digital product or service, as it combines the advantages of remote testing (e.g., convenience, access to geographically diverse participants) with the benefits of live moderation (e.g., real-time feedback, ability to clarify any misunderstandings).

This method is particularly useful when face-to-face testing is not possible or practical, such as when participants are located in different geographic regions or when it is necessary to maintain physical distance, as in the case of remote work or global pandemics. It provides rich qualitative insight into user behavior, preferences, and challenges, enabling researchers to identify usability issues and improvements that can inform the design and development process.

Overall, moderated remote usability testing is a valuable tool in a UX researcher's toolkit, allowing them to gather user feedback and observations in real-time, even when participants are located remotely.

Moderated Virtual Reality User Interviews

Moderated virtual reality user interviews are a method used in user research (UXR) to gather qualitative data and insights about user experiences in virtual reality (VR) environments. This approach involves a trained moderator guiding participants through a series of tasks or scenarios within a VR system, while conducting a structured interview.

The process of conducting moderated virtual reality user interviews typically begins with the moderator explaining the purpose of the study and obtaining informed consent from participants. The moderator then provides instructions on how to use the VR headset and controllers, ensuring that participants feel comfortable and familiar with the equipment.

During the session, the moderator carefully observes participants' interactions, behaviors, and reactions within the VR environment, as well as any challenges or frustrations they may encounter. The moderator may prompt participants with questions to gather more detailed feedback about their experiences, preferences, and suggestions for improvement.

Moderated virtual reality user interviews offer several advantages in user research. They provide an opportunity to directly observe user behavior and reactions in a controlled virtual environment, which can yield rich qualitative data. This method allows researchers to gain a deeper understanding of user experiences, identify usability issues, and gather feedback early in the development process.

Overall, moderated virtual reality user interviews serve as an effective means for uncovering insights and informing the design and improvement of VR experiences, ultimately enhancing user satisfaction and engagement.

Moderation Guide

A Moderation Guide in the context of user research (UXR) refers to a document or set of instructions that outlines the guidelines and procedures for conducting and managing the moderation of user research sessions. The main purpose of a moderation guide is to ensure consistency and effectiveness in the research process by providing the moderator with clear directions and prompts to follow during each session. The moderation guide typically includes a detailed description of the research objectives and goals, the target user group, and the specific tasks or scenarios to be explored during the session. It also outlines the structure and flow of the session, including the introduction, warm-up exercises, task instructions, and debriefing activities. The guide provides the moderator with specific questions and prompts to ask the participants to gather insights and feedback. These questions are designed to elicit valuable information and uncover user behaviors, needs, and preferences. The guide may also include instructions on how to handle certain scenarios or situations that may arise during the session, such as technical issues or participant hesitation. Furthermore, the moderation guide serves as a reference for the moderator to ensure consistency and uniformity across multiple research sessions. It helps maintain a standardized approach to gathering data and enables comparability between different sessions and participants. Overall, a moderation guide is an essential tool for conducting successful user research sessions. It ensures that moderators follow a consistent and systematic process, leading to reliable and meaningful insights that can inform the design and development of user-centric products and experiences.>

Moderation

Moderation is a vital component of user research (UXR) that involves managing and overseeing research sessions to ensure effective and unbiased data collection. It is the responsibility of the moderator to facilitate the research process by creating a conducive environment for participants to express their thoughts, opinions, and behaviors.

The role of the moderator in user research is to guide and control the conversation, ensuring that the session stays on track and the research objectives are met. This involves setting the tone for the session, establishing rapport with participants, and asking open-ended questions to encourage them to share their experiences and insights.

Additionally, a skilled moderator employs active listening techniques to understand and interpret participants' feedback accurately. They remain neutral and objective throughout the session, avoiding bias and leading questions that could influence the participant's responses. Moderators also have the responsibility to address any potential biases that may arise from their own preconceived notions or assumptions.

Furthermore, moderation includes recording and documenting the findings and observations during the research session. This could involve taking notes, capturing audio or video recordings, or using specialized user research tools. The collected data is then analyzed and synthesized to derive meaningful insights that inform design and development decisions.

Multivariate Testing

Multivariate testing, in the context of user research (UXR), refers to a method of conducting experiments to evaluate and optimize various combinations of elements within a design or user interface. This type of testing allows researchers to analyze the impact of multiple variables simultaneously, providing valuable insights into how different factors contribute to the overall user experience.

With multivariate testing, researchers can assess the effects of different combinations of elements such as layout, color scheme, typography, button placement, content, and much more. By creating different variations of these elements and randomly assigning them to participants, researchers can gather data on which combinations lead to the most favorable user outcomes, such as improved task completion rates, higher engagement, or increased conversions.

Mystery Shopping Surveys

Mystery Shopping Surveys in the context of user-research (UXR) refer to a method of gathering information from users about their experiences with a product or service. This research technique involves hiring individuals, known as mystery shoppers, who visit or interact with a business or website to evaluate its customer experience. Mystery shopping surveys are designed to simulate real-world scenarios and capture detailed feedback on various aspects of the user journey.

These surveys are carefully crafted to assess the usability, functionality, and overall user satisfaction of a product or service. They typically include a series of questions that prompt mystery shoppers to provide their opinions, observations, and ratings based on their interactions. By anonymizing the identity of the mystery shoppers, businesses can gather authentic user feedback without bias.

Mystery Shopping

Mystery Shopping is a research methodology used in user research (UXR) to evaluate the quality of service provided by a company or organization from the perspective of a customer. It involves hiring individuals, known as mystery shoppers, who pose as normal customers and interact with the company's products, services, or employees. These mystery shoppers follow predefined scripts or scenarios, designed by the UXR team, to simulate real customer experiences.

The objective of mystery shopping is to gather valuable insights and firsthand experiences that help the UXR team identify strengths, weaknesses, and areas of improvement in the company's customer service, product offerings, and overall user experience. By collecting data on various aspects such as employee behavior, product knowledge, response time, cleanliness, and overall customer satisfaction, mystery shopping provides a comprehensive assessment of the company's performance from a customer's standpoint.

Narrative Inquiry

Narrative inquiry in the context of user research (UXR) refers to a research method that aims to understand the experiences, perspectives, and stories of individuals through the collection and analysis of narrative data. It involves gathering rich, qualitative data from participants through interviews, observations, and other storytelling techniques.

This method allows researchers to explore the lived experiences of users, uncovering their thoughts, emotions, and motivations. By capturing the stories and narratives of users, researchers can gain deeper insights into how individuals interact with products, services, or systems, and how these experiences shape their attitudes and behaviors.

Natural Language Processing (NLP) Model Validation

Natural Language Processing (NLP) Model Validation refers to the process of evaluating the performance and accuracy of a NLP model in the context of user-research (UXR). NLP models are designed to understand and interpret human language, enabling machines to communicate and interact with humans in a more natural and intuitive way.

During the validation phase, UXR professionals assess the NLP model's ability to accurately understand, process, and respond to user inputs. This typically involves testing the model against a variety of user queries, analyzing the model's responses, and comparing them to the expected outcomes. The goal is to measure how well the NLP model performs in delivering the intended user experience and meeting the specific requirements of the user-research project.

Navigation Testing

Navigation testing in the context of user research (UXR) refers to the evaluation and assessment of the effectiveness, efficiency, and user satisfaction with the navigation interface of a website or application. This type of testing aims to understand how easily and successfully users are able to navigate through the different sections, pages, and features of a digital product. During navigation testing, researchers observe and measure users' interactions, behavior, and feedback related to navigating through the product. This includes tasks such as finding specific information, accessing particular features or functionalities, and moving between different parts of the interface. The goal of navigation testing is to identify any potential issues or challenges users may encounter when navigating, as well as pinpoint opportunities for improvement and optimization. By conducting navigation testing, UXR practitioners gain insights into the information architecture, labeling, organization, and overall usability of the navigation system. This helps in identifying any areas that may confuse or frustrate users, as well as understanding their mental models and expectations. The findings from navigation testing can inform design decisions, such as the placement of navigation elements, the visibility of important links, and the overall structure of the interface. This iterative testing process allows designers and developers to refine and enhance the navigation system, ultimately leading to a more user-friendly and intuitive experience. In conclusion, navigation testing plays a crucial role in user research as it helps assess the effectiveness and efficiency of a website or application's navigation interface. By understanding the challenges users face during navigation, designers and developers can improve the overall usability and user experience of the product.>

Net Promoter Score (NPS) Surveys

Net Promoter Score (NPS) Surveys are a commonly used user research method in the field of User Experience Research (UXR). NPS surveys aim to measure customer satisfaction and loyalty by asking a single question: "On a scale of 0 to 10, how likely are you to recommend our product/service to a friend or colleague?"

This question is designed to assess the likelihood of customers referring others to the product or service, which is considered a strong indicator of customer satisfaction and loyalty. NPS surveys typically include an open-ended follow-up question asking respondents to provide reasons for their rating, enabling deeper understanding of their sentiments.

Netnography

Netnography is a research methodology commonly used in the field of user research (UXR) to study and analyze online communities and their behavior in order to gain insights into user needs, preferences, and experiences. It involves the systematic observation, collection, and interpretation of data from online communities, such as social media platforms, discussion forums, and blogs.

Netnography enables researchers to observe and understand how users interact with each other and with online products or services. By immersing themselves in these online communities, researchers can capture authentic and real-time information about users' opinions, behaviors, and motivations. This method allows for a deep understanding of the context in which user experiences occur and helps identify patterns, trends, and social dynamics within these communities.

Networking

Networking in the context of user-research (UXR) refers to the process of building and maintaining professional relationships with individuals or groups within the field of user experience. It involves connecting with fellow researchers, designers, and industry experts to exchange knowledge, insights, and best practices.

Networking is crucial for UXR professionals as it allows them to stay up-to-date with the latest trends, methodologies, and tools in the field. By establishing and nurturing relationships with peers, researchers can tap into a rich network of resources and support, enabling them to ideate, iterate, and innovate more effectively.

Nolt

Nolt is a user research (UXR) tool designed to facilitate the collection and analysis of feedback from users. It provides a platform for conducting and managing user research activities such as surveys, polls, and interviews. With Nolt, researchers can easily create and distribute surveys to collect feedback from targeted user groups.

The tool enables researchers to customize survey questions and formats, making it easy to gather specific and actionable insights. Nolt also allows researchers to analyze and interpret the collected data, presenting it in a clear and visual manner. This helps in identifying patterns, trends, and areas for improvement.

One key feature of Nolt is its collaboration functionality, which allows researchers to involve stakeholders and team members in the research process. They can share access to survey data and analysis, fostering collaboration and ensuring that research insights are effectively communicated and utilized.

Nolt's user-friendly interface and intuitive navigation make it easy for both researchers and participants to engage in the research activities. This results in higher response rates and better quality of feedback.

In summary, Nolt is a versatile user research tool that streamlines the process of collecting, analyzing, and sharing user feedback. Its customizable surveys, visual data analysis, and collaboration features make it a valuable asset for researchers in gaining insights and improving the user experience of products and services.

Non-Functional Testing

Non-functional testing refers to a type of software testing that focuses on evaluating the attributes of a system or application, rather than its specific functionalities or features. In the context of user research (UXR), non-functional testing aims to assess the overall usability, performance, and reliability of a product, primarily focusing on the experience it provides to the end user.

This type of testing typically involves assessing various non-functional aspects such as the product's responsiveness, scalability, security, compatibility, and accessibility. During non-functional testing in UXR, researchers aim to identify potential issues or flaws that could negatively impact the user experience. For example, they may test how the product performs under high load or stress conditions, how secure it is against potential vulnerabilities, or if it is accessible to users with disabilities.

Offline Focus Groups

Offline focus groups are a type of user research method commonly used in the field of user experience research (UXR). They involve bringing together a small group of participants in a physical location to gather qualitative data and insights about a specific product, service, or user experience.

During an offline focus group, a trained facilitator guides the participants through a structured discussion or series of activities related to the research objectives. The facilitator ensures that the conversation stays on track and encourages all participants to contribute their thoughts and opinions.

Offline focus groups offer several advantages in user research. First, they allow for real-time interactions and non-verbal cues, which can provide deeper insights into participants' thoughts, emotions, and behaviors. Second, being in a group setting can stimulate discussion and facilitate the emergence of new ideas and perspectives. Third, offline focus groups can be particularly useful for exploring complex topics or sensitive issues, as participants can independently express their views without fear of being influenced or judged by others.

However, offline focus groups also have limitations. They can be time-consuming and costly to organize, requiring a physical location, recruiting participants, and compensating them for their time. Additionally, the group dynamic might lead to certain individuals dominating the conversation while others remain quiet, potentially biasing the results. Therefore, it's important for the facilitator to actively manage the group dynamics and ensure that all participants have an equal opportunity to contribute.

Offline Surveys

An offline survey in the context of user research (UXR) refers to a survey method conducted without the need for an internet connection. It involves collecting data from participants in an offline environment, typically using pen and paper or electronic devices that can store data locally.

Offline surveys are particularly useful in situations where internet connectivity is limited or unavailable, such as rural areas, remote locations, or events where online access may be restricted. By conducting surveys offline, researchers can still gather valuable insights from participants and obtain data to inform their user-centered designs.

Online Focus Groups

Online focus groups refer to a method of user research (UXR) that involves conducting group discussions with participants through digital platforms. These platforms may include video conferencing tools, online chat rooms, or dedicated online research platforms. The purpose of online focus groups is to gather insights and opinions from users about a particular product, service, or user experience.

As a user research method, online focus groups serve as a means to understand user perspectives, behavior, and preferences. By engaging multiple participants in a group discussion, researchers can uncover shared experiences, patterns, and diverse viewpoints. This interactive format allows for in-depth exploration of topics, encouraging participants to build upon each other's responses and generate new ideas.

Online focus groups offer several advantages in comparison to traditional face-to-face focus groups. Firstly, they eliminate the geographical limitations and logistical challenges associated with physical meetings. Participants can join from anywhere, providing a more diverse pool of individuals to gather insights from. Additionally, online platforms enable researchers to capture and analyze data efficiently, with features such as automatic transcription and real-time chat recording.

However, online focus groups also present certain limitations. The lack of in-person interaction might lead to reduced non-verbal cues and hinder the development of strong group dynamics. Technical issues may arise, impacting the quality of discussions. Moreover, participants' level of comfort and familiarity with online platforms can influence their engagement and contribution.

In summary, online focus groups are a valuable user research method for gathering insights from a group of participants in an interactive and efficient manner. By leveraging digital platforms, researchers can overcome geographical barriers and collect diverse perspectives, although potential limitations in communication quality and participant engagement should be considered.

Online Surveys

An online survey is a user research method commonly used in the field of User Experience Research (UXR) to gather data and insights about users and their preferences, behaviors, and opinions. It involves the collection of responses from participants who are asked a series of questions, typically in a digital format.

The purpose of online surveys in user research is to systematically gather quantitative data that can be analyzed and used to make informed design decisions. By reaching a large number of participants, online surveys allow researchers to obtain a broad range of opinions and perspectives from a diverse user base, yielding valuable insights that can inform product development and improve user experiences.

Open Card Sorting

Open Card Sorting is a user research method used in the field of User Experience Research (UXR) to understand how users categorize and organize information. It involves presenting users with a set of cards or items and asking them to group or sort the items into categories that make sense to them.

The process of Open Card Sorting typically involves the following steps:

1. Preparation: Define the research objectives and develop a set of cards or items to be sorted. The cards can contain different types of information, such as product features, content topics, or website navigation labels.

2. Recruitment: Identify and recruit participants who fit the target user profile. The number of participants can vary depending on the scope of the research.

3. Procedure: During the sorting session, participants are provided with the set of cards and instructions on how to group them. They can create their own categories or use predefined ones. Participants are encouraged to think aloud and explain their thought process while sorting.

4. Data Analysis: Once the sorting sessions are completed, the data collected from participants is analyzed. This analysis involves identifying common patterns, similarities, and differences in how participants organized the cards.

Open Card Sorting can provide valuable insights into users' mental models and help inform the design of information architecture, navigation structures, and content organization. The method allows researchers to understand the users' perspective and uncover potential usability issues or improvements that can enhance the overall user experience.

Optimal Workshop

Optimal Workshop is a user-research platform that provides a set of tools and features aimed at improving the user experience (UX) of digital products and services. It offers a range of software products that help researchers collect, analyze, and interpret data to gain insights into users' behaviors, needs, and preferences.

By using Optimal Workshop, UX researchers can conduct various types of research activities, such as user testing, card sorting, tree testing, and surveys. These activities allow researchers to understand how users interact with a product or service, identify potential usability issues, and make informed decisions based on data-driven insights.

The platform enables researchers to create and manage studies, recruit participants, and collect qualitative and quantitative data. It provides tools for designing and building surveys, creating tasks and scenarios for user testing, and visualizing data through interactive charts and graphs.

Furthermore, Optimal Workshop offers features that facilitate collaborative research, allowing multiple researchers and stakeholders to work together on a project, share insights, and provide feedback. The platform also includes features for remote research, making it easy to conduct studies with participants located anywhere in the world.

In summary, Optimal Workshop is a comprehensive user-research platform that offers a range of tools and features to support UX researchers in collecting and analyzing data, conducting various research activities, and gaining insights to enhance the user experience of digital products and services.

OptimalSort

The OptimalSort method is a user-research technique used in the field of UX research. It involves organizing and categorizing information or items based on how users perceive and interact with them.

In OptimalSort, participants are typically presented with a set of cards or items representing concepts, features, or products. They are then asked to sort these cards into groups or categories that make sense to them. This sorting exercise helps uncover users' mental models and understand how they naturally organize and make sense of the information or items presented to them.

The goal of OptimalSort is to gain insights into users' cognitive processes and decision-making when it comes to organizing and categorizing information. By understanding how users mentally group and categorize items, UX researchers can improve the organization, navigation, and overall usability of products, websites, or interfaces. This method also helps identify patterns and common themes that can inform the design and information architecture of user interfaces.

OptimalSort sessions can be conducted in-person or remotely, depending on the research plan and resources available. The results of the sorting exercise are often analyzed quantitatively and qualitatively, providing valuable data and insights for UX designers and researchers.

Outreach

Outreach in the context of user research (UXR) refers to the process of actively engaging and connecting with participants or target users in order to gather insights and feedback for improving the design and usability of a product or service.

Outreach in user research involves various activities such as recruitment, communication, and scheduling with potential participants. It aims to reach out to a diverse pool of users who represent the target audience or user segments. Outreach also involves establishing a rapport and building trust with participants to create a comfortable and open environment for sharing their experiences and perspectives.

The goals of outreach in user research are to gather valuable data and insights that help the user research team in understanding user needs, behaviors, preferences, and pain points. By reaching out to a wide range of users, UX researchers can ensure that their findings and recommendations are representative of the target user base.

Effective outreach strategies may include utilizing multiple communication channels such as emails, phone calls, social media, and in-person meetings. Clear and concise messaging is crucial in outreach efforts, as it helps potential participants understand the purpose of the research study and the value of their input.

In summary, outreach in user research is a systematic approach to actively engage with users and collect valuable insights that inform the design and development of user-centered products or services.

Panel Surveys

A panel survey, in the context of user research (UXR), refers to a method of data collection that involves a representative group of participants who have agreed to take part in multiple surveys over a period of time. This group of participants, known as a panel, is carefully selected to represent the target audience or user base of a product or service.

The purpose of conducting panel surveys is to gain insights and feedback from a consistent set of participants over a longer duration, enabling researchers to monitor changes in opinions, behaviors, or attitudes over time. By using the same participants for multiple surveys, researchers can better understand patterns, trends, and longitudinal data, which can provide valuable information for decision-making in product design, marketing, and strategic planning.

Panel surveys often utilize a combination of quantitative and qualitative research methods to gather data. These can include questionnaires, interviews, usability testing, and other data collection techniques. The surveys may be conducted online or offline, depending on the accessibility and preferences of the panel members. The frequency of the surveys can vary, from monthly or quarterly to yearly, depending on the research objectives and the pace of change within the target audience.

Panel surveys can provide several benefits for user research. They offer a cost-effective way to collect data from a consistent group of participants, reducing the need for recruiting new participants each time. Panels also allow for the exploration of long-term attitudes, behaviors, and preferences, providing a comprehensive understanding of user journeys and experiences. Additionally, panel surveys enable the tracking of changes and the measurement of the impact of interventions or modifications on user perceptions and actions.

Participatory Action Research (PAR)

Participatory Action Research (PAR) is a research approach commonly used in the field of user research (UXR) that emphasizes active involvement and collaboration with participants in the research process. It aims to address real-world problems by generating practical knowledge and fostering social change.

PAR is rooted in the belief that individuals who are directly affected by a problem or issue have valuable insights and knowledge that can contribute to finding solutions. Unlike traditional research methods, PAR focuses on empowering participants, allowing them to actively participate in all stages of the research, including problem identification, data collection, analysis, and action planning.

Participatory Design

Participatory Design is a user-centered approach to designing products and services that involves active collaboration between designers, researchers, and end-users. It emphasizes the importance of including users in the design process to ensure that their needs, preferences, and perspectives are taken into account.

At its core, Participatory Design focuses on empowering users and giving them a voice in shaping the final product or service. This approach recognizes that users have valuable insights and expertise that can greatly contribute to the design process. By involving them from the beginning, designers can gain a deeper understanding of their needs, goals, and challenges, which can lead to more meaningful and effective solutions.

Pendo

Pendo is a user research (UXR) platform that allows businesses to gather insights about their users and improve their products or services through data-driven decision making.

With Pendo, businesses can capture and analyze user behavior, engage with users through in-app messaging, and collect feedback to gain a deeper understanding of their needs and preferences. The platform provides tools for conducting surveys, A/B testing, and user feedback management, enabling businesses to make informed decisions about product development, feature prioritization, and user experience optimizations.

Perceptual Mapping

Perceptual mapping is a user research technique used in the field of User Experience Research (UXR) to visualize and analyze users' perceptions and preferences towards products or brands. This method helps researchers understand how users perceive and distinguish between different products or brands in relation to specific attributes or characteristics.

Through perceptual mapping, researchers can gather insight into users' mental representations of products or brands and their associations with certain qualities or features. The technique allows for the creation of a graphical representation, typically a two-dimensional map, that enables researchers to visualize and compare users' perceptions and preferences.

Performance Testing

Performance testing is a methodical evaluation of the usability and responsiveness of a user interface or system, conducted in order to measure its efficiency and effectiveness in various scenarios. It aims to assess the performance of the system under different loads and determine its ability to handle a large number of concurrent users or transactions.

During performance testing, specific scenarios are created to imitate real-world conditions and user behavior, such as heavy usage during peak hours or high traffic situations. The system's responsiveness, speed, stability, and scalability are measured and analyzed to identify potential bottlenecks or performance issues that may affect the user experience.

Photo Elicitation

Photo elicitation is a user research method used in the field of User Experience Research (UXR) to gather participants' perspectives, emotions, and experiences based on visual stimuli. It involves showing participants photographs or images and then conducting interviews or discussions to elicit their thoughts, reactions, and associations.

During a photo elicitation session, participants are typically shown a series of carefully selected photographs or images that are relevant to the research topic or study objective. These visuals could be pictures of products, interfaces, environments, or even abstract images that represent a concept. The participants are then encouraged to express their opinions, thoughts, and feelings about the visuals, providing valuable insights into their experiences and perceptions.

Photovoice Interviews

Photovoice interviews are a qualitative research method used in user experience research (UXR) to gather insights and understanding about participants' experiences, preferences, and needs. The process involves participants capturing and discussing photographs that relate to their experiences, allowing them to share subjective viewpoints and uncover hidden dimensions of their lived experiences.

During a photovoice interview, participants are typically provided with cameras or smartphones and encouraged to document moments and contexts relevant to the research topic. These photographs serve as prompts for further exploration during the interview, enabling participants to explain the significance behind each image and express their emotions, opinions, and needs associated with the subject matter.

The approach leverages the power of visual communication, enabling participants to engage in a more efficient and intuitive way to express complex thoughts that might be challenging to articulate verbally. The photographs act as a catalyst for dialogue, creating a collaborative and interactive atmosphere where participants and researchers can co-construct knowledge.

Photovoice interviews are particularly useful in uncovering insights about subjective experiences, cultural factors, and marginalized perspectives. They allow for a deeper understanding of the participants' worldviews, values, and daily routines, providing a rich and comprehensive understanding of their needs and aspirations. By incorporating visuals into the research process, photovoice interviews enhance empathy, enable various perspectives to be heard, and ultimately inform more inclusive and user-centered design solutions.

PingPong

PingPong is a user-research method in the context of UX research (UXR) that involves a back-and-forth interaction between researchers and participants to gain insights, validate assumptions, and refine designs. It is a collaborative approach, allowing researchers to gather valuable information while giving participants an opportunity to express their thoughts, opinions, and experiences.

In PingPong, researchers present participants with a set of questions, prompts, or design concepts relevant to the research objectives. Participants then respond, providing feedback, suggestions, or observations. The researchers, in turn, actively listen, asking clarifying questions, digging deeper into the participant's perspective, and seeking to understand their needs and preferences. This iterative process continues, resembling a game of "ping-pong," as the conversation bounces back and forth between researchers and participants.

Pingboard

Pingboard is a user research tool that allows user researchers to gather and analyze data to inform decision-making and improve the user experience (UX) of a product or service.

With Pingboard, user researchers can conduct various research activities such as surveys, interviews, and usability tests to collect qualitative and quantitative data about users' behaviors, needs, and preferences. The tool provides a platform for managing and organizing research projects, creating and distributing research materials, and capturing and analyzing research findings.

Plan

User research (UXR) is a discipline that involves gathering and analyzing data about user behaviors, needs, and motivations in order to inform the design and development of products, services, or experiences. It is a systematic approach that aims to understand users and their interactions with a particular product or system. Through user research, designers and developers can gain insights that help them make informed decisions about how to create user-centered designs. This involves studying the target audience, conducting user interviews, surveys, and usability tests, and analyzing quantitative and qualitative data. The goal is to identify user needs, pain points, and preferences, and use this knowledge to iterate and improve the user experience. User research plays a crucial role in successful product development by ensuring that designs are intuitive, usable, and meet the needs of the target audience. It allows designers and developers to validate assumptions, uncover usability issues, and discover opportunities for innovation. By involving users throughout the design process, UXR helps create user-friendly interfaces and enhances user satisfaction. Overall, user research is a foundational practice in UX design that emphasizes understanding the users and their context to create products that meet their needs effectively. It provides valuable insights that inform design decisions, resulting in improved user experiences and increased product success.

Platform

A platform, in the context of user research (UXR), refers to the technological infrastructure or framework that supports the collection, analysis, and presentation of data related to user experiences. It provides the necessary tools and resources for conducting research activities and allows researchers to gather insights and make informed design decisions.

A user research platform typically includes various features and functionalities such as survey creation and distribution, participant recruitment and management, data collection and storage, data analysis and visualization, and collaboration tools for team members. These platforms may be web-based or software applications, and they are designed to streamline and optimize the user research process.

PlaybookUX

PlaybookUX is a user-research platform designed to help UX researchers conduct valuable and efficient research studies. It offers a wide range of features and tools that facilitate the gathering and analysis of user insights, ultimately enhancing the decision-making process for product design and development.

The platform allows researchers to create and customize various types of research studies, such as usability tests, interviews, surveys, and card sorts. These studies can be conducted remotely, eliminating geographical limitations and enabling access to a diverse pool of participants. PlaybookUX also provides a seamless participant recruitment process, allowing researchers to recruit and schedule participants for their studies.

When conducting research studies, PlaybookUX offers tools for tasks such as screen recording, session transcription, note-taking, and questionnaires. These features help researchers efficiently collect and analyze user data, enabling them to identify patterns, uncover insights, and make data-driven decisions.

Collaboration is made easy with PlaybookUX's sharing and feedback capabilities. Researchers can securely share study results, videos, and reports with team members and stakeholders, streamlining the collaboration process and ensuring that everyone has access to the same valuable information.

In summary, PlaybookUX is a user-research platform that empowers UX researchers to conduct and analyze research studies efficiently. With its comprehensive set of features, it helps researchers gain valuable insights from users, facilitating informed decision-making in product design and development.

Podcasts

A podcast refers to a digital audio or video file that is available for download or streaming, typically in a series format. It is a form of media content that users can subscribe to and listen to on-demand using a computer, smartphone, or other portable media devices. Podcasts are often created by individuals or organizations who produce regular episodes on a specific topic or theme.

For user researchers (UXRs), podcasts can be a valuable source of information and insights. They offer a rich and diverse range of content related to various subjects, including user experience, design, technology, and industry trends. UXR professionals can listen to podcasts to enhance their knowledge, stay up-to-date with the latest developments, and gain unique perspectives from experts in the field.

Post-Interaction Surveys

Post-interaction surveys, in the context of user research (UXR), refer to the process of gathering feedback from users after they have interacted with a product or system. These surveys are conducted to understand users' experiences, preferences, and satisfaction levels, allowing researchers to gain insights into improving the user experience.

Post-interaction surveys are usually designed to be quick and straightforward, incorporating a set of questions related to specific aspects of the user interaction. These questions can vary depending on the research goals and objectives, but commonly cover topics such as usability, ease of use, satisfaction, and overall impressions. The surveys can be administered through various methods, including online forms, email, in-app pop-ups, or verbally during a research session.

The goal of post-interaction surveys is to collect quantitative and qualitative data that can inform UX improvements. The data gathered from these surveys can help identify pain points, usability issues, or potential areas of improvement within a product or system. By understanding users' perceptions and experiences, researchers can make informed decisions on design modifications, feature enhancements, or overall product changes to create a better user experience.

In conclusion, post-interaction surveys play a crucial role in user research by providing valuable insights into users' experiences and preferences. These surveys allow researchers to collect data that can drive evidence-based decision-making and ultimately lead to improved user experiences.

Preference Ranking Surveys

Preference Ranking Surveys are a type of user-research method used in the field of user experience research (UXR). These surveys are designed to gather insights and data about users' preferences and prioritize their choices according to their preferences.

In a Preference Ranking Survey, participants are presented with a set of items, options, or features that they are asked to evaluate and rank in order of preference. The survey often uses a scale or numerical system to capture the participants' preferences and prioritize their choices accordingly.

These surveys can be conducted through various methods, such as online surveys, interviews, or in-person sessions. The participants' responses are then collected and analyzed to identify patterns and trends in their preferences.

Preference Ranking Surveys provide valuable insights to inform the design and development process of user-centered products or services. By understanding users' preferences and priorities, UX researchers can make informed decisions and prioritize features or improvements that align with the users' needs and desires.

In conclusion, Preference Ranking Surveys are a user-research method used to gather insights and data about user preferences and prioritize their choices. By conducting these surveys, UX researchers can understand users' needs, make informed design decisions, and create user-centered products or services.

Preference Testing Surveys

Preference Testing Surveys, in the context of user research (UXR), are a type of survey used to gather data on user preferences and opinions. These surveys are designed to understand users' subjective preferences for different options, features, or designs, and to determine which options are most preferred or appealing to users. Preference Testing Surveys typically involve presenting users with a set of options or designs and asking them to rank or rate them based on their preference. These surveys allow researchers to collect quantitative data that can be analyzed to understand the relative popularity or preference of different options among the target user group. The goal of conducting Preference Testing Surveys is to gather insights into users' preferences and to inform decision-making in the design and development process. This data allows UX researchers and designers to make informed decisions regarding which features or designs to prioritize, refine, or discard. When conducting Preference Testing Surveys, it is important to carefully define the options being presented and to clearly communicate to users how they should rank or rate them. The survey questions should be unbiased and designed to capture users' true preferences accurately. By conducting Preference Testing Surveys, UX researchers can gather valuable insights about user preferences and make data-driven decisions that align with the needs and preferences of their target audience. This ultimately helps in creating more user-centered and successful products or experiences.>

Preference Testing With Best-Worst Scaling

Preference testing with Best-Worst Scaling is a user research method used to measure the relative preferences of participants for a set of items or options. It is commonly employed in the field of User Experience Research (UXR) to understand user preferences and prioritize features, designs, or products.

In Best-Worst Scaling, participants are presented with a list of items and are asked to select the best and worst options from each set. By forcing participants to make trade-offs and choose the best and worst options, this method provides more nuanced and discriminating results than traditional rating scales.

During the preference test, participants are typically given a series of choice sets, which consist of a subset of the items to be compared. Each choice set may contain three or more items, and participants are asked to indicate the best and worst options. This process is repeated multiple times to gather sufficient data for analysis.

The data collected from Best-Worst Scaling is analyzed using statistical techniques to calculate the preference scores for each item. These scores represent the relative preference or importance of each item within the given set. The higher the score, the more preferred or important the item is considered to be by the participants.

Preference testing with Best-Worst Scaling enables researchers to prioritize features, designs, or products based on the preferences of the target user group. It helps in understanding the key drivers of preference and making informed decisions when designing or improving user experiences.

Preference Testing With Biometrics

Preference testing with biometrics is a user research method used in the field of User Experience Research (UXR) to evaluate and measure user preferences based on physiological and behavioral responses. This approach combines traditional preference testing techniques with the use of biometric data to gain deeper insights into user preferences.

Biometric measures such as heart rate, skin conductance, eye tracking, facial expressions, and brain activity are collected while participants interact with a product, interface, or experience. These measures provide objective and quantitative data that can be used to understand users' emotional and cognitive responses, engagement levels, attention, and overall preferences.

Preference Testing With Choice Modeling

Preference Testing with Choice Modeling is a user-research methodology used in the field of User Experience Research (UXR) to understand and measure the preferences of users when provided with different choices. It involves presenting users with multiple options and asking them to select their preferred choice.

This methodology uses choice modeling techniques to analyze the data collected from the users' choices. Choice modeling is a statistical technique that helps in understanding the factors influencing users' preferences. It helps identify the trade-offs users make when presented with different choices, allowing researchers to quantify the relative importance of different attributes or features.

Preference Testing With Conjoint Analysis

Preference testing with conjoint analysis is a user research method commonly used in UX design to understand user preferences and decision-making processes. It involves presenting users with a series of hypothetical scenarios or product features and asking them to make choices or indicate their preferences.

Conjoint analysis breaks down a product or service into its individual characteristics, allowing researchers to assess not only which factors influence preference but also the relative importance of each factor. For example, if testing a new smartphone, researchers might consider factors such as screen size, camera quality, brand reputation, and price. By systematically varying these factors and analyzing users' choices, researchers can determine the impact of each attribute on user preferences.

Preference Testing With Discrete Choice Experiments

Preference testing with discrete choice experiments is a research technique used in user experience research (UXR) to understand user preferences and decision-making processes. It involves presenting users with a series of hypothetical scenarios or choices and asking them to select their preferred option.

In this type of research, users are typically presented with two or more alternatives, each described by a set of attributes or features. The goal is to determine which combination of attributes users find most desirable or preferable. By systematically varying the attributes and levels presented, researchers can gather data on the relative importance of different attributes and the trade-offs users are willing to make.

Preference Testing With Emotional Response Analysis

Preference testing with emotional response analysis is a user research method used in the field of user experience research (UXR). It involves evaluating participants' preferences and emotional responses towards different aspects of a product or interface to gather insights and inform design decisions.

The process typically begins by selecting a representative group of participants, who are then presented with various design options or variations. These options can include different color schemes, layout configurations, icon styles, or even different product features. The participants are asked to rate their preference for each option, usually on a scale or through a likert-like questionnaire.

Alongside the preference ratings, emotional response analysis is conducted to capture participants' subconscious reactions to the different design options. This can be done through methods such as biometric measurements (e.g., heart rate, skin conductance) or self-reporting of emotional states (e.g., feeling happy, frustrated, or annoyed).

The combination of preference testing and emotional response analysis provides valuable insights into users' subjective reactions towards different design elements. It helps identify what aspects of a product or interface are most appealing or effective, and what elicits positive or negative emotional responses. These insights can then guide design decisions, allowing for the creation of more user-centered and emotionally engaging experiences.

Preference Testing With Eye Tracking

Preference testing with eye tracking is a user research method in the field of User Experience Research (UXR) that aims to determine users' preferences and interest by using eye tracking technology. Eye tracking technology allows for the measurement and recording of eye movements, gaze points, and fixation duration, providing valuable insights into user attention and visual behavior. In a preference testing study with eye tracking, participants are presented with different stimuli, such as websites, images, or digital interfaces. The eye tracking device captures their eye movements and records the areas of the stimuli that capture their attention the most. Through the analysis of the eye tracking data, researchers can identify which elements of the stimuli participants look at first, spend the most time viewing, or find most engaging. The primary goal of preference testing with eye tracking is to understand how users engage and interact with different design variations or content formats. It helps researchers gain insights into users' visual behavior, perception, and preferences, which can inform design decisions and improve user experience. The data collected from eye tracking studies can be analyzed using different metrics, such as fixation duration, fixation count, or heatmaps. These metrics provide quantitative and qualitative measures of users' visual attention and preferences. Preference testing with eye tracking can be utilized in various UX research scenarios, such as evaluating the effectiveness of different website layouts, comparing the impact of design variations on user engagement, or assessing the effectiveness of visual content in communicating information. By understanding and addressing users' preferences, organizations can create more user-centered and engaging designs and experiences.>

Preference Testing With Implicit Association Tests (IAT)

Preference Testing with Implicit Association Tests (IAT) is a user-research method commonly used in the field of User Experience Research (UXR). It aims to measure the implicit biases and preferences of users towards certain concepts or attributes.

The IAT is based on the principle that people often hold unconscious associations and biases that can influence their behaviors and decision-making. It is designed to capture these implicit associations by measuring the speed and accuracy of users' responses during a series of association tasks.

Preference Testing With MaxDiff Analysis

Preference testing with MaxDiff analysis is a user research method used in UX research to determine user preferences or prioritize features or designs. MaxDiff analysis is a quantitative technique that helps researchers identify the most preferred and least preferred items from a set of options.

This method involves presenting participants with a set of options or features and asking them to select the most preferred and least preferred options from each group. The goal is to understand the relative importance or preference of each item within the set.

Preference Testing With Predictive Modeling

Preference Testing with Predictive Modeling, in the context of user research (UXR), refers to the practice of using statistical models and data analysis techniques to gain insights into user preferences. It involves collecting user feedback and data on their preferences and using predictive modeling to analyze and predict their future behavior or choices.

Preference testing is crucial in user research as it helps UX researchers understand what users like, dislike, and prioritize. It aids in the decision-making process for product design and development, as well as marketing strategies. By understanding user preferences, researchers can tailor their products and experiences to align with user expectations and needs.

Preference Testing With Van Westendorp Price Sensitivity Meter

Preference testing with the Van Westendorp Price Sensitivity Meter is a user research method used to determine the price range that is most acceptable to users for a particular product or service. This method helps to understand the price sensitivity of users and their preferences when making purchase decisions. Van Westendorp Price Sensitivity Meter is named after its creator, Peter Van Westendorp.

The process involves conducting surveys with potential users and asking them to provide their willingness to pay at different price points. Four questions are typically asked:

1. At what price would you consider the product/service to be so expensive that you would not consider buying it?

2. At what price would you consider the product/service to be priced so low that you would feel the quality is not good enough?

3. At what price would you consider the product/service to be getting expensive but would still consider buying it?

4. At what price would you consider the product/service to be a bargain?

By collecting responses to these four questions, the Van Westendorp Price Sensitivity Meter can determine the price ranges that are considered too expensive, too cheap, getting expensive but still acceptable, and a bargain. From these ranges, the optimal price point and the price at which demand is maximized can be identified.

Preference testing with the Van Westendorp Price Sensitivity Meter is particularly valuable in pricing decisions and market research studies. It helps businesses understand the price expectations and trade-offs that users are willing to make, aiding in pricing strategies, product positioning, and competitive analysis.

Preference Testing

Preference testing, in the context of user-research (UXR), is a method used to determine the user's preferences or likes/dislikes for a specific product, feature, or design element. It helps researchers gain insights into the user's subjective opinions and preferences in order to inform the development or improvement of a product or service.

During preference testing, participants are typically presented with different options or variations of a product or design and are asked to indicate their preferences, often using a rating scale or by ranking the options in order of preference. The goal is to understand which option or variation is preferred by the majority of users and why.

Presentation Deck

A presentation deck in the context of user research (UXR) refers to a set of slides or visuals used to convey findings, insights, and recommendations derived from user research activities. It serves as a means of communicating research findings to stakeholders, such as product managers, designers, and developers, in a succinct and visually engaging manner.

The presentation deck typically includes important information gathered during the research process, such as research objectives, methodology, and participant demographics. It may also include visuals such as charts, graphs, and images that help illustrate key findings and trends observed during user research sessions. The primary purpose of a presentation deck in user research is to effectively communicate the user insights and findings in a manner that is easy to understand, digest, and act upon for stakeholders. It should provide a clear narrative that highlights the most significant findings and their implications for the design and development of a product or service. In addition to presenting research findings, the presentation deck may also include recommendations for improving the user experience based on the insights from the research activities. These recommendations may be related to changes in the product design, features, or overall user journey. Overall, the presentation deck plays a crucial role in bridging the gap between user research and decision-making, as it provides a platform for researchers to share their findings, insights, and recommendations with stakeholders in a concise and visually compelling format.

Presentation

User research, or UXR, is a systematic investigation method employed by UX designers and researchers to gain thorough insights into users and their behaviors, needs, and preferences. It involves collecting and analyzing qualitative and quantitative data from users to inform the design and development of user-centered solutions.

Through user research, UXR practitioners aim to understand users' goals, motivations, and challenges, as well as their interactions with products or services. They employ various techniques such as surveys, interviews, usability testing, observation, and data analysis to gather meaningful and actionable data.

Price Elasticity Testing

Price elasticity testing is a user research method used in the field of user experience research (UXR) to determine the sensitivity of users towards changes in pricing. It involves conducting experiments or surveys to examine how users' behaviors and preferences are influenced by price variations.

By analyzing and measuring price elasticity, UXR professionals can gain insights into the price points at which users are more likely to make a purchase, switch to a competitor, or abandon a product or service altogether. This information allows businesses to make informed decisions about pricing strategies and optimize their offerings based on user needs and preferences.

Prodpad

Prodpad is a user research tool specifically designed for user experience research (UXR). It enables UX researchers to collect, analyze, and manage user feedback, allowing them to gain actionable insights and make informed decisions.

With Prodpad, UXR professionals can conduct user research studies, such as usability testing, surveys, and interviews, to gather valuable feedback from users. The tool provides a centralized platform for storing and organizing this feedback, making it easier for researchers to access and analyze the data.

One of the key features of Prodpad is its user feedback management functionality. It allows researchers to categorize and prioritize user feedback based on various criteria, such as severity, impact, and frequency. This categorization helps prioritize the most critical issues and identify patterns or trends in user feedback.

In addition, Prodpad offers collaboration tools that enable UXR professionals to work together efficiently. Researchers can share user feedback with other team members, collaborate on analysis, and track the progress of research activities.

Overall, Prodpad streamlines the user research process, empowering UXR professionals to effectively collect and analyze user feedback. By leveraging this tool, researchers can make data-driven decisions that improve the user experience of the products they are working on.

Product Placement Testing

Product Placement Testing, in the context of user research (UXR), refers to the process of evaluating the effectiveness and impact of product placements in various media formats, such as movies, TV shows, or online content. It involves conducting studies and gathering data to understand how users perceive and engage with these product placements, with the goal of informing marketing and advertising strategies.

During product placement testing, researchers typically use a range of quantitative and qualitative research methods to gather insights from users. These methods may include surveys, interviews, focus groups, eye-tracking studies, or observational research. The data collected through these methods allows researchers to measure user attention, recall, and brand recognition in relation to specific product placements.

Productboard

Productboard is a user-research (UXR) tool designed to support UXR professionals in the process of collecting, organizing, and analyzing user data. It provides a centralized platform where UXR teams can efficiently manage all aspects of their research projects.

With Productboard, UXR professionals can streamline the process of gathering user insights by organizing and structuring research findings in a systematic manner. The tool allows users to create and manage various types of research artifacts, such as interview transcripts, survey results, and usability test recordings, in a single location.

Productboard offers features that enable UXR professionals to categorize and tag research data, making it easy to search and retrieve specific information. This helps to ensure that UXR teams can efficiently access and leverage valuable user insights when designing and optimizing products.

The platform also facilitates collaboration within UXR teams and with other stakeholders. Users can invite team members to contribute to research projects, assign tasks, and track progress. This promotes a more cohesive and coordinated approach to user research, enhancing efficiency and productivity.

Furthermore, Productboard provides powerful analytics capabilities, allowing UXR professionals to derive meaningful insights from their research data. Users can generate customizable reports and visualizations to communicate research findings effectively to stakeholders, supporting evidence-based decision-making.

In summary, Productboard is a comprehensive user-research tool that empowers UXR professionals to streamline the research process, collaborate effectively, and derive valuable insights for designing and optimizing products.

Project Management

Project Management in the context of user research (UXR) refers to the discipline of planning, organizing, and controlling the various activities and resources required to effectively carry out user research projects. It involves the application of specific processes, techniques, and tools to achieve the project goals and deliver valuable insights that inform the design and development of user-centered products and services.

At its core, project management in user research involves the following key elements:

1. Planning: This encompasses defining the research objectives, scope, and deliverables, as well as identifying the appropriate research methods and tools. It involves creating a project plan that outlines the timeline, resource requirements, and milestones.

2. Organizing: This involves allocating and coordinating the necessary resources, such as human resources, budget, and equipment, to ensure smooth execution of the research activities. It includes setting up the research environment, selecting and recruiting participants, and managing logistics.

3. Controlling: This refers to monitoring the progress of the research project and making adjustments as necessary to keep it on track. It involves regular communication and collaboration with stakeholders to ensure that their expectations are met and risks are mitigated effectively.

By effectively managing user research projects, organizations can maximize the value of their user insights and ensure that they are incorporated into the design and development process. This helps drive user satisfaction, engagement, and overall product success.

Prototype Validation

Prototype validation in the context of user-research (UXR) refers to the process of evaluating and testing a prototype with users to gather feedback and insights in order to improve its design and functionality. It is a crucial step in the product development lifecycle, as it allows designers and researchers to assess the viability and effectiveness of the prototype before investing time and resources into the development of the final product.

During prototype validation, UXR professionals conduct various user tests and observations to understand how users interact with the prototype, identify usability issues, and measure user satisfaction and performance. These tests can range from simple click-through tasks to more complex scenarios that simulate real-world usage.

Publications

Publications in the context of user research (UXR) refer to written materials that document and communicate the findings, insights, and recommendations found in user research studies. These materials are essential for sharing the knowledge gained from the research process and informing design and decision-making processes. Publications can take various forms, including research reports, white papers, case studies, and academic papers. They typically follow a structured format and include sections such as an executive summary, research objectives, methodology, findings, analysis, and recommendations. The content is presented in a clear and concise manner, often supported by visuals like charts, graphs, and user quotes. The purpose of publications is to provide a comprehensive and reliable account of the research conducted. They serve as a record of the research process, ensuring that the insights and observations are accurately documented and can be referenced in the future. Publications also help to disseminate the research findings to stakeholders, such as designers, product managers, and executives, who can utilize the insights to inform their decision-making processes. In addition, publications in UXR often contribute to the broader UX research community. They can be shared through conferences, journals, industry events, or online platforms to facilitate knowledge exchange and foster a culture of learning and improvement within the field. By openly sharing research outcomes, practitioners can collectively advance their understanding of user behaviors, preferences, and needs, ultimately leading to the creation of better user experiences. Overall, publications are crucial in the user research process, enabling researchers to communicate their findings effectively, drive informed decision-making, and contribute to the continual growth and development of the UX research discipline.>

Qualaroo

Qualaroo is a user research tool commonly used in the field of user experience research (UXR). It allows researchers to gather feedback from website visitors through targeted surveys and questionnaires. The tool is designed to help researchers gain insights into user behavior, preferences, and needs, which can inform the design and development of user-friendly digital products.

With Qualaroo, researchers can create and customize surveys that appear to users as pop-ups, chat bubbles, or slide-ins based on defined triggers, such as time on page or user actions. These surveys can be used to collect both qualitative and quantitative data by asking open-ended or multiple-choice questions. Researchers can also use skip logic to guide users through a survey based on their responses, ensuring a personalized and efficient research experience.

Qualaroo provides researchers with options to target specific user segments or personas, allowing for more focused and relevant feedback. It also offers features such as A/B testing, where different versions of a survey can be compared to determine the most effective questions or design elements.

The collected data from Qualaroo surveys can be analyzed using its built-in reporting and analytics tools. Researchers can interpret the data, identify patterns or trends, and generate actionable insights. These insights can then be shared with stakeholders, such as designers, developers, or product managers, to inform decision-making and improve the overall user experience of a website or digital product.

Qualitative Data

Qualitative data refers to non-numerical data that is gathered through user research methods in the field of user experience research (UXR). It focuses on understanding and explaining the underlying reasons, motivations, and insights behind user behavior and preferences.

This type of data is collected through various research techniques such as interviews, focus groups, observations, and user testing. It is often descriptive in nature and provides deeper insights into user experiences, emotions, attitudes, and perceptions. Unlike quantitative data, which can be measured and analyzed statistically, qualitative data is subjective and context-dependent, requiring interpretation and analysis based on patterns, themes, and underlying meanings.

Quantitative Data

Quantitative data, in the context of user research (UXR), is a type of data that is collected and analyzed using numerical values and statistical methods. It involves gathering information through structured surveys, questionnaires, usage metrics, and other measurable sources.

Quantitative data is used in UXR to obtain objective insights and statistical evidence about user behavior, preferences, and experiences. It aims to quantify user opinions, actions, and patterns through numerical measurements and statistical analyses.

Quantitative Insights

Quantitative insights in the context of user-research (UXR) refer to data-driven findings and analysis obtained from measurable and numerical data. These insights are derived through quantitative research methods that involve systematically collecting and analyzing large sets of numeric data related to user behavior, preferences, and experiences.

During the user-research process, quantitative insights are obtained by conducting surveys, questionnaires, or experiments that involve large sample sizes. The data collected typically consists of metrics such as response times, click-through rates, task success rates, ratings, and demographic information. These numeric data points can provide insights into user patterns, trends, preferences, and satisfaction levels.

Quantitative insights are particularly useful in identifying statistical relationships, making generalizations about user behavior, and generating reliable predictions. Using statistical analysis techniques, such as correlation or regression analysis, quantitative insights can help establish cause-and-effect relationships, test hypotheses, and make evidence-based decisions.

However, it is essential to complement quantitative insights with qualitative insights, which involve more in-depth explorations of user perceptions and motivations. By combining both qualitative and quantitative methods, researchers can obtain a comprehensive understanding of user experiences, uncover usability issues, and inform design improvements.

Quru

A user research (UXR) is a systematic process of gathering and analyzing qualitative and quantitative data about users to gain insights into their behaviors, needs, and preferences.

By conducting user research, UX researchers aim to understand the target audience's motivations, goals, and pain points in order to design and improve products or services that meet their requirements and expectations.

ROI Analysis

ROI analysis, in the context of user research (UXR), refers to the examination of the return on investment that can be expected from conducting user research activities. It involves assessing the potential benefits and costs associated with conducting user research, in order to determine the value and impact it may have on a business or organization.

The primary goal of ROI analysis in UXR is to determine whether investing resources, such as time, money, and personnel, into conducting user research is justified and will provide a positive return. This analysis takes into account various factors, including the potential impact on user satisfaction, product usability, and overall business success.

ROI Measurement

ROI Measurement in the context of user research (UXR) refers to the assessment and quantification of the Return on Investment (ROI) for user-centered design and research efforts.

This evaluation allows organizations to determine the effectiveness and value of their investments in UXR activities. ROI measurement in UXR aims to provide insights into the impact and benefits of user research on business goals and outcomes.

ROI

ROI, or Return on Investment, is a key metric used in user research (UXR) to evaluate the effectiveness and efficiency of a project or initiative. It measures the return or gain that is generated from the investment made in user research activities.

ROI helps UXR professionals demonstrate the value and impact of their work to stakeholders and decision-makers within an organization. By quantifying the benefits and outcomes achieved, ROI provides a clear indication of the success and worthiness of user research efforts.

Rapid Prototyping

Rapid prototyping is a user-focused iterative design approach used in user-research (UXR), which involves creating quick and low-fidelity representations of a product or system to gather feedback and validate design decisions.

In the context of user-research, rapid prototyping allows researchers and designers to quickly generate multiple versions of a product or system and test them with users. It helps to uncover usability issues, gather user feedback, and iterate on the design based on user needs and preferences. The primary goal of rapid prototyping is to reduce the time and cost in the overall design process by identifying and resolving design problems early on.

Real-Time Experience Tracking

Real-Time Experience Tracking, in the context of user-research (UXR), refers to the process of continuously monitoring and measuring user interactions and behaviors during their engagement with a product, service, or digital platform.

By employing real-time experience tracking, researchers can gather immediate and dynamic insights into how users navigate, engage, and respond to different elements and features of a product or service. This approach allows for the collection of rich and authentic data that can inform and guide the design, development, and optimization of user experiences.

Real-time experience tracking typically involves the use of various research methods and tools such as analytics, heatmaps, clickstream analysis, session replay, and user feedback. These tools provide researchers with detailed information about users' interactions, including the paths followed, time spent on particular elements, clicks, scrolls, and user-generated feedback or comments.

Through real-time experience tracking, researchers can uncover patterns, pain points, and opportunities for improvement in real-time or near real-time, enabling iterative design and continuous optimization of the user experience. This approach helps ensure that the product or service meets users' needs, preferences, and expectations, ultimately leading to enhanced user satisfaction, engagement, and loyalty.

Recommendations

User research (UXR) is a discipline within the field of user experience (UX) that focuses on understanding the needs, behaviors, and preferences of users through various research methods. UXR plays a crucial role in informing the design and development of products, services, and interfaces to ensure they meet user expectations and deliver a positive user experience. Through conducting user research, UXR professionals gather qualitative and quantitative data to gain insights into how users interact with a product or service. This involves employing techniques such as interviews, surveys, usability testing, and observation to collect data on user needs, motivations, pain points, and preferences. The insights gathered from user research provide valuable information to guide the design process. UXR professionals analyze and interpret research findings to uncover patterns, identify opportunities for improvement, and inform decision-making. By understanding user perspectives, goals, and challenges, they can make informed design choices that effectively address user needs and enhance the overall user experience. In addition to informing design decisions, user research also helps validate assumptions and reduce risks associated with developing new products or features. By testing prototypes and gathering feedback from users, UXR professionals can validate design solutions, identify areas of improvement, and ensure that the final product aligns with user expectations. Overall, user research is essential in creating user-centric designs that prioritize the needs and goals of the target audience. By incorporating user feedback and insights, organizations can deliver products and services that are intuitive, enjoyable, and meet users' expectations.>

Recruitment Plan

A recruitment plan in the context of user research (UXR) refers to a strategic approach for identifying and selecting participants for research studies or usability testing. It involves outlining the goals, objectives, and criteria for recruiting participants who represent the target user demographic or user segments.

The recruitment plan typically begins with clearly defining the research objectives and the specific user profiles or personas that need to be included in the study. This helps in determining the ideal participants who can provide relevant insights and feedback. The plan may involve collaborating with various stakeholders, such as product managers, designers, and engineers, to understand the research goals and requirements.

Once the criteria and objectives are established, the recruitment plan outlines the methods and channels for reaching potential participants. This may include various approaches such as contacting existing users, utilizing online platforms, or reaching out to user communities. The plan also specifies the desired sample size and any incentives or compensation offered to participants.

The recruitment plan further includes a timeline, indicating the start and end date for recruiting participants, as well as the dates for the research sessions or interviews. It also defines the roles and responsibilities of the team members involved in the recruitment process, such as the recruiter or the person responsible for screening and selecting participants.

In conclusion, a recruitment plan in UXR is a systematic strategy that outlines the methods, objectives, criteria, timeline, and stakeholders involved in identifying and selecting participants for research studies or usability testing.

Recruitment

Recruitment in the context of user research (UXR) refers to the process of identifying and selecting individuals to participate in user research studies. These studies aim to gain insights into users' needs, preferences, and behaviors in order to inform the design and development of products and services.

Recruitment involves various steps, including identifying the target user group, defining specific criteria for participant selection, and reaching out to potential participants. The goal is to ensure that the recruited participants align with the target user group to effectively represent the broader user population.

During the recruitment process, researchers may utilize different methods, such as online surveys, interviews, or inviting specific users from existing customer databases. The participants may be compensated for their time and effort, fostering their motivation to provide genuine feedback.

Recruitment is a crucial aspect of user research as it directly impacts the quality and validity of the findings. The selected participants should possess the necessary characteristics and behaviors that align with the research objectives. By recruiting diverse participants, researchers can ensure a comprehensive understanding of users' needs and perspectives, leading to more inclusive and user-centered design decisions.

Overall, recruitment in user research plays a vital role in gathering relevant data and insights to enhance the user experience of products and services. It enables researchers to bridge the gap between the user and the design team, facilitating the creation of more effective and user-friendly solutions.

Regression Testing For AI Models

Regression Testing for AI Models is a user-research practice in which previously tested aspects of an AI model are retested to ensure that any modifications or updates to the model have not introduced new defects or regression bugs that could adversely impact the user experience (UX). It involves systematically rerunning a set of test cases on the modified AI model to determine if it continues to produce the expected outputs, behavior, and performance.

The primary objective of Regression Testing for AI Models is to detect and prevent unintended consequences or regressions that may have been introduced during the evolution or enhancement of an AI model. By retesting the model against a representative set of input data, scenarios, and expected outcomes, UXR teams can identify any discrepancies, anomalies, or unexpected changes in the model's behavior or performance.

Regression Testing

Regression Testing, in the context of user-research or UX research, refers to the process of retesting a product or feature after making changes or updates to the existing design or functionality. This testing is conducted to ensure that the changes or updates have not introduced any new bugs, errors, or usability issues and that the previous functionality is still intact.

During regression testing, the focus is on verifying the stability and reliability of the product or feature, as well as assessing its impact on the overall user experience. This type of testing is crucial in user-research as it helps in maintaining the quality and consistency of the user interface and user interactions.

Remote Diary Studies

Remote diary studies refer to a user research method in which participants are asked to document their experiences, thoughts, and behaviors related to a specific product, service, or task over a designated period of time. This approach allows researchers to gather detailed and authentic insights into how users engage with a product or service in their daily lives.

In a remote diary study, participants typically use a combination of written entries, photos, videos, or audio recordings to capture their experiences and provide feedback. Researchers provide participants with guidelines or prompts to encourage reflection on specific aspects of their experience. This method enables researchers to understand the user's context, motivations, challenges, and goals, resulting in valuable qualitative data.

Remote Testing

Remote Testing is a user research method commonly employed in the field of User Experience Research (UXR) to gather insights and feedback from participants who are geographically dispersed, without the need for them to be physically present at a testing facility. It involves conducting usability tests, interviews, surveys, or other research activities remotely using various digital tools and technologies.

Remote Testing offers several advantages over traditional in-person testing. It eliminates the need for travel for both researchers and participants, making it more convenient, cost-effective, and accessible. It allows researchers to reach a larger and more diverse pool of participants, enabling them to collect a wider range of perspectives and insights. Furthermore, remote testing enables researchers to conduct studies in participants' natural environments, which may provide more accurate and realistic feedback.

There are several methods and techniques used for remote testing, including screen sharing, video conferencing, remote task completion, and online surveys. These tools and technologies enable researchers to observe participants' interactions with digital interfaces, capture their thought processes, and gather their feedback and opinions.

However, remote testing also has its limitations. Not being able to observe participants' non-verbal cues or body language may impact the understanding of their experiences. Technical issues such as internet connectivity or software glitches could potentially disrupt the testing process. Additionally, selecting and recruiting remote participants who accurately represent the target user group can be challenging.

In conclusion, remote testing is a valuable user research method that allows researchers to collect insights and feedback from geographically dispersed participants. It provides convenience, cost-effectiveness, and a broader participant pool, making it an essential tool in the field of User Experience Research.

Remote Usability Testing

Remote usability testing is a user research method commonly used in the field of user experience research (UXR). It involves conducting usability tests on digital products or services with participants who are located remotely from the researchers or facilitators. This method allows for valuable insights to be gathered about the user experience of a product or service, regardless of geographical constraints.

In a remote usability test, participants are typically given a set of tasks to complete on a digital prototype or an existing product, while their interactions and thoughts are recorded remotely using various tools such as screen sharing, video recordings, or session logging software. The researcher can observe the participant's actions and listen to their thought process, providing valuable insights into how users interact with the product and identifying any pain points or areas for improvement.

This method offers several advantages over traditional in-person usability testing. It allows researchers to test with a wider pool of participants, including those from different geographic regions or with diverse backgrounds. It also eliminates the need for participants to travel, making it more convenient and cost-effective for both researchers and participants. Remote usability testing also enables researchers to gather insights in a familiar context, as participants are using their own devices and environments.

However, remote usability testing also has its limitations. The lack of physical presence during the session may hinder non-verbal cues and in-depth observation. Technical issues such as poor internet connection or unfamiliarity with remote tools can also affect the overall test experience. Researchers must carefully plan and design the remote usability test to mitigate these limitations and ensure accurate and useful results.

Repertory Grid Interview

A repertory grid interview is a user-research technique used in the field of UX research to understand people's mental models and perceptions about a particular topic or system. It is a structured interview approach that helps researchers gain insights into how users think and prioritize various elements or attributes related to a specific product, service, or experience.

In a repertory grid interview, participants are presented with a grid-like structure consisting of rows and columns. Each column represents a specific attribute or characteristic of the topic being studied, while each row represents individual instances or examples. Participants are then asked to rate or rank these instances based on the given attributes. The purpose is to uncover the underlying cognitive processes and decision-making criteria used by users.

This technique allows researchers to gain a deeper understanding of users' mental frameworks, perceptions, and preferences. By analyzing the patterns and associations participants make in the grid, researchers can identify common themes, outliers, or conflicts in users' thinking. This information can be valuable for informing design decisions, identifying usability issues, or tailoring experiences to match users' mental models.

Overall, the repertory grid interview is an effective method in user-research as it provides a structured approach to explore the complexities of users' cognition, helping UX researchers gain insights into users' perspectives and improve the overall user experience.

Repertory Grid Technique

Report

User research (UXR) is a methodical approach to understanding the needs, behaviors, and motivations of users in order to inform the design and development of products or services. It involves gathering and analyzing qualitative and quantitative data to gain insights into user experiences and preferences, and using these insights to make informed design decisions.

UXR encompasses various research methods, such as interviews, observations, surveys, and usability testing. These methods are used to collect data about users' interactions with a product or service, their goals and tasks, and their pain points or areas of satisfaction. By studying user behavior and preferences, UXR helps identify areas for improvement and guides the creation of user-centered designs.

Reporting

Reporting in the context of user research (UXR) refers to the process of summarizing and presenting data and insights gathered from user research activities. It involves organizing and presenting information in a clear and concise manner to facilitate decision-making and inform the design and development of user-centric products and services.

The purpose of reporting in user research is to communicate the findings, observations, and recommendations to stakeholders, such as designers, developers, product managers, and other decision-makers. The report should provide a comprehensive overview of the research objectives, methodologies, participants, and key findings.

The reporting process typically includes the following components:

1. Introduction: This section provides an overview of the research objectives, scope, and methodologies used. It sets the context for the research and explains the rationale behind the

research questions and methodologies.

2. Participant profile: This section provides information about the participants involved in the research, including their demographics, roles, and any relevant background information. This helps stakeholders understand the target audience and the context in which the research was conducted.

3. Research findings: This section presents the key insights and findings derived from the research activities, such as interviews, surveys, usability tests, and observations. The findings should be organized logically and supported by relevant quotes, data, or visuals.

4. Recommendations: This section provides actionable recommendations based on the research findings. It outlines potential design improvements, feature enhancements, or changes that should be considered to address user needs, preferences, and pain points.

By effectively reporting user research findings, stakeholders can gain a deeper understanding of user needs and expectations, make informed design decisions, and ultimately create better user experiences.

Repository

A repository, in the context of user research (UXR), is an organized and centralized location where user data and research findings are stored and managed. It serves as a comprehensive database that houses all the relevant information collected during the user research process, including user interviews, surveys, observations, and usability test results.

Within a repository, user researchers can easily access and retrieve valuable insights to inform and guide the design and development of products or services. This systematic approach ensures that user research findings are both accurate and readily available for analysis, interpretation, and decision-making purposes.

Retail Audits

Retail audits refer to a systematic examination and evaluation of various factors related to the retail environment and customer experience. This process is typically conducted by user researchers (UXRs) to gather insights and data that inform decision-making and improvement strategies for retail businesses.

During retail audits, UXR professionals assess different aspects of the retail environment, including store layout, product displays, signage, pricing, customer service, and overall brand experience. They observe and analyze how customers interact with the store and its offerings, aiming to understand their needs, preferences, and pain points. The data collected through retail audits helps UXR teams identify areas requiring enhancement or optimization, contributing to the creation of better retail experiences.

Reverse Card Sorting

Reverse card sorting is a user research method utilized in the field of User Experience Research (UXR). It involves presenting users with a set of predefined categories and various cards containing items or concepts related to those categories. Instead of asking users to sort the cards into the categories, the roles are reversed, and users are asked to assign categories to each card.

This method aims to uncover users' mental models and the way they naturally categorize information. By tasking users to assign categories to the cards, rather than providing predetermined categories for sorting, it allows for a more open-ended approach that reflects users' own thinking and understanding.

Roadmap

A roadmap is a strategic document that outlines the direction and goals for a specific project or initiative. In the context of user research (UXR), a roadmap is a plan that guides the progression of research activities to achieve the desired outcomes.

The UXR roadmap serves as a high-level overview of the research goals, objectives, and timeline. It helps teams gain clarity on the research activities needed to meet user needs and business objectives. The roadmap is typically created in collaboration with stakeholders, product managers, designers, and researchers.

A well-designed roadmap identifies and prioritizes research activities based on their relevance, impact, and feasibility. It maps out key milestones and deliverables to ensure that the research is conducted in a systematic and efficient manner. The roadmap serves as a reference for the UXR team, allowing them to align their efforts, resources, and timelines accordingly.

Moreover, the UXR roadmap helps communicate the research strategy to different stakeholders involved in the project. It provides them with a clear understanding of the research objectives, potential outcomes, and the expected impact on the product or service being developed. The roadmap also facilitates collaboration and coordination among different teams by ensuring that everyone is on the same page regarding the research priorities and timelines.

Roadmunk

Roadmunk is a user-research (UXR) tool that enables organizations to effectively plan and visualize their product development roadmap. It is a web-based platform designed to assist product managers, stakeholders, and UXR professionals in creating, managing, and presenting roadmaps.

With Roadmunk, UXR teams can centralize and organize their user research findings, insights, and recommendations. The tool allows users to create different research categories or themes, such as usability testing, focus groups, surveys, and interviews, and record specific details about each study, including objectives, methodologies, participant demographics, and key findings.

Roadmunk provides a user-friendly interface with customizable templates and drag-and-drop functionality, making it easy to create and update roadmap visualizations. Users can visualize their research data in a timeline or swimlane style, using configurable themes, colors, and icons to represent different research activities and stages. This enables stakeholders and team members to easily understand the progression of research and its impact on product development decisions.

Furthermore, Roadmunk offers collaboration and sharing features, allowing multiple stakeholders to contribute to and review the roadmap. It also provides integration capabilities with other tools commonly used in the product development process, such as Jira and Trello, facilitating seamless workflow management.

In summary, Roadmunk is a valuable UXR tool for planning, organizing, and visualizing user research activities and insights. It streamlines the product development process, enhances communication and collaboration among stakeholders, and ultimately helps organizations make data-driven decisions to create user-centered products and experiences.

Role-Playing

Role-Playing in the context of user-research (UXR) refers to a technique used to simulate and understand user experiences in a controlled and interactive environment. It involves assigning participants specific roles or personas and asking them to act out scenarios that represent real-world interactions with a product, service, or interface.

During a role-playing session, participants are encouraged to empathize with the assigned roles, assuming their characteristics, goals, motivations, and behaviors. This enables researchers to gain insights into how users might interact with a product or service, allowing them to identify pain points, usability issues, and potential improvements.

The main objective of role-playing in user-research is to replicate and examine user experiences in a simulated environment. By immersing participants in interactive scenarios, researchers can observe how users navigate through different tasks, make decisions, and ultimately achieve their goals. This method helps generate qualitative data, including behavioral patterns, emotional responses, and cognitive processes, all of which are crucial for understanding user needs and preferences.

Role-playing is particularly useful for exploring user interactions in situations that are difficult or costly to recreate in a real-world setting. It allows researchers to examine user behavior, preferences, and problem-solving strategies when faced with various challenges. Through this technique, user-researchers can gain valuable insights that inform the design and development of user-centered products and services.

Scenarios And Storytelling

Scenarios and storytelling are methodologies commonly used in user research (UXR) to understand and empathize with users, as well as to generate insights and ideas for designing user-centered experiences.

Scenarios are fictional stories or narratives that describe a specific context, situation, or problem that users may encounter when interacting with a product or service. They often include details about the user's goals, motivations, actions, and emotions. Scenarios help researchers and designers build a shared understanding of user needs and behaviors, and they serve as a tool for evaluating and refining design concepts.

Storytelling, on the other hand, is the act of communicating information or experiences through the use of stories. In the context of user research, storytelling involves collecting and sharing real-life user stories to capture their experiences, emotions, and perceptions related to a specific product or service. These stories can be gathered through interviews, observations, or other qualitative research methods. Storytelling helps researchers and designers gain deep insights into users' behaviors, needs, pain points, and motivations.

Both scenarios and storytelling are essential tools in user research as they enable the researcher to step into the shoes of the users and understand their needs, desires, and frustrations. By using these methodologies, researchers can uncover opportunities for improvement, identify areas of usability concerns, and generate ideas for innovative design solutions. Ultimately, scenarios and storytelling help create user-centered experiences that meet the needs and expectations of the target users.

Scroll Heatmap Analysis

A scroll heatmap analysis is a user research method used in UX research to understand how users interact with a webpage or website by tracking their scrolling behavior. This analysis provides insights into how users navigate through a webpage, where their attention is focused, and how far they scroll down the page.

Scroll heatmaps are generated by tracking user scrolling activity and visually representing the data in a heatmap format. The heatmap uses color gradients to highlight areas that receive more or less attention from users. The hotter areas indicate high engagement, while cooler areas indicate less engagement.

Security Testing

Security testing is a systematic evaluation process carried out to measure the effectiveness of security measures implemented within a system or application, with the objective of identifying vulnerabilities and potential threats that could compromise the confidentiality, integrity, and availability of user data and resources.

Within the context of user research (UXR), security testing involves assessing the security aspects of user experiences to ensure privacy and protect sensitive user information. It aims to identify potential risks that may affect user trust and confidence in using a particular system or application. User researchers employ security testing to uncover potential vulnerabilities, such as weak authentication mechanisms, data leakage, or insecure data transmission, that could be exploited by malicious actors.

Self-Administered Surveys

Self-administered surveys are a research method commonly used in user research (UXR) to gather data from participants. This type of survey allows participants to complete the survey on their own, without the presence or assistance of a researcher.

Self-administered surveys can be conducted through various mediums, such as online forms, paper questionnaires, or mobile applications. Participants are provided with a set of standardized questions to answer, allowing researchers to collect quantitative or qualitative data depending on the survey objectives.

In user research, self-administered surveys are often used to gain insights into user preferences, behaviors, or feedback regarding a specific product or service. These surveys can be sent to a large number of users simultaneously, making them a cost-effective and efficient method for gathering data. Self-administered surveys can also be conducted at different stages of the user journey, such as before or after using a product or interacting with a website.

However, it is important to take into consideration potential biases associated with self-administered surveys. Participants may interpret questions differently, leading to inconsistent or inaccurate responses. Additionally, participants who are less motivated or engaged may not complete the survey, resulting in a potential sampling bias. Measures should be taken to minimize these biases, such as clear and concise instructions, randomization of question order, and incentivizing participation.

Semantic Differential Scale

Semantic Differential Scale is a user-research method commonly used in the field of User Experience Research (UXR). It is a quantitative technique that assesses the perceived meaning of concepts or objects in terms of their underlying dimensions. In the context of UXR, the Semantic Differential Scale helps researchers understand how users perceive and evaluate specific aspects of a product or service. It provides insights into users' attitudes, opinions, and preferences, allowing researchers to gather data that can inform design decisions and improve user experience. The scale typically consists of a series of bipolar adjectives anchored at each end of a continuum. Users are asked to rate a concept or object on each adjective, indicating their perception of its position along the continuum. The adjectives chosen should represent the key attributes of the concept or object being evaluated. For example, if researchers are studying users' perception of a mobile app's usability, they might ask participants to rate the app on adjectives such as "difficult" and "easy," "frustrating" and "satisfying," or "intuitive" and "counterintuitive." By collecting ratings on these adjectives, researchers can gain insights into users' perceptions of the app's usability. To conduct a Semantic Differential Scale study, researchers typically use surveys or questionnaires. The responses are then analyzed quantitatively to identify trends, patterns, and areas where improvements can be made. By employing the Semantic Differential Scale in UXR, researchers can understand the subjective meanings users associate with concepts or objects, facilitating the development of user-centered designs that meet users' expectations and preferences.>

Sensory Analysis

Sensory analysis is a research methodology used in user research (UXR) to evaluate users' perceptions and experiences of a product or service through their senses. It involves the systematic measurement and interpretation of users' responses to sensory stimuli, such as visual, auditory, tactile, gustatory, and olfactory cues.

The primary objective of sensory analysis in UXR is to gain insights into how users perceive and interact with a product or service in terms of its sensory attributes. This includes understanding how different design elements, such as color, shape, texture, sound, taste, and smell, impact users' overall experience and satisfaction.

Sensory analysis can be conducted using various techniques, including qualitative and quantitative methods. Qualitative techniques involve observing and documenting users' subjective feedback, thoughts, emotions, and behaviors related to the sensory aspects of the product or service. This can be done through interviews, focus groups, or user diaries.

Quantitative techniques, on the other hand, aim to gather measurable data on users' sensory experiences through rating scales, surveys, or psychophysical tests. These methods provide more objective and statistically significant results, allowing researchers to make data-driven decisions about product or service improvements.

By implementing sensory analysis in UXR, researchers can identify both positive and negative aspects of a product or service's sensory attributes. This knowledge can then be used to inform the design and development process, ensuring that the final product meets users' expectations and creates a positive user experience.

Sentiment Analysis

Sentiment Analysis is a technique used in user research (UXR) to analyze and understand the emotional responses and attitudes of users towards a particular product, service, or experience. It involves the process of extracting and categorizing sentiments expressed in user feedback, such as reviews, comments, or social media posts, to gain insights into user satisfaction, preferences, and pain points.

By applying Sentiment Analysis in UXR, researchers can uncover valuable information that helps shape the design and development of user-centered products and services. It allows them to identify patterns, trends, and sentiments that are often difficult to determine through traditional qualitative data analysis. This technique helps researchers to understand the overall sentiment distribution of users' reactions, whether they are positive, negative, or neutral, and enables them to prioritize and address users' concerns and issues effectively.

Session Replay Analysis

Session replay analysis refers to the process of reviewing recorded user sessions to gain insights into user behavior and user experience (UX) on a digital platform. These recorded sessions are typically captured using session replay tools or software that record the user's interactions, including mouse movements, clicks, and keystrokes. Through session replay analysis, user researchers (UXRs) can observe how users navigate through a website or app, identify pain points, and understand user expectations and interactions with various features. This analysis helps UXR teams uncover usability issues, understand user frustrations, and gather data to inform design improvements. By closely examining session replays, UXR professionals can identify patterns and trends in user behavior, such as common paths or actions taken by users, recurring errors, and roadblocks that hinder smooth user experiences. This data can be used to optimize user flows, simplify processes, and enhance overall user satisfaction. Furthermore, session replay analysis enables UXR teams to validate or invalidate hypotheses, gauge the effectiveness of design changes, and measure the impact of UX improvements. By observing real-time user interactions, UXR professionals can make data-driven decisions to create user-centered designs and enhance the overall usability of digital products. In summary, session replay analysis allows UXR teams to gain valuable insights into user behavior, identify pain points, improve user experience, and optimize digital platforms by studying recorded user sessions. This data-driven approach helps drive customer-centric design decisions, ultimately leading to improved user satisfaction and better overall product performance.>

SessionCam

SessionCam is a comprehensive user-research (UXR) tool that enables businesses to gather valuable insights into user behavior and interactions on their websites. With SessionCam, researchers can systematically collect and analyze data on how users engage with their platform, helping them identify areas of improvement and optimize the user experience.

Through its advanced session replay technology, SessionCam captures and records user sessions, providing researchers with a visual representation of exactly how visitors navigate and interact with the website. This allows UXR professionals to gain an in-depth understanding of user behavior, identify pain points, and uncover usability issues.

SessionStack

SessionStack is a user-research tool that provides valuable insights into user behavior and experience on websites or web applications. It captures and records user interactions on a website, allowing researchers and UX professionals to gain a deeper understanding of how users navigate, engage, and interact with a particular digital platform.

By recording every user session, SessionStack provides detailed playback functionality, enabling researchers to view and analyze user interactions in a chronological order. This allows them to identify patterns, uncover pain points, and detect areas of improvement in the user experience. Through SessionStack, researchers can also observe real-time user interactions, providing them with a comprehensive perspective of how users interact with the website.

Shadowing

Shadowing in the context of user research (UXR) refers to the act of observing and documenting a user's behavior and interactions while they are using a product, service, or system. This research method involves closely following and studying users in their natural environment, typically without interfering or influencing their actions. The goal of shadowing is to gain insights into users' needs, expectations, pain points, and usage patterns.

During shadowing, a user researcher closely observes users as they navigate through a website, app, or physical product, taking notes and capturing significant moments of their experience. Researchers pay attention to the user's actions, gestures, facial expressions, verbal expressions, and any other behaviors or cues that may provide insight into their thoughts, feelings, or frustrations.

Shadowing is often conducted as part of the early stages of a UX research project, as it helps researchers understand how users engage with a product or service in real life. This method enables researchers to gain a deep understanding of user needs and challenges, which can inform the design and development of user-centered solutions.

By shadowing users, researchers can uncover usability issues, pain points, and areas where the user experience can be improved. This method can also reveal unexpected user behaviors or preferences, providing valuable insights that might not be captured through other research methods such as surveys or interviews.

Shopper Insights

Shopper Insights refers to the collection, analysis, and interpretation of data related to the behavior, preferences, and needs of shoppers or consumers. This research approach is commonly used in user research (UXR) to gain a deep understanding of user behavior and decision-making processes in the context of shopping experiences and interactions with products or services.

Through the application of various UXR methods such as surveys, interviews, observations, and usability testing, shopper insights aim to uncover key insights about shopping habits, motivations, pain points, and satisfaction levels. Researchers explore factors that influence shoppers' choices, such as price, product features, brand reputation, convenience, and emotions. The objective is to identify patterns, trends, and drivers of shopping behavior, allowing businesses to make informed decisions and improvements in their offerings to better meet the needs and expectations of their target audience.

Silent Observation

Silent observation is a user research technique commonly used in the field of user experience research (UXR) to gain insights into users' behaviors, preferences, and needs without direct interaction or interference from the observer. It involves carefully observing users as they naturally engage with a product, system, or service, allowing the researcher to understand how users interact with the product and identify any pain points, usability issues, or areas for improvement.

During silent observation, the researcher remains silent and takes notes or records the session through audio or video capturing methods. This technique aims to minimize the impact of the observer's presence, ensuring that users behave as naturally as possible. By avoiding direct interaction, users are more likely to engage with the product or service in a way that reflects their normal usage patterns and preferences.

Slido

Slido is an online audience interaction tool commonly used in user research (UXR). It provides a platform for researchers to gather real-time feedback, opinions, and insights from their target audience using polls, surveys, and Q&A sessions.

With Slido, researchers can create interactive sessions and engage with participants through various channels, including live events, webinars, and virtual meetings. The tool allows for seamless integration with popular video conferencing platforms, making it easy to incorporate audience interaction into remote sessions.

In the context of UXR, Slido enables researchers to gather valuable data, validate hypotheses, and gain a deeper understanding of user needs and preferences. By conducting polls, researchers can quickly collect quantitative data and identify patterns or trends within their target audience. Surveys offer a more in-depth approach, allowing researchers to delve into specific topics and gather qualitative insights.

The Q&A session feature provided by Slido enables researchers to address participants' questions and concerns directly, fostering a collaborative environment and enhancing engagement. It also allows participants to vote on the most relevant and interesting questions, ensuring that the session focuses on the topics that matter most to the audience.

Smartlook

Smartlook is a user research tool specifically designed for User Experience Researchers (UXRs). It provides valuable insights into how users interact with websites or mobile apps, helping UXR professionals understand user behavior and improve overall user experience.

As a user research tool, Smartlook offers a variety of features to assist in conducting user research. It allows UXR professionals to record user sessions, capturing their screen, clicks, mouse movements, and other interactions. This enables researchers to gain a better understanding of user behavior in real-time, identifying pain points, and areas of improvement.

Additionally, Smartlook provides heatmaps, which visually represent the most frequently clicked areas on a website or app. This information allows UXR professionals to optimize the placement of important elements and improve overall user engagement.

Furthermore, Smartlook offers conversion funnels, which enable UXR professionals to track user journeys from entry to conversion. By analyzing these funnels, researchers can identify bottlenecks in the user flow and make data-driven decisions to enhance conversion rates.

In summary, Smartlook is a valuable tool that provides UXR professionals with the ability to record user sessions, analyze heatmaps, and track conversion funnels. By leveraging these features, researchers can gain valuable insights into user behavior, identify areas of improvement, and ultimately enhance the overall user experience of websites and mobile apps.

Social Media Listening

Social media listening, in the context of user research (UXR), refers to the process of monitoring and analyzing social media conversations and interactions to gain insights about user opinions, preferences, and experiences.

Through social media listening, user researchers can gather valuable information about how users perceive and engage with a product, brand, or industry. By analyzing social media posts, comments, reviews, and other user-generated content, researchers can uncover patterns, sentiments, and trends that provide a deeper understanding of user needs, desires, and pain points.

The data collected through social media listening can be used to identify emerging themes, identify pain points, and gauge overall sentiment towards a brand or product. This information can then help inform the design and development of user-centered solutions, as well as inform marketing strategies and communication efforts.

Additionally, social media listening can be used to track and assess the impact of marketing campaigns, product launches, or other business initiatives. By monitoring social media conversations, researchers can measure the reach and effectiveness of their efforts, identify areas for improvement, and make data-driven decisions.

Split Testing

A split test, also known as an A/B test or bucket test, is a user research method used in the field of UX research. It involves comparing two or more versions of a design or feature to determine which one performs better in terms of meeting user needs and achieving business goals.

The process of split testing begins by identifying the specific element or feature to be tested, such as a headline, layout, or call-to-action button. Two or more variants of the element are created, with each variant being presented to a separate group of users. These groups, known as the control group and the experimental group, are randomly assigned to ensure unbiased results.

During the test, data is collected and analyzed to evaluate user interactions, behaviors, and preferences. Various metrics, such as click-through rates, conversion rates, or completion rates, are used to measure the performance of each variant. The statistical significance of the results is then determined to identify whether the observed differences are statistically meaningful or simply due to chance.

Split testing provides valuable insights into user preferences and can help inform design decisions, improve user experience, and optimize conversion rates. By comparing different design options, UX researchers and designers can identify the most effective elements and make data-driven decisions to enhance the overall user experience of a product or service.

Sprint User Interviews

User interviews are a qualitative research method conducted in user experience research (UXR) to gather firsthand information from individuals who represent the target audience or user base. These interviews are conducted in a structured or semi-structured format, allowing researchers to gather rich, in-depth insights about users' needs, preferences, behaviors, attitudes, and challenges related to a product or service.

The purpose of user interviews in UXR is to gain a deep understanding of users' goals, motivations, and pain points, which can help inform the design and development process. By conducting interviews, researchers can uncover valuable insights that may not be obtainable through other research methods, such as observation or analytics. User interviews provide an opportunity to directly engage with users, allowing researchers to ask open-ended questions, probe for more details, and understand the underlying reasons behind users' behaviors and opinions.

Stakeholders

A stakeholder in the context of user-research (UXR) refers to an individual or a group of individuals who have a vested interest or influence in a project, product, or service that is being developed. Stakeholders may include internal members of an organization, such as executives, managers, designers, and developers, as well as external parties, such as users, customers, clients, and partners.

As the primary focus of user research is to understand and meet the needs, goals, and expectations of users, stakeholders play a crucial role in shaping the research process and its outcomes. They provide valuable insights, knowledge, and requirements that inform and guide the design and development decisions. By involving stakeholders in the research, user researchers can ensure that the final product or service aligns with the overall vision, strategy, and objectives of the stakeholders.

Storytelling Interviews

Storytelling interviews in the context of user research (UXR) refer to a qualitative research method used to gain a deeper understanding of users' experiences and perceptions. Unlike traditional interviews that focus on eliciting specific information, storytelling interviews aim to uncover the stories and narratives behind users' experiences with a particular product or service.

During a storytelling interview, the researcher adopts a narrative approach to encourage participants to share their experiences in the form of a story. The interviewee is given the freedom to express themselves and share their thoughts, emotions, and personal anecdotes related to their use of the product or service. The researcher acts as a facilitator, asking open-ended questions to encourage the interviewee to provide a rich and detailed account of their experience.

Storytelling interviews are valuable in user research as they provide insights into the user's context, motivations, and needs on a deeper level. By focusing on narratives, researchers can uncover not only what users do but also why and how they do it. This helps in gaining a holistic understanding of the user experience and can inform the design and development of user-centered solutions. Additionally, storytelling interviews can reveal the emotional aspects of the user's experience, providing valuable insights into their overall satisfaction and engagement.

Strategy

User research (UXR) is a systematic process of understanding the needs, behaviors, preferences, and motivations of users to inform the design and development of products, services, or systems. It involves collecting and analyzing data through various research methods, such as interviews, observations, surveys, and usability testing, to gain insights into user experiences and perceptions. The primary goal of user research is to bridge the gap between the intended design of a product and the actual needs and behaviors of its target users. By conducting user research, designers and developers can identify and prioritize user requirements, uncover pain points and difficulties, evaluate the usability and effectiveness of a product, and gather valuable feedback for iterative improvements. User research encompasses both qualitative and quantitative methods. Qualitative research techniques, such as user interviews and observations, provide rich, in-depth insights into users' thoughts, feelings, and behaviors. On the other hand, quantitative research methods, including surveys and analytics, generate numerical data to measure, quantify, and validate user behavior patterns. The findings from user research help inform design decisions, guide usability improvements, and ultimately contribute to the creation of user-centered products and experiences. By involving users throughout the design process, UXR ensures that products meet their needs, are intuitive to use, and provide a positive user experience. In summary, user research is a systematic approach to gain a deep understanding of users' needs, behavior, and preferences. It enables designers and developers to make informed decisions, prioritize user requirements, and create products that meet users' needs and expectations.

Stress Testing

Stress Testing, in the context of user research (UXR), refers to a method of evaluating the usability and user experience of a design or product under extreme or challenging conditions. It involves intentionally subjecting the design to various stressful scenarios to observe how it performs and identify potential weaknesses or points of failure.

The purpose of stress testing in user research is to uncover any usability issues that may arise when the design is used in real-world conditions that are demanding or less than ideal. By simulating these stress-inducing situations, researchers can gather insights into areas where the design may not meet users' needs or expectations, highlighting areas for improvement.

Structured Walkthrough

A structured walkthrough in the context of user research (UXR) is a systematic process used to evaluate and improve the user experience of a product or service. It involves a detailed examination of the user interface, functionality, and overall design to identify potential issues or areas of improvement. During a structured walkthrough, a team of researchers, designers, and stakeholders come together to review the product or service. The process typically follows a predefined set of steps to ensure consistency and accuracy: 1. Preparation: The team familiarizes themselves with the goals and objectives of the study, as well as any relevant background information about the users and their needs. 2. Scenario development: A series of hypothetical user scenarios are created to simulate real-world usage of the product or service. These scenarios help guide the evaluation process and provide context for the participants. 3. Execution: The team systematically goes through each scenario, interacting with the product or service and documenting their observations. They pay attention to user interactions, user interface elements, error messages, and any other relevant aspects. 4. Findings and analysis: The team collaboratively discusses and consolidates their findings, noting both positive aspects and areas that require improvement. They may use various qualitative and quantitative research methods to support their observations. 5. Recommendations: Based on the findings and analysis, the team develops actionable recommendations for improving the user experience. These recommendations may include changes to the design, user interface, functionality, or any other relevant aspects. A structured walkthrough provides valuable insights into the strengths and weaknesses of a product or service from a user's perspective. It helps identify usability issues, improve user satisfaction, and guide iterative design and development processes.>

Success Stories

Success Stories in the context of user research (UXR) refer to real-life examples or case studies that demonstrate how user research has been instrumental in achieving desired outcomes or goals for a product or service. These stories highlight the positive impact of user research on a project's success and help to illustrate the value of incorporating user insights and perspectives into the design and development process.

Success Stories in UXR typically involve the identification and understanding of user needs, pain points, and preferences through various research methods such as interviews, surveys, usability testing, or ethnographic studies. The insights gained from these research efforts are then used to inform decision-making, shape product strategy, improve user experience, and drive business outcomes.

For example, a success story could showcase how a UXR team conducted in-depth user interviews to uncover a specific pain point in a mobile banking app. Based on these insights, the design team made iterative improvements to the app's navigation and layout, resulting in a significant decrease in user frustrations and an increase in customer satisfaction. This ultimately led to higher usage rates and increased revenue for the banking institution.

Success Stories in UXR are valuable tools for both practitioners and stakeholders as they provide tangible evidence of the impact and benefits of user research. They help to build credibility, justify investment in UXR, and inspire organizations to prioritize user-centric design practices. Overall, Success Stories in UXR reinforce the importance of understanding and empathizing with users to create products and services that truly meet their needs and expectations.

Summative Assessment Surveys

A summative assessment survey in the context of user-research (UXR) is a formal method used to evaluate and measure the overall success or effectiveness of a product, service, or user experience. It is typically conducted at the end of a project or specific stage to gather feedback and data from users or participants.

The purpose of a summative assessment survey is to provide quantitative insights and metrics that help researchers and stakeholders assess the overall satisfaction, usability, and performance of a product or experience. This type of survey aims to determine the extent to which the objectives and goals of the project have been achieved, as well as identify areas for improvement.

Summative Usability Testing

The summative usability testing is a formal evaluation method used in user-research (UXR) to assess the overall usability of a product or system. It is typically conducted towards the end of the development process to gather quantitative data and measure the effectiveness, efficiency, and user satisfaction of the product.

This type of testing involves observing users as they perform specific tasks on the product, such as completing a purchase, signing up for an account, or navigating through different sections. The goal is to identify any usability issues, pain points, or areas of confusion that may impact the user experience.

During summative usability testing, researchers often use various metrics and measurements to quantify the performance and user satisfaction, such as task success rate, completion time, error rate, and subjective ratings. The test sessions are carefully planned and executed, following a predefined protocol to ensure consistency and reliability of the results.

The findings and insights from summative usability testing are then used to refine and improve the product's design and functionality. By identifying usability issues and areas for improvement, the testing helps to validate design decisions, prioritize enhancements, and ultimately enhance the overall user experience.

Survey Design

A survey design refers to the process of creating a structured set of questions or prompts that are used to collect data and insights from users in order to understand their needs, preferences, and behaviors. In the context of user research (UXR), survey design plays a crucial role in gathering quantitative and qualitative data to inform the design and development of user-centered products and experiences.

The goal of survey design in user research is to gather specific information from a targeted user group that can be analyzed and used to make informed decisions. The design of the survey should be carefully planned and executed to ensure the collection of accurate and relevant data.

When designing a survey for user research, it is important to carefully consider the following factors:

The target audience: Defining the specific group of users that the survey aims to gather insights from. This includes considering demographics such as age, gender, location, and any other relevant characteristics that may impact the user's experience.

The research objectives: Clearly outlining the goals and objectives of the survey. This includes identifying the specific information or insights that need to be gathered in order to address the research objectives.

The survey structure: Creating a logical and organized structure for the survey questions. This includes using appropriate question types, such as multiple choice, rating scales, open-ended, or Likert scale questions, to effectively capture the desired information.

The wording and phrasing: Using clear, concise, and neutral language in the survey questions to avoid biased or leading responses. It is important to ensure that the questions are easy to understand and answer.

The order and flow: Designing the survey in a way that ensures a smooth and logical progression of questions. This includes considering the order of questions, grouping related questions together, and avoiding any potential confusion or repetition.

The survey design process involves iterative testing and refining to ensure that it effectively elicits the desired responses and meets the objectives of the user research. By carefully considering these factors, survey design provides a valuable method for collecting user insights and shaping user experiences.

Surveys

A survey is a research method used in user-research (UXR) to collect information and data from individuals in order to gain insights about their opinions, preferences, behaviors, and experiences. It involves asking a series of questions, which can be both open-ended and closed-ended, to a specific group of people, also known as respondents or participants.

The main purpose of conducting surveys in user-research is to gather quantitative and qualitative data that can help UX researchers understand user needs, expectations, and motivations. By analyzing the responses obtained from surveys, researchers can identify patterns, trends, and commonalities among the respondents, which can be used to inform the design and development of user-centered products or services.

Surveys can be administered through various channels and mediums such as online platforms, email, mobile applications, telephone calls, or in-person interviews. The questions asked in surveys can cover a wide range of topics, including user demographics, product usability, satisfaction levels, attitudes towards certain features or functionalities, and suggestions for improvement.

Survey methodologies can vary depending on the research objectives and the target audience. Common survey types used in UXR include cross-sectional surveys, which gather data at a single point in time, and longitudinal surveys, which collect data over an extended period. Surveys can also employ different question formats, such as multiple-choice, rating scales, Likert scales, and open-text responses.

Overall, surveys are a valuable tool in user-research as they provide a structured and systematic approach to collect data from a large number of users, enabling researchers to gain insights, make data-driven decisions, and improve the user experience of products or services.

Survicate

Survicate is a user-research (UXR) tool that enables companies to gather valuable feedback from their users, helping to better understand their needs and improve the overall user experience.

With Survicate, businesses can easily create and distribute surveys, questionnaires, and feedback forms to their audience. These can be customized to fit specific research objectives, allowing companies to gather targeted insights and data. The tool supports various question formats, including multiple choice, open-ended, rating scales, and more, providing flexibility in data collection.

Survicate also offers different distribution methods, such as pop-ups, embedded forms, email campaigns, and website surveys. This allows for reaching users at various touchpoints throughout their journey, capturing feedback at the right moment. The tool integrates with popular platforms like Gmail, WordPress, Shopify, and more, streamlining the data collection process.

Furthermore, Survicate provides powerful analytics and reporting features to interpret the gathered data. These include real-time visualizations, customizable dashboards, and cross-tabulations, enabling businesses to uncover patterns, insights, and correlations effortlessly. The insights can help identify pain points, assess user satisfaction, and inform decision-making processes.

In summary, Survicate is a comprehensive user-research tool that empowers companies to collect feedback directly from their user base. By leveraging this tool, businesses can gain valuable insights, optimize their products, and enhance the overall user experience, ultimately driving customer satisfaction, loyalty, and business growth.

Synthesis

User Research (UXR) is a systematic process of gathering and analyzing data with the purpose of understanding user needs, behaviors, and motivations. It involves various qualitative and quantitative research methods to inform the design and development of user-centered products and services.

UXR aims to uncover insights that help organizations make informed decisions about their products and improve the overall user experience. By collecting and interpreting user data, UXR practitioners gain a deeper understanding of users' goals, preferences, pain points, and interactions with a product or service.

Task Analysis

User research (UXR) is a systematic approach used in the field of user experience (UX) design to understand users' behaviors, needs, motivations, and goals. It involves gathering qualitative and quantitative data from actual users to inform the design and development process.

Through various research methods, UXR aims to uncover insights about users' preferences, pain points, and expectations in order to create user-centered products and services. It helps designers and organizations gain a deep understanding of their target audience, enabling them to make informed decisions to improve user satisfaction and overall user experience.

Tealeaf

Tealeaf is a user-research tool that provides valuable insights into user behavior and helps improve user experience (UX) design. Developed by IBM, Tealeaf records and captures user interactions on websites and mobile applications, allowing UX researchers to analyze and understand user behavior in-depth.

Tealeaf offers a range of features and functionalities that enable UX researchers to identify pain points, areas of friction, and opportunities for optimization in the user journey. It captures and enables replay of user sessions, including mouse movements, clicks, taps, scrolling, and form inputs. This detailed view of user interactions helps researchers uncover user intent, understand user struggles, and identify potential usability issues.

With Tealeaf, UX researchers can segment and filter user sessions based on various criteria like device type, location, user actions, and user demographics. This allows for targeted analysis and helps identify patterns and trends in user behavior. The tool also provides heatmaps and session replays, further enhancing the understanding of how users engage with a website or application.

Tealeaf integrates with other UX research tools and analytics platforms, making it easier to combine quantitative and qualitative data for a comprehensive understanding of user behavior. The insights gained from Tealeaf can be used to make data-driven decisions, enhance UX design, and optimize the user journey, ultimately leading to improved user satisfaction and business outcomes.

Telephone Surveys

Telephone surveys are a user-research method used in the field of user experience research (UXR) to gather quantitative data from a selected sample of participants. This method involves conducting structured interviews over the phone, where a researcher asks a series of pre-determined questions to collect information and insights related to a specific research objective.

Telephone surveys offer several advantages in user research. Firstly, they provide a relatively quick and cost-effective way to collect data from a large number of participants. Unlike in-person interviews, telephone surveys do not require travel or physical presence, making them more convenient for both researchers and participants. Additionally, telephone surveys allow researchers to reach a geographically diverse group of participants, eliminating location constraints.

Furthermore, telephone surveys can be used to gather both qualitative and quantitative data, depending on the type of questions asked. Open-ended questions can provide in-depth insights and opinions from participants, while closed-ended questions with predefined response options allow for easier data analysis and comparison. Moreover, telephone surveys are flexible, as they

119

can be conducted during various times of the day to accommodate different participants' schedules.

However, telephone surveys also have limitations. They may be subject to response bias, as people who do not have access to phones or prefer not to participate in surveys may be excluded from the sample. Additionally, the lack of visual cues during phone interviews may limit the researcher's ability to observe non-verbal expressions and emotions, potentially impacting data collection. Nevertheless, when used effectively, telephone surveys can provide valuable insights into user behaviors, preferences, and attitudes, helping inform the design and improvement of products, services, and experiences.

Text Analytics

Text analytics, in the context of user-research (UXR), refers to the process of extracting valuable insights and meaningful patterns from textual data collected during user research activities. It involves utilizing various computational techniques to analyze and interpret text-based information in order to gain a deeper understanding of user behavior, preferences, and attitudes.

Text analytics encompasses several key components, including natural language processing (NLP), sentiment analysis, and topic modeling. NLP techniques are used to preprocess and clean textual data, enabling further analysis. Sentiment analysis focuses on determining the emotional tone and sentiment expressed within the text, allowing researchers to comprehend users' opinions and attitudes towards a particular product, service, or experience. Topic modeling helps to identify and categorize recurring themes or topics discussed within the text, providing researchers with insights into users' interests and priorities.

Thematic Analysis

Thematic analysis in the context of user research (UXR) is a qualitative data analysis method used to identify and interpret recurrent patterns or themes in interview transcripts, observation notes, survey responses, or other types of data collected from users. The goal of thematic analysis is to gain a deeper understanding of users' experiences, perceptions, behaviors, and needs.

The process of thematic analysis typically involves several steps. Firstly, the researcher familiarizes themselves with the data by transcribing interviews, creating summaries, or reviewing notes. Then, the researcher generates initial codes, which are short labels or tags that represent different aspects of the data. These codes can be descriptive or interpretive and are used to categorize segments of the data that share similar content or meaning.

Next, the researcher organizes the codes into potential themes, which are broader patterns or structures that encompass multiple codes. Themes are generated through a process of comparison and grouping, focusing on identifying similarities and differences between codes. The researcher examines the relationships between themes and codes, refining and revising them as necessary.

Once the themes are finalized, the researcher writes a report that includes a description of each theme, supported by relevant quotes or examples from the data. The report aims to provide a rich and nuanced understanding of the data, highlighting key findings, insights, and implications for the design or improvement of user experiences.

Think-Aloud Protocols

A Think-Aloud Protocol is a qualitative research method used in User Experience Research (UXR) to gain insights into users' thought processes and decision-making while they interact with a product or system. It involves instructing participants to verbalize their thoughts and reactions out loud as they perform a series of tasks or engage in specific activities.

During a Think-Aloud session, participants are encouraged to express their thoughts, feelings, intentions, and uncertainties in real-time. They are asked to share any observations, opinions, understandings, or difficulties they encounter during the task. This technique is primarily used to understand how users perceive, interpret, and interact with a product, identifying areas of success, confusion, or frustration.

The data collected from Think-Aloud Protocols provides researchers with invaluable insights into users' mental models, expectations, biases, and preferences. By capturing participants' unfiltered thoughts and behaviors, researchers can identify usability issues, validate design decisions, and generate ideas for improvement. This method is particularly effective for uncovering usability problems that may not be apparent through other research methods.

Think-Aloud Protocols can be conducted in various settings, such as usability labs, remote sessions, or natural environments. They can be used at different stages of product development, from early conceptualization to post-launch evaluation. The researcher's role is to facilitate the session, encourage participants to think out loud, and ask probing questions whenever necessary to elicit more detailed insights.

In summary, Think-Aloud Protocols provide researchers with in-depth insights into users' cognitive processes, helping to inform user-centered design decisions and enhance the overall user experience of a product or system.

Thought Leadership

Thought leadership in the context of user research (UXR) refers to the ability of a practitioner to become an authority and provide unique insights and perspectives within the field.

As a thought leader in user research, a practitioner demonstrates a deep understanding of user behavior, needs, and motivations. They stay up-to-date with current industry trends, research methods, and emerging technologies. Through their expertise, they are able to offer innovative and valuable solutions to design challenges and improve the overall user experience.

Time-On-Page Analysis

Time-on-Page Analysis is a user research method used in the field of User Experience Research (UXR) to measure the amount of time users spend on a specific webpage or content within a website. It aims to understand user engagement and behavior by analyzing the duration users spend on a page or specific elements within that page.

By tracking the time-on-page metric, researchers can gain insights into user interactions, such as reading, scrolling, or engaging with multimedia content. This analysis helps identify patterns and behaviors that can be used to improve website design, content layout, and overall user experience.

Tools Evaluation

User research tools are software applications or platforms that assist UX researchers in collecting, analyzing, and interpreting data during the research process. These tools facilitate the systematic gathering of user insights, enabling researchers to make informed design decisions. One commonly used user research tool is surveys. Surveys allow researchers to collect large-scale quantitative data from a wide audience. By asking multiple-choice or open-ended questions, researchers can gather information about user preferences, behavior, and demographics. Surveys can be conducted online or in-person, providing flexibility in data collection methods. Another important user research tool is interviews. Interviews enable researchers to conduct in-depth conversations with individual users or groups. Through open-ended questions and follow-up probes, researchers can gain a deeper understanding of user experiences, motivations, and needs. By incorporating empathy and active listening, researchers can obtain rich qualitative data that informs the design process. Observation tools, such as eye-tracking software or screen recording tools, help capture and analyze user behavior and interactions. These tools allow researchers to monitor users' actions, mouse movements, gaze patterns, and clicks, providing valuable insights into user engagement and usability. Usability testing platforms are also vital user research tools. These tools facilitate the evaluation of prototypes or existing interfaces by allowing researchers to observe users interact with the product. Researchers can identify areas of improvement, usability issues, and pain points by observing users' actions and collecting their feedback. In conclusion, user research tools are indispensable resources for UX researchers. These tools aid in collecting both quantitative and qualitative data through surveys, interviews, observation, and usability testing. By harnessing the power of these tools, researchers can make data-driven decisions that enhance the user experience.>

Tools

Tools refer to the various hardware and software resources used by user researchers (UXRs) to collect, analyze, and interpret data in order to gain insights into the needs, preferences, and behaviors of users. These tools enable UXR professionals to conduct effective research and make informed design decisions.

UXR tools can be classified into different categories based on their specific purposes and functionalities. Some common types of tools used in user research include:

1. Communication Tools: These tools facilitate effective communication and collaboration among researchers, stakeholders, and participants. Examples include messaging platforms, video conferencing software, and project management tools.

2. Data Collection Tools: These tools help UXR professionals collect data from users through various methods such as surveys, interviews, and usability testing. They may include online survey platforms, interview tools, screen recording software, and eye-tracking equipment.

3. Data Analysis Tools: These tools enable researchers to analyze and make sense of the collected data. They may range from basic spreadsheet software to advanced statistical analysis tools, data visualization platforms, and qualitative analysis software.

4. Prototyping and Design Tools: These tools aid in creating and refining design prototypes and mockups. They can include wireframing software, prototyping tools, graphic design software, and interactive user interface (UI) design tools.

Overall, the use of appropriate tools in user research is crucial for generating accurate and reliable insights, understanding user needs, and creating user-centered products and experiences.

Touchstone Tours

Touchstone Tours is a user-research service that specializes in gathering valuable insights from users to inform the design and development of digital products and experiences. This service is essential for businesses that aim to create user-centered designs and enhance user satisfaction.

Through various research methodologies, such as user interviews, surveys, and usability testing, Touchstone Tours collects qualitative and quantitative data regarding user behaviors, needs, and preferences. This data is then analyzed and synthesized to identify patterns, trends, and opportunities for improvement.

The main goal of Touchstone Tours is to bridge the gap between businesses and their target users by uncovering deep insights into their needs, motivations, and pain points. This allows businesses to make informed decisions in their product development process, ultimately leading to more successful and impactful digital experiences.

Touchstone Tours follows a user-centered approach, prioritizing the user's perspective and considering their feedback throughout the design and development process. By conducting user research, businesses can understand their users better, identify areas for improvement, and ensure that their products are intuitive, user-friendly, and meet the needs of their target audience.

Trade Show Testing

Trade show testing, in the context of user research (UXR), refers to the process of conducting usability evaluations and gathering feedback from users during trade shows or similar events.

During a trade show, organizations often showcase their products or services to a large number of attendees. It provides an opportune moment for UX researchers to interact with potential users and collect valuable insights regarding the usability and desirability of their offerings.

Training Program

A user research (UXR) training program refers to a structured set of activities and learning experiences designed to equip individuals with the necessary skills and knowledge to conduct effective user research in the field of user experience (UX). The program aims to develop participants' understanding of user-centered design principles and methodologies, and enhance their abilities to gather meaningful insights from users to inform the design and development process.

The UXR training program typically covers a range of topics related to user research, including research planning, recruitment and selection of participants, data collection techniques (such as interviews, surveys, and usability testing), data analysis and synthesis, and reporting and communication of research findings. Participants are guided through theoretical concepts and best practices, and are given opportunities to engage in hands-on exercises and real-world projects to apply their learning in practical situations.

The program employs a combination of instructional methods, including lectures, group discussions, case studies, role-playing exercises, and practical assignments. Participants are encouraged to engage in critical thinking and reflective practice to build their expertise in user research. The training program may be delivered in different formats, such as live workshops, online courses, or a blend of both, to accommodate different learning preferences and geographical constraints.

By participating in a UXR training program, individuals can develop the skills and confidence needed to effectively conduct user research, leading to improved user experiences and better-informed design decisions. The program also provides a platform for individuals to connect with other professionals in the field, fostering a community of practice and enabling knowledge sharing and collaboration among practitioners.

Training

User research (UXR) refers to the systematic investigation of users' behaviors, needs, and motivations in order to inform the design and development of user-centered products or services. It involves gathering and analyzing qualitative and quantitative data to gain insights into users' experiences, preferences, and challenges.

In the context of user-centered design, user research plays a crucial role in understanding the target user base, their goals, and the context in which they will interact with a product or service. This information helps designers identify and prioritize design requirements, make informed design decisions, and validate design concepts.

User research typically involves various methods and techniques such as interviews, surveys, observations, usability testing, and data analysis. These methods provide valuable data about users' attitudes, behaviors, motivations, and needs, which can then be used to identify pain points, uncover opportunities for improvement, and guide iterative design processes.

The insights gained from user research empower designers to create intuitive and effective user interfaces, optimize user flows, and enhance overall user satisfaction. Furthermore, by involving users in the design process, user research helps ensure that the end product meets the needs and expectations of its target audience, leading to increased user adoption and loyalty.

In conclusion, user research is a fundamental practice within the field of user experience design. It enables designers to gain a deep understanding of users and their needs, resulting in the creation of user-centered products and services that effectively meet those needs.>

Tree Testing

Tree testing is a user-research method commonly used in the field of User Experience Research (UXR). It involves evaluating the information architecture (IA) and navigation structure of a website or application by testing how well users are able to find specific items or complete tasks within the system.

The technique gets its name from the analogy of a tree, where the root represents the homepage and the branches represent the different categories and subcategories. Tree testing focuses on the structural organization rather than the visual design or content of the interface, allowing researchers to isolate and evaluate the effectiveness of the IA and navigation elements.

During a tree testing session, participants are presented with a simplified text-based representation of the website's navigation structure, consisting of a hierarchical tree diagram. They are then given specific tasks to complete, such as finding a particular product or locating relevant information. Participants navigate through the tree structure by selecting nodes that they believe will lead them to the desired destination.

The goal of tree testing is to identify any issues or inconsistencies in the IA and navigation that may hinder users' ability to find information or complete tasks efficiently. Data collected during tree testing sessions can provide valuable insights for improving the organization and labeling of website categories, subcategories, and navigation paths.

Treejack

Treejack is a user research tool commonly used in the field of user experience research (UXR) to evaluate and optimize the information architecture (IA) of a website or application. It provides a quantitative analysis of how well users can navigate through the structure of a website or application and find specific pieces of information.

The Treejack tool allows researchers to create and administer tree tests, which involve presenting users with a hierarchical structure of a website or application and asking them to navigate to a specific item or category. Participants are provided with a series of tasks or questions and are asked to click on the path they would take to find the requested item. This process allows researchers to gather data on how users perceive and comprehend the structure and organization of information on a website or application.

Trends

Trends in user-research (UXR) refer to the patterns and shifts in behaviors, preferences, and attitudes of users and consumers that can be observed over a period of time. These trends provide valuable insights into the evolving needs and expectations of users, allowing UX researchers and designers to make informed decisions and create more user-centered experiences.

By identifying and analyzing trends in UXR, researchers can gain a deeper understanding of user behaviors, motivations, and pain points. This understanding helps in identifying opportunities for improving user experiences, identifying areas that require further investigation, and predicting future user needs.

Triad Interviews

Triad interviews, in the context of user research (UXR), refer to a method of conducting qualitative interviews with multiple participants simultaneously. Unlike traditional one-on-one interviews, triad interviews involve three participants: a moderator and two users. The purpose of triad interviews is to gather richer insights and perspectives by promoting interaction and discussion among participants. By bringing together two users who share a similar context or have contrasting experiences, triad interviews allow for the exploration of similarities, differences, and the dynamics that arise during discussions. During a triad interview, the moderator acts as a facilitator and guide, ensuring that the conversation remains focused and productive. The moderator encourages participants to share their thoughts, experiences, and opinions, while also providing equal opportunities for each participant to speak. The dynamics between participants often lead to the emergence of new insights and ideas that may not have arisen in a one-on-one interview setting. Triad interviews are particularly valuable in user research as they provide a more comprehensive understanding of users' behaviors, preferences, and needs. By observing the interactions and listening to the discussions, researchers can uncover underlying motivations, explore potential pain points, and gain deeper insights into user experiences with a product or service. In conclusion, triad interviews offer an effective approach to user research by fostering interaction and discussion among multiple participants. Through these interviews, researchers can gain valuable insights that can inform the design and development of user-centered products and services.>

TryMyUI

TryMyUI is a user-research platform that enables businesses and organizations to gather feedback and insights about their digital products and services. Specifically designed for usability testing, TryMyUI offers a comprehensive suite of tools and features that aid in evaluating the user experience (UX) of websites, applications, and other digital interfaces.

With TryMyUI, researchers can create and administer tasks for participants to complete while interacting with a digital product. These tasks are carefully crafted to simulate real-life scenarios and user journeys, allowing researchers to observe and understand how users navigate through the interface, interpret information, and complete desired actions.

The platform offers various testing modes, including remote usability testing, moderated testing, and unmoderated testing, providing flexibility and convenience for researchers and participants. TryMyUI also supports screen and audio recording during testing sessions, capturing valuable footage of participants' behaviors, interactions, and comments.

TryMyUI's robust analytics and reporting capabilities enable researchers to analyze and interpret the collected data, identifying usability issues, pain points, and areas of improvement in their digital products. These insights can inform design decisions, guide iterative development, and ultimately enhance the overall user experience.

Through its user-friendly interface and intuitive workflows, TryMyUI streamlines the process of conducting user research, making it accessible to both seasoned UX professionals and those new to the field. With its diverse range of testing options, comprehensive data collection, and analysis features, TryMyUI serves as an invaluable tool for any organization seeking to optimize the usability of their digital products and ensure a positive user experience.

Typography Testing

Typography testing is a user-research method in which the visual aspects of text, such as font, size, spacing, and formatting, are evaluated for their impact on user experience. It involves studying how the design choices of typography affect readability, comprehensibility, and overall user perception and satisfaction.

Typography plays a crucial role in shaping the user's interaction and understanding of digital and print content. By conducting typography testing, UX researchers gather valuable insights into the preferences and needs of users related to how text is presented. This method helps researchers and designers make informed decisions about typography and its impact on usability and aesthetics.

UXCam

UXCam is a user research tool that allows researchers to gain insights into user behavior by capturing and analyzing user interactions within mobile apps. It provides valuable data for user experience research (UXR) teams to understand how users navigate through an app, identify pain points, and uncover opportunities for improvement.

With UXCam, researchers can record and replay user sessions to observe how specific users interact with an app. This feature enables them to see exactly what users see and understand the context in which certain actions are taken. By watching session recordings, researchers can pinpoint usability issues, track user flows, and identify areas where users may get stuck or frustrated.

The tool also captures various data points such as time spent on screens, touch gestures, device orientation, and user inputs. This data helps researchers identify common patterns and behaviors, allowing them to make informed decisions based on real user actions rather than assumptions or guesswork.

UXCam offers additional features such as customizable events and funnels, heatmaps, and user feedback collection. These features further enhance the depth of insights available to researchers. Funnel analysis allows researchers to track specific user journeys and identify drop-off points, while heatmaps provide visual representations of where users engage most within an app.

In conclusion, UXCam is a valuable user research tool for UXR teams, providing detailed insights into user behavior within mobile apps. It allows researchers to observe and analyze user interactions, identify usability issues, and make data-driven decisions to improve the user experience.

Unmoderated Remote Usability Testing

Unmoderated remote usability testing is a type of user research method in which participants carry out tasks or interact with a website or application remotely, without any direct guidance or observation from a facilitator.

In this method, participants are given specific tasks to perform on their own, typically using their own devices and in their own environments. They are usually provided with a set of instructions and asked to think aloud as they complete the tasks. Their interactions and feedback are then recorded and analyzed by the researchers.

Unmoderated Virtual Reality User Interviews

An unmoderated virtual reality user interview refers to a user research method where participants engage in virtual reality experiences without the presence or guidance of a moderator or researcher. This type of user interview allows participants to freely explore and interact with a virtual environment, providing valuable insights into their experience, perception, and usability of the virtual reality content or application.

Unlike moderated user interviews, unmoderated virtual reality user interviews do not involve real-time interaction or direct guidance from a researcher. Instead, participants independently navigate the virtual reality environment and provide feedback on their experience through various means, such as post-task questionnaires or self-reporting tools embedded within the virtual reality application. It enables researchers to collect user data remotely and at scale.

Usability Benchmarking Surveys

Usability benchmarking surveys in the context of user research (UXR) refer to structured questionnaires designed to assess the usability of a product or system. These surveys are typically conducted to measure the efficiency, effectiveness, and satisfaction of users when interacting with a particular design. The goal of usability benchmarking surveys is to gather objective data and feedback from users to evaluate the usability of a product and identify areas for improvement.

Usability benchmarking surveys are usually conducted in a controlled testing environment or remotely, depending on the research objectives and constraints. The surveys are designed to capture both quantitative and qualitative data, utilizing a combination of closed-ended questions and open-ended prompts to gather insights. Closed-ended questions allow for easy analysis and comparison of responses, while open-ended prompts provide users with the opportunity to provide detailed feedback and suggestions.

Usability Benchmarking

Usability benchmarking is a form of user research that involves evaluating the usability of a product or system against a set of predetermined criteria. This process is used to measure the effectiveness, efficiency, and satisfaction of users when interacting with a product or system, and it helps to identify areas for improvement.

During usability benchmarking, researchers typically define a set of tasks or scenarios that users will perform while interacting with the product or system. These tasks are designed to reflect the most common and critical user activities. Users are then observed and measured as they attempt to complete the tasks, and their interaction with the product or system is assessed based on various usability metrics.

Usability Heuristic Evaluation

A usability heuristic evaluation is a systematic and structured method used in user research (UXR) to assess the user-friendliness and overall quality of a digital product or system. This evaluation method involves a team of usability experts or researchers who inspect the product and identify any usability issues or violations of established usability principles or heuristics.

The evaluation is conducted based on a set of predefined usability heuristics, which are guidelines or best practices derived from previous research and industry standards. These heuristics help evaluate the product's interface design, functionality, and overall user experience. Commonly used heuristics include visibility of system status, match between system and the real world, user control and freedom, consistency and standards, error prevention, flexibility, aesthetic and minimalist design, help and documentation, and more.

During a heuristic evaluation, the evaluators assess the product interface and interactions, taking notes of potential issues or violations of the chosen heuristics. These issues are typically categorized and prioritized based on severity and impact on the user experience. The evaluation results are then compiled into a report, which includes recommendations for improving the product's usability.

By conducting a usability heuristic evaluation, UX researchers can gain valuable insights into the strengths and weaknesses of a digital product from a usability perspective. These evaluations help identify areas for improvement, inform design decisions, and ultimately enhance the user experience of the product for its target audience.

Usability Heuristics

The usability heuristics, in the context of user-research (UXR), refer to a set of general principles or guidelines that are used to evaluate the usability of user interfaces. These heuristics help identify and address potential usability issues or problems within a system or application.

Usability heuristics are typically used as a framework for conducting heuristic evaluations, where evaluators assess the interface against a predefined list of usability heuristics. The results of these evaluations can provide valuable insights and recommendations for improving the user experience of a product.

Usability Lab

A usability lab is a controlled environment used in user research (UXR) to observe and assess user interactions with a product or system. It provides a dedicated space where researchers can conduct experiments, interviews, and usability tests to measure the ease of use and user experience of a product.

The usability lab typically consists of a room equipped with video cameras, microphones, and screen recording software to capture user behavior and interactions. The lab may also have eye-tracking devices and biometric sensors to gather additional data on user attention, emotions, and physiological responses.

In a usability lab, participants are invited to perform specific tasks or explore a product while being observed by researchers. This controlled setting allows researchers to measure and analyze user behavior, identify pain points, and understand user expectations and preferences.

Usability labs play a crucial role in the iterative design process, where user feedback and insights are used to improve the usability and user experience of a product. Through the data collected in a usability lab, researchers can identify areas of improvement, validate design decisions, and ultimately create more user-friendly and intuitive products.

Usability Metrics Analysis

Usability metrics analysis is a method used in user research (UXR) to assess the usability of a product or system. It involves the measurement and evaluation of various metrics that provide insights into how effectively and efficiently users can interact with the product or system to achieve their goals.

The primary objective of usability metrics analysis is to collect data that helps researchers understand the user experience and identify areas for improvement. This analysis focuses on capturing both quantitative and qualitative metrics to provide a comprehensive view of usability.

Usability Metrics

Usability metrics are quantitative measures used in user research (UXR) to evaluate the effectiveness, efficiency, and satisfaction of a specific user interface or product. These metrics provide insights into how easy and intuitive a system is for users to interact with, helping to identify areas for improvement and measure the success of design changes.

There are various usability metrics that can be utilized depending on the research objectives and the nature of the user interface being tested. Some commonly used metrics include:

1. Task success: Measures the percentage of users who successfully complete a specific task within a given timeframe. This metric helps identify any usability issues that may hinder users from achieving their goals efficiently.

2. Time on task: Measures the average time it takes for users to complete a task. Longer times may indicate usability problems or a steep learning curve that could be optimized for improved user experience.

3. Error rate: Measures the number or percentage of errors made by users during the completion of a task. High error rates may indicate confusing or misleading design elements that need to be addressed.

4. Satisfaction: Measures user satisfaction with the system or interface using questionnaires or surveys. This metric provides subjective feedback on the overall usability and user experience, complementing the objective data gathered from other metrics.

By collecting and analyzing these usability metrics, user researchers can gain valuable insights into the strengths and weaknesses of a user interface or product, helping inform design decisions and improve the overall user experience.

Usability Scorecards

A usability scorecard is a tool used in user research (UXR) to assess the usability of a product or system. It provides a structured way to evaluate the user experience by focusing on key usability factors.

Usability scorecards are typically created by UXR professionals and follow a standardized format. They consist of a set of criteria or guidelines that are relevant to the specific context of the product or system being evaluated. These criteria are formulated based on established usability principles and best practices.

The purpose of a usability scorecard is to objectively measure the extent to which a product or system meets the expected usability standards. It allows UXR professionals to evaluate different aspects of the user experience, such as ease of use, learnability, efficiency, error prevention, and user satisfaction.

During a usability evaluation, the UXR professional assesses the product or system against each criterion in the scorecard. They may use various research methods, such as usability testing, expert reviews, or heuristic evaluations. The results of the evaluation are then recorded in the scorecard, using a rating scale or checklist format.

By using usability scorecards, UXR professionals can gather data and insights that help identify specific usability issues and areas for improvement. The scorecards provide a standardized way to compare and track usability performance over time and across different products or systems.

Usability Surveys

A usability survey is a user-research method used in the field of User Experience Research (UXR) to assess the usability of a product or service. It involves collecting feedback from users based on their experience with using the product or service in order to evaluate its effectiveness, efficiency, and overall user satisfaction.

During a usability survey, participants are typically asked to complete a series of tasks or scenarios using the product or service, while their interactions are observed and recorded. These tasks are designed to simulate real-world usage and allow researchers to identify any usability issues, such as navigation difficulties, clarity of instructions, or confusing user interfaces.

The survey may also include open-ended questions to gather qualitative feedback on users' opinions, preferences, and suggestions for improvement. This qualitative data helps researchers gain deeper insights into users' experiences and can provide valuable context to complement the quantitative data gathered from task completion metrics and ratings.

Usability surveys can be conducted remotely or in-person, depending on the research goals and available resources. Remote surveys are often conducted through online platforms or applications, while in-person surveys may involve setting up a controlled environment for user testing.

The findings from usability surveys inform design decisions and help UX designers and researchers make data-driven improvements to enhance the overall user experience of the product or service. By identifying and addressing usability issues, organizations can increase user satisfaction, reduce user frustration, and ultimately improve the success and adoption of their products or services in the market.

Usability Test With Eye Tracking

Usability Test with Eye Tracking is a user-research method used to evaluate the effectiveness and efficiency of a website or application by measuring and analyzing user eye movements and fixations. It is commonly utilized in the field of User Experience Research (UXR) to gather insights on how users interact with a digital interface and to identify potential usability issues.

During a Usability Test with Eye Tracking, participants' eye movements are tracked using specialized eye-tracking hardware or software. This technology allows researchers to understand where users are looking, how long they focus on certain visual elements, and how their gaze patterns relate to their navigation and decision-making process.

By combining eye-tracking data with other qualitative and quantitative data, researchers can gain a deeper understanding of users' cognitive processes, attention patterns, and preferences. This method provides valuable insights into how users perceive and process visual information, helping designers and developers optimize the user interface to enhance usability, readability, and overall user satisfaction.

Overall, Usability Test with Eye Tracking is a powerful tool in UXR that allows researchers to objectively measure and evaluate the user experience. Through the analysis of eye movement data, researchers can identify areas of improvement to create more intuitive and user-friendly digital products, ultimately enhancing user satisfaction and loyalty.

Usability Test With Facial Expression Analysis

A usability test with facial expression analysis is a user research technique used to evaluate the usability of a website, application, or product by analyzing users' facial expressions during their interaction with it. This method aims to gain valuable insights on users' emotional responses, engagement levels, and overall experience to inform the design and optimization of the user interface.

During the test, participants are observed and recorded while they perform specific tasks or scenarios using the product. Their facial expressions are closely monitored and analyzed using computer vision or facial recognition technology to detect and interpret various emotions such as happiness, frustration, confusion, or surprise. These expressions can provide valuable indications of the users' cognitive processes, satisfaction, and ease of use.

Usability Testing For Augmented Reality (AR) Apps

Usability testing for Augmented Reality (AR) apps refers to a user research method that aims to evaluate the effectiveness, efficiency, and user satisfaction of AR applications. This type of testing involves observing and gathering user feedback to identify any usability issues and assess the overall user experience of the app. During usability testing, participants are asked to perform specific tasks using the AR app while researchers closely observe their interactions. These tasks are designed to simulate real-life scenarios to understand how users engage with the app and accomplish their goals. Researchers take note of any difficulties or challenges users encounter while using the app and also collect qualitative feedback about their experience. The main objective of this testing is to identify usability issues and areas for improvement in the AR app. Usability testing helps the development team understand how users navigate, interact with virtual content, and complete tasks in the app. It provides insights into the effectiveness of user interfaces, the intuitiveness of gesture-based interactions, the accuracy of object recognition, and the overall user satisfaction. The usability testing process typically includes planning, participant recruitment, test execution, data collection, analysis, and reporting. The findings from this testing method help guide the iterative design process, allowing designers and developers to fine-tune the AR app and enhance the user experience. In conclusion, usability testing for Augmented Reality (AR) apps is a crucial user research method in the field of User Experience (UX). By observing user interactions and collecting feedback, this testing facilitates the identification of usability issues, guiding the improvement of AR app design and user satisfaction.>

Usability Testing For Dating Apps

Usability testing for dating apps is a user-research method in the field of UX design that aims to evaluate the ease of use and effectiveness of dating applications. It involves observing and analyzing how users interact with the app, identifying any usability issues, and collecting feedback to improve the overall user experience.

The primary objective of usability testing is to understand how users navigate through the app, accomplish specific tasks, and overcome any obstacles or frustrations they encounter. By conducting this type of testing, UX researchers can identify areas where the app may be confusing, difficult to navigate, or inefficient, and then make informed design decisions to address these issues.

Usability Testing For E-Commerce Platforms

Usability testing for e-commerce platforms is a user-research method used to evaluate the effectiveness, efficiency, and satisfaction of an e-commerce website or application. It involves gathering feedback from real users by observing and analyzing their interactions with the platform, with the goal of identifying usability flaws and areas for improvement.

In the context of user experience research (UXR), usability testing plays a crucial role in uncovering usability issues, understanding user behavior, and validating design decisions. By observing users navigating through the e-commerce platform, researchers can assess how well the platform meets users' needs, how easily users can complete tasks, and how user-friendly the overall experience is.

Usability Testing For E-Learning Platforms

Usability testing for e-learning platforms refers to the process of evaluating the user-friendliness and effectiveness of an online learning platform. It involves conducting research to identify any usability issues that may hinder user experience and learning outcomes.

In the context of user research (UXR), usability testing plays a crucial role in understanding how users interact with an e-learning platform. It helps gather insights into how learners navigate through the interface, interact with the content, and accomplish their goals.

Usability Testing For Entertainment Apps

Usability testing for entertainment apps is a user research method aimed at evaluating the effectiveness, efficiency, and user satisfaction with an entertainment app's interface. The goal of this type of testing is to uncover potential usability issues and gather feedback on the overall user experience in order to improve the app's design and functionality.

This form of testing involves observing and analyzing how users interact with the app while performing certain tasks or scenarios representative of the app's typical usage. Test participants are typically asked to complete specific tasks, such as finding and playing a video, browsing content, or customizing settings, while their actions, preferences, and difficulties are recorded and analyzed.

The insights gained from usability testing help identify areas where the app may be confusing, unintuitive, or difficult to use. This information is crucial for making informed design decisions and refining the app's interface, navigation, and feature set to better meet the needs and expectations of its target audience.

Usability testing for entertainment apps can uncover various usability issues, such as unclear labeling, confusing navigation, inefficient workflows, and slow loading times. By providing qualitative and quantitative feedback, this testing method informs the iterative design process, allowing designers and developers to identify and prioritize improvements that will enhance the user experience and ultimately increase user satisfaction and retention.

Usability Testing For Financial Apps

Usability testing for financial apps is a user research technique that evaluates the ease of use, efficiency, and user satisfaction of financial applications. It involves observing and collecting data on how users interact with the app, identifying any usability issues, and making improvements to enhance the overall user experience.

The goal of usability testing is to uncover any usability problems that may hinder users from achieving their goals efficiently and effectively within the financial app. By conducting usability testing, UX researchers can gather insights about users' perceptions, behaviors, and preferences, which can help inform the design and development of the app.

Usability Testing For Fitness And Wellness Apps

Usability testing for fitness and wellness apps is a user-research method aimed at evaluating the effectiveness and efficiency of these applications in meeting the needs and goals of their users. It involves observing and analyzing how real users interact with the app, identifying usability issues, and gathering insights to guide iterative design improvements.

During usability testing, participants are tasked with completing specific scenarios or tasks within the app while their interactions, actions, and feedback are closely observed by the researcher. The focus is on understanding how easily users can navigate the app, accomplish their desired goals, and whether they encounter any obstacles or confusion along the way.

Through usability testing, UX researchers aim to identify areas where the app can be enhanced to provide a more user-friendly experience. This includes identifying points of friction or confusion in the app's interface, uncovering areas where the app may not align with user expectations or mental models, and collecting feedback on specific features or functionalities. Usability testing can provide valuable insights into how the app can be improved to enhance overall user satisfaction, increase engagement, and facilitate better adoption of fitness and wellness practices.

By conducting usability testing for fitness and wellness apps, organizations can make data-driven decisions to improve the user experience, ensure the app meets the needs of its target audience, and increase the likelihood of user retention and success in their health and wellness journeys.

Usability Testing For Food Delivery Apps

Usability testing for food delivery apps is a user-research method that aims to evaluate the ease of use and effectiveness of these apps from the perspective of the end-users. It involves observing and gathering feedback from users as they interact with the app, with the goal of identifying any usability issues and improving the overall user experience (UX).

During usability testing, participants are given specific tasks to complete within the food delivery app while researchers observe and take notes on their actions and feedback. These tasks can range from simple activities like searching for and selecting a restaurant to more complex actions like placing an order or tracking its delivery. The testing process may also involve conducting interviews or surveys to gather more subjective insights from the participants.

The main objective of usability testing for food delivery apps is to identify and address any usability issues that may hinder users from successfully and efficiently using the app to order food. This could include issues such as confusing navigation, unclear instructions, slow loading times, or difficulties with the payment process. By identifying these problem areas, designers and developers can make necessary changes and improvements to enhance the overall usability and user satisfaction of the app.

Ultimately, the purpose of usability testing is to ensure that the food delivery app meets the needs of its users, providing them with a smooth and enjoyable experience when using the app to order food. By conducting usability testing, app developers can make data-driven decisions to improve the app's design, functionality, and overall user experience.

Usability Testing For Healthcare Apps

Usability testing for healthcare apps is a user-research methodology used to evaluate the ease of use and effectiveness of healthcare applications. It involves gathering feedback from end users by observing their interactions with the app and analyzing their experience. The primary objective of usability testing is to identify any usability issues or barriers that may hinder users from efficiently and accurately utilizing the app.

This type of testing typically involves selecting a representative group of users who closely resemble the target audience for the healthcare app. These users are then given specific tasks to perform within the app while their interactions are closely observed and recorded. The tasks may range from simple actions such as navigating through the app to more complex actions like inputting and retrieving patient information. Observers collect data on various aspects such as time taken to complete tasks, number of errors made, and user feedback during the testing session.

The data collected from usability testing is then analyzed to identify areas of improvement in the app's design and functionality. Common usability issues include confusing or unclear navigation, unintuitive workflows, and complex terminology. By addressing these issues, healthcare app developers can enhance the overall user experience, increase user satisfaction, and improve the app's effectiveness in supporting healthcare professionals and patients.

Usability Testing For Healthcare Devices

Usability testing for healthcare devices is a method of user research (UXR) that aims to evaluate the ease of use and effectiveness of medical devices in a healthcare setting. It involves observing and collecting data from users as they interact with the devices, with the goal of identifying usability issues and improving the overall user experience.

During a usability test, a representative group of healthcare professionals or patients is selected to participate. They are asked to perform specific tasks using the device while researchers observe and take notes. The tasks are designed to simulate real-life scenarios that users would encounter, allowing researchers to evaluate the device's functionality and efficiency.

The data collected during a usability test includes observations of user behavior, feedback from participants, and performance metrics such as success rates, task completion times, and errors. This data is then analyzed to identify patterns and insights regarding the device's usability. The findings from the usability test can inform iterative design improvements and help ensure that the device meets the needs and expectations of its intended users.

Overall, usability testing for healthcare devices plays a crucial role in improving the safety and effectiveness of medical technologies. By involving users in the testing process, it enables designers and manufacturers to create devices that are intuitive, efficient, and user-friendly, ultimately leading to better healthcare outcomes for patients and healthcare professionals.

Usability Testing For IoT (Internet Of Things) Devices

Usability testing for IoT devices is a user research method used to evaluate and measure the effectiveness, efficiency, and satisfaction of the user interface and overall user experience of internet-connected products. The focus of this testing is to ensure that the device is easy to use, intuitive, and provides value to its users.

During usability testing, participants are recruited to interact with the IoT device and perform specific tasks to evaluate its usability. The testing process can include various techniques such as user observation, task scenarios, surveys, interviews, and performance measurements.

Usability Testing For Language Learning Apps

Usability testing for language learning apps is a user research method in the field of user experience research (UXR). It involves evaluating the user-friendliness and effectiveness of language learning apps through gathering feedback from users and observing their interactions with the app.

During the usability testing process, participants are given specific language learning tasks to complete using the app. The researcher carefully observes and records participants' actions, interactions, and feedback, focusing on aspects such as ease of use, effectiveness in facilitating language learning, and overall user satisfaction.

The primary goal of usability testing for language learning apps is to identify and address any usability issues or areas for improvement. This process helps developers and designers understand how users navigate through the app, interpret instructions, and interact with the learning content. Through usability testing, researchers can gather valuable insights into users' preferences, behaviors, and challenges, enabling them to make informed decisions regarding app design enhancements and optimizations.

Usability testing sessions often involve a combination of qualitative and quantitative research methods, such as observing participants' behaviors, collecting feedback through surveys or interviews, and analyzing performance metrics. The findings from usability testing provide actionable insights and recommendations to enhance the design, functionality, and overall user experience of language learning apps.

Usability Testing For Mobile Games

Usability Testing for Mobile Games refers to the process of evaluating the overall user experience and ease of use of a mobile game specifically designed for handheld devices such as smartphones and tablets. It is a user-research method conducted by UX researchers to assess the effectiveness, efficiency, and satisfaction of players while interacting with the game.

During usability testing, players are observed and recorded as they navigate through the game, complete tasks, and provide feedback on their experience. The tests can be conducted in a controlled lab environment or remotely through screen sharing or video conferencing tools. The primary goal is to identify any usability issues, areas of improvement, and gather insights that can guide the game's design and development.

Usability Testing For Navigation Apps

Usability testing for navigation apps is a user research method used to evaluate the effectiveness and efficiency of a navigation app's design and functionality. It involves observing and gathering feedback from users as they use the app to complete specific tasks related to navigation. The goal is to identify any usability issues or areas for improvement in the app's interface and features.

During usability testing, participants are typically given a set of predefined tasks to complete using the navigation app. These tasks may include finding and selecting a destination, getting directions, adjusting settings, or exploring different features. Researchers closely observe and record participants' interactions with the app, taking note of any difficulties, confusion, or errors encountered.

The collected feedback and observations are then analyzed to pinpoint problem areas and areas of strength within the navigation app. Usability testing helps identify user pain points, usability barriers, and areas where the navigation app can be improved to enhance the user experience. Based on the findings, design recommendations can be made to optimize the navigation app's interface, features, and overall usability.

Usability testing for navigation apps is crucial in gaining insights into how users interact with the app and whether it meets their navigation needs effectively. By involving real users in the testing process, designers and developers can ensure that the navigation app is intuitive, user-friendly, and provides a seamless experience for users in reaching their destinations.

Usability Testing For News And Media Apps

Usability testing for news and media apps refers to the process of evaluating the ease of use and user satisfaction with these applications. It involves observing and collecting data from actual users as they interact with the app, with the goal of identifying any usability issues and making improvements to enhance the user experience.

During usability testing, participants are given specific tasks to perform within the app, such as finding and reading news articles, navigating through different sections, or sharing content on social media. They are encouraged to think aloud and provide feedback on their experience, highlighting any difficulties, confusion, or frustrations they encounter.

The main objectives of usability testing in the context of news and media apps include:

1. Assessing the app's ease of use: Usability testing helps determine how easily users can navigate through the app, find relevant content, and perform desired actions. It identifies any design or interface issues that may hinder users from achieving their goals efficiently.

2. Identifying user pain points: Usability testing helps uncover where users struggle or get stuck within the app. This could be due to unclear labels, confusing navigation, or other factors that hinder the user's ability to complete their tasks successfully.

3. Collecting user feedback: Usability testing provides an opportunity to gather direct feedback from users about their overall experience with the app. This feedback helps understand user preferences, expectations, and perceptions, which can inform future iterations and enhancements.

By conducting usability testing for news and media apps, organizations can improve the usability and user satisfaction, leading to increased engagement, retention, and ultimately achieving their goals of delivering relevant and compelling news content to users.

Usability Testing For Photography Apps

Usability testing for photography apps is a user research method that aims to evaluate the ease of use, user satisfaction, and overall user experience of photography apps. It involves observing and collecting data from users who are given specific tasks to perform using the app, with the purpose of identifying any usability issues or areas for improvement.

The process of usability testing typically involves selecting a representative group of participants who are the target users of the photography app. These participants are given a set of tasks to complete while using the app, such as capturing and editing photos, applying filters and effects, organizing and sharing photos, and accessing settings and preferences. The participants' interactions with the app are observed and recorded, and their feedback and opinions are collected through interviews, questionnaires, or other methods.

Usability Testing For Productivity Apps

Usability testing for productivity apps refers to the process of observing and evaluating how efficiently and effectively users can interact with these applications to perform tasks and achieve their goals. It is a user-research method employed in the field of user experience research (UXR) to assess the usability and user-friendliness of productivity apps.

This type of testing typically involves selecting representative users and providing them with specific tasks to complete using the productivity app. The users' interactions with the app are closely observed, and their feedback and behavior are recorded and analyzed for insights into potential usability issues or areas of improvement.

Usability Testing For Smart Appliances

Usability testing for smart appliances is a user research method used to evaluate the effectiveness, efficiency, and satisfaction of using smart appliances. It aims to identify usability issues and gather user feedback in order to improve the user experience (UX) of these devices.

During usability testing, participants are asked to perform specific tasks using the smart appliances, while their interactions and experiences are observed and recorded. The testing process often involves the following steps:

1. Test planning: Defining the objectives, test scenarios, and specific tasks that participants will be asked to perform. This stage also includes selecting the appropriate testing methods and recruitment of participants.

2. Testing sessions: Participants are given clear instructions to perform various tasks using the smart appliances. Observers closely watch and take notes on their interactions, difficulties encountered, and feedback. Data, such as task completion time, errors made, and participant satisfaction, may also be collected.

3. Data analysis: The recorded observations, feedback, and collected data are analyzed to identify patterns, common issues, and opportunities for improvement. This analysis helps to prioritize and address usability concerns.

4. Iterative design: Usability testing is often an iterative process, where design changes are made based on the findings of each testing session. The revised design is then tested again to validate the improvements and identify any remaining issues.

By conducting usability testing for smart appliances, designers and manufacturers can gain valuable insights into how users interact with their products and make informed decisions for enhancing the user experience. Ultimately, this research method contributes to the development of more intuitive, efficient, and satisfying smart appliances that align with user needs and expectations.

Usability Testing For Smart Home Devices

Usability testing for smart home devices is a user research technique used to evaluate the ease of use, effectiveness, and overall user experience of smart home devices. It involves observing and collecting feedback from users as they interact with the devices in their own environment.

The goal of usability testing is to identify any usability issues, pain points, or areas of improvement in the smart home device's design, functionality, and user interface. This research is crucial in ensuring that the device meets the needs and expectations of its intended users.

During the usability testing process, participants are typically given specific tasks to complete using the smart home device, such as setting up a schedule or adjusting the temperature. Their interactions, feedback, and overall experience are carefully observed and recorded by the UX researcher. This allows for a comprehensive understanding of how users navigate and interact with the device, as well as any challenges they may encounter along the way.

Usability testing for smart home devices can be conducted in various settings, such as controlled lab environments, participants' homes, or simulated home environments. The research findings and insights gathered from usability testing can guide iterative design improvements, inform product development decisions, and ultimately contribute to creating smart home devices that are user-friendly, intuitive, and enjoyable to use.

Usability Testing For Smart Vehicles

Usability testing for smart vehicles is a user research technique used to evaluate the ease of use and overall user experience of a smart vehicle's user interface and features. The goal of usability testing is to identify any usability issues or roadblocks that may hinder users from effectively and efficiently interacting with the smart vehicle.

During usability testing, participants are given specific tasks to perform using the smart vehicle's interface, such as setting up navigation, adjusting the temperature, or connecting to a mobile device. Their interactions and experiences are observed and recorded by a researcher, who collects both qualitative and quantitative data on their performance, satisfaction, and any difficulties encountered.

Usability Testing For Social Media Apps

Usability testing for social media apps is a user research method used to assess the ease of use and overall user experience of social media applications. It involves observing and collecting data from users as they interact with the app, with the objective of identifying usability issues and gathering insights to inform design improvements.

During the usability testing process, participants are given specific tasks to perform within the social media app, such as creating a post, following a user, or searching for a specific topic. While they complete these tasks, their interactions, behaviors, and feedback are recorded and analyzed. This allows researchers to understand the users' mental models, their ability to navigate the app's interface, and any pain points or frustrations they encounter.

Usability Testing For Travel And Booking Apps

Usability testing for travel and booking apps is a user research methodology aimed at evaluating the ease of use and effectiveness of these applications. It involves observing and analyzing how real users interact with the app, identifying usability issues, and gathering feedback to inform design improvements.

During the usability testing process, participants are given specific tasks to complete using the travel and booking app while researchers observe their actions, experiences, and difficulties they encounter. The goal is to uncover any usability problems, such as confusing navigation, unclear instructions, or technical glitches, that hinder users from achieving their goals effectively, efficiently, and satisfactorily.

Researchers use various methods to conduct usability testing, such as in-person sessions, remote sessions, think-aloud protocols, or focus groups, depending on the research objectives and constraints. They might employ screen recording software, eye-tracking technology, or heat maps to capture participants' interactions and gather additional quantitative and qualitative data for analysis.

Through usability testing, researchers obtain insights into users' needs, preferences, and pain points, enabling them to identify areas of improvement and prioritize design enhancements. This iterative process helps ensure that travel and booking apps are user-friendly, intuitive, and meet the needs of their target audience, resulting in increased user satisfaction, engagement, and conversion rates.

Usability Testing For Virtual Reality (VR) Apps

Usability Testing for Virtual Reality (VR) Apps refers to the process of evaluating the effectiveness and efficiency of virtual reality applications in terms of user experience. It involves systematically observing and collecting data on users' interactions with the VR app to identify any usability issues or difficulties they encounter during the interaction.

The main objective of usability testing is to assess the ease of use and user satisfaction of the VR app. By conducting usability testing, user researchers can gain insights into how well the VR app meets the needs and expectations of its intended users. It helps to identify areas of improvement and suggests possible enhancements or modifications to enhance the overall user experience.

Usability Testing For Weather Apps

Usability testing for weather apps refers to the process of evaluating the user-friendliness and effectiveness of weather applications through direct observation and feedback from users. It is a user research method conducted by User Experience Researchers (UXRs) to ensure that the app meets the needs and expectations of its target audience.

During usability testing, participants are given specific tasks to perform within the app while the UXR observes their interactions, listens to their feedback, and collects data on their overall experience. The purpose is to identify any usability issues, usability barriers, or areas of improvement that may hinder users from effectively using the weather app.

Usability Testing With Assistive Technologies

Usability testing with assistive technologies is a user research method that evaluates the accessibility and user-friendliness of a digital product or service for individuals with disabilities. This testing approach involves observing and gathering feedback from users who rely on assistive technologies such as screen readers, magnifiers, voice recognition software, or alternative input devices.

The primary goal of usability testing with assistive technologies is to ensure that individuals with disabilities can effectively and efficiently use the product or service. This method focuses on identifying barriers and challenges that may hinder the user experience for this specific user group, allowing for necessary improvements and optimizations to be made. By directly involving users with disabilities, researchers gain valuable insights into their needs, preferences, and pain points.

Usability Testing With Augmented Reality (AR) Devices

Usability testing with augmented reality (AR) devices is a user research method used to assess the effectiveness, efficiency, and overall user experience of AR devices and applications. This type of testing involves observing and measuring how users interact with AR devices in real-world scenarios, with the goal of identifying usability issues and making improvements to enhance the user experience.

During a usability test with AR devices, a researcher typically sets up a controlled environment where participants are given specific tasks to complete using the AR device. The researcher observes and records the participants' interactions, collecting qualitative and quantitative data on factors such as task completion time, error rates, and user satisfaction.

This type of testing provides valuable insights into the usability and user experience of AR devices, allowing designers and developers to identify areas for improvement and make informed design decisions. By understanding how users interact with the AR interface, researchers can uncover usability issues such as navigation difficulties, unclear instructions, or ineffective gestures, and work towards designing more intuitive and user-friendly experiences.

Overall, usability testing with AR devices plays a crucial role in ensuring that these technologies are accessible and enjoyable for users. By testing and refining the user experience, designers and developers can create AR applications that are intuitive, efficient, and aligned with users' needs and expectations.

Usability Testing With Biometric Analysis

A usability testing with biometric analysis is a user research method in the field of user experience research (UXR) that involves measuring and analyzing the physiological and emotional responses of participants while they interact with a product, interface, or website. This type of testing combines traditional usability testing techniques, such as observation and participant feedback, with biometric measurements to provide deeper insights into user behavior and engagement.

During a usability testing with biometric analysis, participants are typically equipped with various biometric sensors, such as electroencephalography (EEG) for measuring brainwave activity, electrodermal activity (EDA) sensors for measuring skin conductance and sweat gland activity, and eye-tracking devices for monitoring gaze patterns. These sensors provide objective data that can be used to understand the cognitive workload, emotions, attention, and physiological responses of participants during different tasks.

Usability Testing With Eye Tracking

Usability testing with eye tracking is a user research method that involves measuring and analyzing eye movements and gaze patterns of participants as they interact with a product or interface.

During the testing session, participants are equipped with special eye-tracking hardware, such as eye-tracking glasses or a monitor-mounted device. This technology allows for the precise measurement of where participants are looking, how long they dwell on specific elements, and the sequence of their eye movements.

The primary goal of usability testing with eye tracking is to gather insights into how users visually interact with a product or interface, with the aim of optimizing its design and enhancing the overall user experience. By understanding users' visual behavior, designers and researchers can identify areas of a product that might be confusing, difficult to find, or inefficient to use.

Eye tracking data can reveal valuable insights, such as the locations on a page that attract the most attention, the order in which users look at elements, and the areas that are frequently skipped over. This information can inform decisions about layout, content prioritization, and visual hierarchy.

Usability testing with eye tracking is often conducted alongside traditional usability testing methods, such as think-aloud protocols or task-based scenarios. Combining eye tracking with qualitative feedback can provide a comprehensive understanding of users' behaviors, thoughts, and emotions as they navigate through a product.

Usability Testing With Eye-Tracking Heatmaps

Usability testing with eye-tracking heatmaps is a user research method used in the field of user experience research (UXR). It involves the use of eye-tracking technology to capture and analyze users' eye movements and fixations while they interact with a digital interface.

The process begins by recruiting participants who represent the target user group for the product or website that is being tested. These participants are then asked to complete a series of tasks using the interface, while their eye movements are recorded using an eye-tracking device. The eye-tracking data is then used to generate visualizations called heatmaps.

Heatmaps provide insights into where users are looking and how their attention is distributed across the interface. They are created by aggregating the eye-tracking data from multiple participants and overlaying it onto a visual representation of the interface. The resulting heatmap shows areas of the interface that have received the most attention, indicated by areas of high fixations and longer gaze durations.

By analyzing these heatmaps, UX researchers can identify patterns and trends in users' visual attention. This information can be used to evaluate the effectiveness of the design, identify areas of usability issues, and inform iterative improvements. Usability testing with eye-tracking heatmaps provides objective data about users' visual attention, complementing other qualitative research methods such as interviews and observation.

Usability Testing With Facial Expression Analysis

Usability Testing with Facial Expression Analysis refers to a user research technique in which facial expressions are analyzed to evaluate the usability of a product or interface. It involves capturing and analyzing users' facial expressions during a usability testing session to gain insights into their emotional reactions and experiences.

During the testing process, participants are asked to interact with a product or interface while their facial expressions are recorded using video or other facial analysis technology. This allows researchers to capture details such as smiles, frowns, raised eyebrows, or other facial movements that indicate positive or negative emotional responses.

By combining traditional usability testing methods, such as observation and think-aloud protocols, with facial expression analysis, researchers can gain a deeper understanding of the users' emotional states and the impact of these emotions on their overall experience. Facial expressions can provide valuable information about usability issues, user frustrations, or moments of delight that may not be fully captured through verbal feedback alone.

This technique can help identify areas for improvement in the design and functionality of a product or interface. It can also assist in validating design decisions and optimizing user experiences. By analyzing facial expressions, designers and researchers can gain insights into the emotional satisfaction or dissatisfaction that users may experience when interacting with a product, enabling them to make informed decisions for enhancing usability and user satisfaction.

Usability Testing With Surveys

Usability testing with surveys is a user research method utilized in the field of user experience research (UXR) to gather feedback and insights on the usability and user satisfaction of a product or service. This method involves the use of surveys to collect data from participants, typically after they have interacted with the product or service being tested.

The main objective of usability testing with surveys is to evaluate the user experience of a system by measuring its usability, ease of use, and overall user satisfaction. Surveys are a cost-effective and efficient way of gathering quantitative data, allowing researchers to collect feedback from a large number of participants in a relatively short period of time.

During usability testing with surveys, participants are typically asked a series of questions about their experience using the product or service. These questions can cover various aspects of the user experience, such as the ease of navigation, clarity of instructions, and overall satisfaction. By collecting feedback through surveys, researchers can identify pain points, areas of improvement, and gain insights into user preferences.

The data collected from usability testing with surveys can be analyzed to identify patterns and trends, allowing researchers to make data-driven decisions and recommendations for improving the user experience. Surveys can also be used to measure changes in user satisfaction over time, such as after implementing design changes or updates to the product or service.

In conclusion, usability testing with surveys is a valuable method in user experience research, providing insights into the usability and user satisfaction of a product or service. By collecting quantitative data through surveys, researchers can make informed decisions to enhance the overall user experience.

Usability Testing With Virtual Reality (VR) Devices

Usability testing with virtual reality (VR) devices is a user-research method that evaluates the effectiveness, efficiency, and satisfaction of a VR application or product from a usability standpoint. VR devices are immersive technologies that create a computer-generated environment, allowing users to interact with digital content in a three-dimensional space.

In the context of user-research (UXR), usability testing with VR devices involves observing and analyzing users' interactions, behaviors, and feedback while they perform tasks or scenarios within a VR environment. The goal is to identify usability issues, gather insights, and make data-driven decisions to improve the user experience.

Usability Testing With Wearable Devices

Usability Testing with Wearable Devices is a user research method used in the field of User Experience Research (UXR). It involves evaluating the ease of use and effectiveness of wearable devices through observation and feedback from participants.

In this testing process, a group of participants is selected to represent the target users of the wearable device. They are asked to perform specific tasks using the device while their interactions and experiences are carefully observed and recorded.

The main objective of this testing is to identify any usability issues or challenges users may face when using the device. It focuses on assessing the overall user experience, such as the device's interface, navigation, and interaction patterns.

During the testing, participants are encouraged to think aloud, expressing their thoughts, frustrations, and suggestions. This provides valuable insights into their understanding of the device and helps identify areas for improvement.

Usability testing with wearable devices can be conducted in various settings, such as controlled lab environments or real-world situations. The choice of setting depends on the research goals and the context in which the device is expected to be used.

The findings from this testing help inform the design and development of wearable devices, ensuring they meet the needs and expectations of users. It also assists in making informed decisions for iteration and optimization, leading to improved user satisfaction and device performance.

Usability Testing With Web Analytics

Usability testing with web analytics is a user-centered research method that combines qualitative data gathered from usability tests with quantitative data collected through web analytics tools. This approach helps UX researchers gain a comprehensive understanding of user behavior, preferences, and interactions on a website or digital product.

During usability testing, participants are asked to perform specific tasks on the website while their actions, observations, and feedback are carefully observed and recorded. This qualitative data provides valuable insights into the users' overall experience, highlighting pain points, areas of confusion, and moments of delight.

Web analytics tools, on the other hand, collect quantitative data about user behavior, such as the number of visits, pageviews, click-through rates, bounce rates, and conversion rates. This data helps UX researchers identify broader patterns and trends, understand user flows, and evaluate the overall performance of the website.

By combining both qualitative and quantitative data, usability testing with web analytics enables UX researchers to make data-driven decisions and prioritize improvements that align with user needs and goals. The qualitative insights offer context and a deeper understanding of users' motivations and frustrations, while the quantitative data provides a broader overview and statistical evidence.

This research method allows organizations to identify specific pain points within the user experience and make informed design decisions to improve usability, increase engagement, and optimize the overall user journey. By continuously conducting usability testing with web analytics, organizations can iterate on their designs, measure the impact of changes, and ensure continuous improvement based on real user feedback and behavior.

140

Usability Testing

Usability testing is a user research method used in the field of user experience research (UXR). It involves evaluating a product, system, or interface by observing real users as they interact with it.

The primary goal of usability testing is to identify usability issues and gather feedback to improve the design and functionality of a product. It aims to understand how users perceive and interact with a system, their pain points, and areas where they may experience confusion or frustration.

During a usability test, participants are given specific tasks to complete using the product or interface. They are observed and their actions, behaviors, and feedback are recorded. This information helps researchers identify areas where the product may be difficult to use, or where users may make mistakes or encounter obstacles in achieving their goals.

Usability testing provides valuable insights into user expectations, preferences, and behavior. It helps validate design decisions, uncover usability issues, and make informed design improvements. By involving real users in the testing process, it ensures that the product is designed with the user's needs and expectations in mind.

Overall, usability testing is an essential part of the user-centered design process. It enables designers and researchers to understand how users interact with products and make informed decisions to enhance usability and improve the overall user experience.

UsabilityHub

UsabilityHub is a platform that is commonly used in user-research (UXR) to gather feedback and insights on digital products and designs through a variety of research methods.

With UsabilityHub, researchers can conduct usability tests, run surveys, and get fast feedback from a diverse group of participants. The platform offers a range of tools and features that facilitate the process of gathering user feedback, making it a valuable resource in the field of UX research.

UsabilityTools

UsabilityTools refers to a set of tools and techniques used in the field of user research (UXR) to evaluate and improve the usability of digital products or services. Usability, in the context of user experience (UX), refers to the ease of use and effectiveness of a product in meeting the needs and goals of its users.

These tools are designed to gather data and insights about user behavior and interactions, allowing researchers and designers to identify pain points, understand user needs, and make informed design decisions. UsabilityTools often include a range of qualitative and quantitative methods, such as usability testing, card sorting, tree testing, heatmapping, and surveys.

Usabilla

Usabilla is a user research tool that allows UX researchers to collect feedback and gather insights from users to improve the user experience of a digital product. It provides a platform for conducting usability testing, surveys, and gathering customer feedback, which can be used to inform design decisions and optimize the user interface.

With Usabilla, UX researchers can create and deploy targeted surveys to specific user segments, enabling them to gather feedback on specific aspects of the user experience. The tool also enables researchers to conduct remote usability testing, allowing participants to interact with a prototype or website while researchers observe and collect data. This remote testing capability is particularly useful in situations where in-person testing is not feasible or practical.

Usabilla offers various features to help UX researchers analyze and interpret feedback data. It provides visualizations and analytics that allow researchers to easily identify patterns and trends in feedback responses. The tool also allows researchers to make annotations and tag feedback, facilitating collaboration and organization within research teams.

In addition to collecting qualitative feedback, Usabilla also offers quantitative metrics such as Net Promoter Score (NPS) and Customer Effort Score (CES) to measure user satisfaction and loyalty. These metrics can provide valuable insights into the overall user experience and help prioritize areas for improvement.

Overall, Usabilla is a user research tool that enables UX researchers to gather feedback and insights from users, helping them improve the user experience of digital products through data-driven decision making.

User Behavior Analysis

User behavior analysis, in the context of user research (UXR), refers to the systematic study and interpretation of how individuals interact with digital products and services. It involves gathering and analyzing data on user actions, reactions, and patterns to gain insights into their preferences, motivations, and needs. Through the use of various research methods such as surveys, interviews, observations, and usability testing, user researchers aim to understand why users behave the way they do when using a product or service. They seek to uncover the underlying factors that influence user behavior, including cognitive processes, emotional responses, and environmental/contextual variables. The analysis of user behavior involves examining both qualitative and quantitative data. Qualitative data provides in-depth insights into user experiences, thoughts, and feelings, while quantitative data offers statistical information about user actions and usage patterns. By combining these two types of data, researchers can develop a comprehensive understanding of user behavior and make informed design decisions. The findings from user behavior analysis are essential for improving the overall user experience of a product or service. By identifying pain points, usability issues, and areas of confusion, researchers can suggest design changes and enhancements that better align with user preferences and expectations. This iterative process helps create user-centered designs that are intuitive, efficient, and enjoyable to use. User behavior analysis is a crucial component of the user-centered design process, providing invaluable insights that guide decision-making and ensure that digital products and services meet user needs effectively.

User Behavior

User behavior refers to the actions, habits, and patterns exhibited by individuals when they interact with a system, product, or service. In the context of user research (UXR), the study of user behavior aims to understand how users perceive, think, and use a particular product or service. UXR focuses on observing and analyzing user behavior to gain insights that can inform the design and improvement of user experiences.

By studying user behavior, UX researchers can identify pain points, uncover usability issues, and gain a deeper understanding of users' needs and preferences. This knowledge allows designers and developers to create user-centric experiences that align with users' mental models and goals. In UXR, various research methods, such as interviews, surveys, and usability testing, are employed to gather data on user behavior.

User Centricity

User centricity in the context of user research (UXR) refers to a research approach that places the needs, goals, and preferences of users at the forefront of the research process. It emphasizes understanding and empathizing with the users, ensuring that their experiences, perspectives, and feedback inform the design and development of products, services, or systems.

User centricity involves adopting a mindset of putting the user first, aiming to create user-centric solutions that address their pain points, enhance their satisfaction, and align with their expectations. It involves conducting thorough research to uncover user insights, which are then used to guide the decision-making process. This research may include methods such as interviews, surveys, observations, and user testing.

By adopting a user-centric approach, UXR professionals can gain a deep understanding of the target users' motivations, behaviors, and needs. This understanding enables them to design more intuitive, relevant, and engaging user experiences. User centricity emphasizes the importance of involving users throughout the design and development process, seeking their feedback, and iterating based on their input.

In summary, user centricity in user research is a mindset and approach that prioritizes the needs and preferences of users. It involves conducting research to gain user insights and using those insights to inform the design and development of user-centric solutions.

User Consent Forms

User Consent Forms

User consent forms are a crucial component of user research (UXR). They are formal documents that outline the purpose, scope, and potential risks of a study, as well as seek the participant's voluntary permission to participate. These forms are designed to ensure that participants fully understand the nature of the research, including how their personal data may be collected, used, and shared. User consent forms are typically used in a variety of user research activities such as interviews, usability testing, surveys, and ethnographic studies.

User Data Privacy

User data privacy in the context of user-research (UXR) refers to the protection and control of an individual's personal information that is collected, processed, and stored during the research process. It involves ensuring that the user's data is handled in a way that respects their rights, maintains confidentiality, and minimizes any potential risks or harm to the individual.

When conducting user-research activities, it is crucial to handle user data in an ethical and responsible manner. This includes obtaining informed consent from participants, clearly stating the purpose and scope of data collection, and providing transparency about how the data will be stored, used, and shared. Additionally, researchers must implement appropriate security measures to protect user data from unauthorized access, breaches, or misuse.

User data privacy in UXR also means giving individuals the right to access, rectify, and delete their personal information. Participants should have the ability to control their data and make informed decisions about its use. This includes providing clear opt-in and opt-out mechanisms, as well as respecting participants' preferences regarding data sharing with third parties.

Overall, user data privacy in UXR ensures that participants' personal information is treated with respect, integrity, and confidentiality throughout the research process. By upholding strong ethical standards and implementing robust security measures, researchers can build trust with their participants and contribute to a more responsible and privacy-conscious user-research practice. >

User Data

User data, in the context of user research (UXR), refers to the information collected about individuals during the process of researching and studying user behavior, preferences, and experiences. It encompasses all the data points and details obtained from users through various research methods, such as interviews, surveys, and user testing.

During user research, practitioners aim to understand users' needs, goals, and motivations in order to design or improve products, services, or experiences. User data provides valuable insights into user behavior patterns, pain points, and areas of satisfaction. It helps UXR professionals make informed decisions and drive successful design choices.

User Delight

User Delight refers to the emotional satisfaction and positive experience derived by a user when interacting with a product, service, or application. It is a key objective of user-centered design and user experience research (UXR) to understand and enhance user delight, as it directly contributes to user loyalty and overall success of a product.

User delight is achieved when a product or service surpasses user expectations and meets their needs effectively, providing a seamless and enjoyable experience. It goes beyond mere usability and encompasses elements such as aesthetics, efficiency, and delightfulness. It is about creating products that not only perform their intended function but also evoke positive emotions and create a memorable experience for the user.

User Empathy Maps

An empathy map is a user research tool used in the field of User Experience Research (UXR) to gain a deeper understanding of the thoughts, feelings, and behaviors of a particular user or user group. It is a visual representation that helps researchers and designers empathize with the users they are studying, enabling them to create more user-centric and effective solutions.

The empathy map consists of four quadrants that focus on different aspects of the user's experience: 'Says', 'Thinks and Feels', 'Does', and 'Pains and Gains'. In each quadrant, researchers gather qualitative data based on observations, interviews, or other research methods to build a comprehensive understanding of the user's motivations, needs, and challenges.

The 'Says' quadrant captures the explicit statements or quotes made by the user, providing insight into their verbalized thoughts, desires, or frustrations. The 'Thinks and Feels' quadrant delves into the user's emotions, beliefs, attitudes, and perceptions, aiming to uncover implicit thoughts or underlying motivations. The 'Does' quadrant seeks to understand the user's observable actions, behaviors, and interactions in various contexts and scenarios. Finally, the 'Pains and Gains' quadrant addresses the user's pain points, barriers, challenges, as well as their motivations, goals, and desired outcomes.

By visually organizing and analyzing these collected data points, the empathy map helps researchers and designers gain a holistic view of the user, allowing them to identify patterns, uncover insights, and generate actionable implications for product or service improvement. The empathy map serves as a valuable tool in informing the design process and ensuring that user needs are effectively addressed within the final solution.

User Empathy

User empathy in the context of user-research (UXR) refers to the ability of a researcher to understand, share, and validate the feelings, needs, perspectives, and behaviors of the users they are studying. In other words, it is the capacity to put oneself in the shoes of the user, to deeply understand their motivations, desires, challenges, and preferences, in order to design products or services that truly cater to their needs.

Being empathetic in user-research involves actively listening, observing, and engaging with users to gain insights into their experiences and emotions. It requires setting aside any assumptions or biases and approaching the research with an open mind. By doing so, researchers can uncover valuable information that helps to inform design decisions and enhance the overall user experience.

User Engagement

User engagement in the context of user research (UXR) refers to the level of interaction, involvement, and interest exhibited by the users during the research process. It measures the extent to which users actively participate, provide feedback, and contribute to the research objectives. User engagement is crucial in obtaining reliable and meaningful insights that can inform the design and development of user-centered products and services. When conducting user research, user engagement can be attained through various techniques such as interviews, surveys, usability testing, and observation. These methods allow researchers to gauge the users' level of interest, motivation, and willingness to share their thoughts and experiences. By actively involving users throughout the research process, researchers can identify pain points, uncover unmet needs, and gain a comprehensive understanding of user behaviors and preferences. High levels of user engagement are indicative of meaningful research outcomes. It suggests that users are invested in the research process and are more likely to provide honest and valuable feedback. Engaged users are not only willing to share their thoughts but also actively contribute ideas and suggestions for improvement. This collaborative approach fosters a sense of ownership and empowers users to shape the future development of products and services. On the other hand, low user engagement can hinder the effectiveness of user research. It may result in incomplete or biased data, leading to missed opportunities for identifying critical user insights. Therefore, it is essential for user researchers to employ strategies that promote user engagement, such as clear communication, empathy, and creating a supportive and non-intimidating research environment. In conclusion, user engagement plays a vital role in user research. It determines the quality and reliability of the insights derived from the research process. Engaging users actively and fostering a collaborative approach can help researchers gain a deeper understanding of user needs, preferences, and behaviors, ultimately leading to the development of superior user experiences.

User Expectations

User expectations, in the context of user research (UXR), refer to the implicit or explicit assumptions and anticipations that users have regarding a particular product or service. These expectations are shaped by various factors such as previous experiences, cultural norms, personal beliefs, and marketing messages. Understanding user expectations is crucial for UX designers and researchers as it enables them to create products and experiences that meet or exceed user needs and desires. By identifying and analyzing user expectations, designers can ensure that their designs are intuitive, efficient, and enjoyable for users. User expectations can be categorized into different dimensions, such as functionality, performance, aesthetic appeal, ease of use, and reliability. For example, users may expect a mobile banking app to have secure login methods, fast transaction processing, a visually appealing interface, easy navigation, and reliable customer support. To uncover user expectations, UXR professionals employ various research methods, including user interviews, surveys, usability testing, and contextual inquiries. These methods help researchers gain insights into users' mental models, goals, and preferences. Additionally, analyzing user feedback, complaints, and support requests can provide valuable input for understanding and managing user expectations. By aligning product design and development with user expectations, companies can enhance user satisfaction, build user trust and loyalty, and differentiate themselves from competitors. Failing to meet user expectations can lead to frustration, negative user experiences, and disengagement, resulting in a loss of customers and negative brand perception. Hence, user expectations serve as a critical guideline for UX design and play a vital role in shaping the success of a product or service.

User Experience Design

User Experience Design (UXD) is a discipline within the field of User Research (UXR) that aims to improve the overall experience of a user while interacting with a product or service. It involves designing and optimizing the usability, accessibility, and desirability of a digital or physical product to meet the needs and expectations of its users.

UXD encompasses various research methodologies and processes, including user research, interaction design, information architecture, and visual design. It entails understanding the users' behaviors, needs, and goals to create intuitive and meaningful experiences. By conducting user research, designers gather valuable insights about users' preferences, pain points, and motivations, which inform the design decisions throughout the product development lifecycle.

UX designers employ a user-centered approach, ensuring that the design decisions are driven by user needs rather than personal preferences or assumptions. They apply usability principles, such as simplicity, learnability, and consistency, to create intuitive and efficient interfaces. Through wireframing, prototyping, and conducting iterative usability testing, UX designers refine and validate their designs to ensure a seamless and engaging user experience.

Ultimately, the goal of UXD is to create products that are not only functional but also enjoyable to use. A well-executed user experience can lead to increased user satisfaction, higher engagement, improved conversion rates, and ultimately, business success. By understanding and empathizing with users, UX designers can create meaningful and impactful experiences that meet their needs and exceed their expectations.

User Experience (UX) Testing

User Experience (UX) Testing is a research method employed in User Experience Research (UXR) to evaluate and validate the usability and user satisfaction of a product or service. It involves observing users as they interact with the product or service and collecting relevant data to assess its effectiveness in meeting user needs and goals. UX testing typically involves the creation of realistic scenarios or tasks for users to complete while using the product or service. These scenarios are designed to simulate real-world situations and allow researchers to observe how users navigate through the interface, make decisions, and overcome challenges. By observing users in this way, researchers can gain insights into their behaviors, preferences, and pain points. Data collected during the testing process can include both qualitative and quantitative information. Qualitative data can be gathered through methods such as user interviews or think-aloud protocols, where users verbalize their thoughts and feelings as they interact with the product or service. This provides valuable insights into users' perceptions, emotions, and subjective experiences. Quantitative data can be collected through metrics like task completion rates, time taken to complete tasks, or error rates, providing more objective measures of usability and performance. The findings from UX testing are used to identify areas of improvement in the product or service. By pinpointing usability issues or areas of user dissatisfaction, designers and developers can make informed decisions about how to enhance the user experience. Iterative testing and refinement of the design based on user feedback is common practice in UX research, as it allows for continuous improvement and ensures that the final product meets user needs and expectations. In conclusion, UX testing is a crucial component of the user research process, providing valuable insights into user behavior and preferences to enhance the overall user experience.

User Feedback

User research (UXR) is a systematic process of gathering, analyzing, and interpreting data about users and their preferences with a product or service. It aims to understand users' behaviors, needs, and preferences to inform the design and development of user-centered solutions. UXR plays a crucial role in shaping the user experience by identifying user pain points, uncovering usability issues, and validating design decisions.

The process of user research involves a range of qualitative and quantitative methods, such as interviews, surveys, observation, and usability testing. These methods help UXR professionals gather insights into how users interact with a product or service, what their goals and motivations are, and how they perceive and make sense of their experiences. By examining the user's journey, UXR can identify opportunities for improvement and guide decision-making throughout the design process.

User Flow Testing

User flow testing is a user-research method that aims to evaluate the user experience (UX) by examining the sequence of steps or actions taken by users to complete a specific task or achieve a desired goal within a digital product or website. It involves observing and analyzing how users navigate through different screens, interact with various elements, and make decisions along the way.

During user flow testing, researchers focus on understanding the efficiency, effectiveness, and satisfaction of the user journeys within the product. This involves identifying potential usability issues, friction points, and areas of improvement in the overall user experience. By closely observing the users' interactions and soliciting their feedback, researchers gain insights into their preferences, expectations, and pain points.

User flow testing typically involves conducting usability tests, interviews, or surveys with representative users who are tasked with completing specific scenarios or workflows. Researchers may use various techniques, such as screen recording, eye-tracking, or thinking-aloud protocols, to capture and analyze users' behavior, decision-making process, and subjective experiences throughout the task.

The findings from user flow testing can inform design decisions, help prioritize improvements, and enhance the overall user experience of the digital product. By identifying areas of confusion, frustration, or inefficiency in the user journey, organizations can make informed decisions to refine the interface, simplify interactions, and ultimately provide a more seamless and intuitive experience for their users.

User Flow

User Flow is a term used in user-research (UXR) to describe the path that a user takes through a website or application in order to complete a specific task. It provides a visual representation of the steps and decisions that a user makes from the beginning to the end of their interaction with a digital product.

A user flow helps UX researchers and designers understand how users navigate a digital product, what their motivations and goals are, and any obstacles they encounter along the way. By examining user flows, researchers can identify areas of friction, confusion, or inefficiency, and make informed decisions to improve the overall user experience.

User Frustrations

User frustrations in the context of user research (UXR) refer to the negative emotions, difficulties, or obstacles experienced by users when interacting with a product, service, or system. These frustrations can occur during the initial discovery phase, the onboarding process, or even after extended usage. They manifest as negative experiences, such as confusion, annoyance, or dissatisfaction, and can have a significant impact on the overall user experience.

User frustrations can arise due to a variety of factors, including design flaws, functionality issues, complex navigation, slow load times, lack of clear instructions, or poor error handling. These frustrations can lead to decreased user engagement, increased abandonment rates, or even negative word-of-mouth referrals, which ultimately affect the success and adoption of a product or service.

It is essential for UX researchers to identify and understand user frustrations through various research methods, such as interviews, usability testing, or surveys. By uncovering these frustrations, researchers can provide valuable insights to the design and development teams, enabling them to make informed decisions to address and mitigate the identified issues.

By actively addressing and resolving user frustrations, companies can improve the overall user experience, increase user satisfaction, and ultimately achieve their business goals. User frustrations, when properly analyzed and addressed, can serve as opportunities for improvement, helping organizations create more user-centric products and services.

User Goals

User goals are the specific objectives and intentions that users have when interacting with a product or service. They represent the desired outcomes that users seek to achieve or the problems they aim to solve. Understanding user goals is essential in user research (UXR) as it helps inform the design and development of effective and user-centered solutions. User goals can vary widely depending on the context and the nature of the product or service being studied. They can include functional goals, such as completing a task or finding specific information, as well as social or emotional goals, such as building relationships or feeling a sense of accomplishment. Identifying and prioritizing user goals is a crucial part of user research. This is typically done through various methods, such as interviews, surveys, and usability testing. By gathering insights into user goals, researchers can gain a deeper understanding of user needs, motivations, and behaviors. This knowledge can then be used to guide the design process, ensuring that the product or service effectively supports users in achieving their goals. In summary, user goals are the desired outcomes or problems that users aim to address when using a product or service. User research is conducted to understand these goals in order to design user-centered solutions that meet user needs and expectations.

User Incentives

147

User incentives refer to the rewards, benefits, or motivations provided to users in exchange for their participation in user-research activities and studies. These incentives can take various forms, such as monetary compensation, gift cards, discounts, or exclusive access to products or experiences. The purpose of offering these incentives is to encourage users to engage and actively participate in user-research, which is essential for obtaining valuable insights and feedback. By providing a tangible benefit or reward, researchers can increase the likelihood of users dedicating their time and effort to provide meaningful input and data. User incentives play a crucial role in ensuring a diverse and representative pool of participants in user-research studies. Offering incentives helps attract a wider range of users, including individuals from different backgrounds, demographics, and levels of experience. This diversity is vital for gathering insights that accurately reflect the target user base and needs. When determining the type and amount of incentives to offer, researchers must consider factors such as the complexity and duration of the research activities, the level of effort required from participants, and the target user profile. It is crucial to strike a balance between providing a sufficient incentive to motivate participation without creating biases or compromising the objectivity of the research. In summary, user incentives are rewards or benefits provided to users in exchange for participation in user-research activities. These incentives help attract and encourage a diverse pool of users, ensuring more accurate and valuable insights for UX research endeavors.

User Insights

User Insights in the context of user research (UXR) refer to the valuable and meaningful observations, interpretations, and understanding gained through the process of studying and analyzing user behavior, attitudes, and experiences. These insights provide crucial information and data that contribute to the development, improvement, and optimization of user-centered design and products.

User insights are derived from various research methods and techniques used in UXR, including interview-based studies, contextual inquiries, usability testing, surveys, and analytics data analysis. By closely observing and engaging with users, researchers are able to gather first-hand information about their needs, preferences, motivations, and pain points. This qualitative and quantitative data is then analyzed to uncover patterns, trends, and key findings that shed light on user behaviors, expectations, and potential barriers or opportunities.

The insights gained from user research enable designers and developers to make informed decisions and shape their solutions in ways that directly address user needs and goals. By understanding users' mental models, context of use, and preferences, designers can create intuitive and user-friendly interfaces and interactions. User insights also help refine and iterate designs through continuous feedback and validation, ensuring that products meet user expectations and provide a seamless and enjoyable user experience.

In conclusion, user insights derived from user research are vital for informing user-centered design decisions, improving overall user experience, and guiding the development and optimization of products and services.

User Interaction

User interaction in the context of user research (UXR) refers to the communication and engagement between users and researchers during the research process. It encompasses the methods and techniques used to gather insights and feedback from users, as well as the reciprocal exchange of information between the two parties.

During user interaction in UXR, researchers aim to understand the needs, preferences, and behaviors of users by observing, interviewing, and involving them in various research activities. This interaction can occur through different channels, such as face-to-face meetings, remote sessions, or online surveys, depending on the nature of the research and the target audience.

The goal of user interaction in UXR is to gather qualitative and quantitative data that can inform the design and development of products or services. By actively engaging with users, researchers can uncover valuable insights, discover pain points, identify usability issues, and gain a deeper understanding of user motivations and expectations.

Through user interaction, researchers can validate or challenge assumptions, refine designs, and ultimately create experiences that are tailored to meet user needs. It also establishes a user-centered approach, ensuring that the end product aligns with user goals, enhances usability, and delivers a positive user experience.

User Interface Design

User Interface Design is a critical aspect of user-research (UXR) that focuses on creating an effective and visually appealing interface for digital products. It involves designing the layout, structure, and overall aesthetics of software applications, websites, and other interactive platforms to enhance user experience.

The primary goal of User Interface Design is to ensure that the graphical elements and interactive features of a digital product are intuitive, accessible, and user-friendly. This involves understanding the target audience, their needs, and the context in which they will interact with the product. User researchers conduct various methods such as surveys, interviews, and usability testing to gather insights and understand user preferences and behavior.

Based on these findings, user interface designers use their creativity and expertise to create wireframes, prototypes, and mockups that align with the users' expectations and goals. They focus on arranging visual elements, such as buttons, icons, text, and images, in a logical and visually pleasing manner. The designers also pay attention to factors like color schemes, typography, and overall visual hierarchy to guide users through the interface.

User interface designers collaborate closely with developers, as their designs need to be implemented effectively. They provide detailed specifications and guidelines to ensure that the final product meets the desired standards of usability and visual appeal. Additionally, they continuously gather feedback from users and make iterative improvements to the interface design based on their preferences and needs.

User Interface (UI) Testing

User Interface (UI) testing in the context of user research (UXR) refers to the evaluation and assessment of the visual elements and interactions within a digital product or application. Its primary objective is to ensure that the user interface meets the intended design goals and provides a seamless experience to the users. UI testing involves examining various aspects of the interface, such as layout, typography, color schemes, iconography, and navigation elements. It focuses on identifying any inconsistencies, errors, or usability issues that may hinder the user's ability to interact with the product effectively. This testing process often involves the use of prototypes, wireframes, or mock-ups that simulate the final product before it is fully developed. The purpose of UI testing is to validate the design choices made during the user interface design phase and to verify that the interface is clear, intuitive, and visually appealing. It helps identify areas where improvements can be made in terms of usability, accessibility, and overall user experience. UI testing can be conducted through various qualitative and quantitative methods, such as usability testing, eye-tracking studies, expert evaluations, and heuristic evaluations. These methods involve gathering feedback from representative users or experts to gain insights into their perceptions, preferences, and challenges while interacting with the interface. By conducting UI testing as part of user research, designers and developers can ensure that the user interface aligns with the needs, expectations, and behaviors of the target users. This iterative process of evaluation and refinement ultimately contributes to the creation of user-centered and user-friendly digital products.

User Interviews Script

User interviews are a qualitative research technique commonly used in user experience research (UXR). They involve conducting structured or semi-structured interviews with individual users to gain insights into their attitudes, preferences, behaviors, and needs related to a specific product or service.

The primary goal of user interviews is to gather in-depth information directly from users, allowing researchers to understand their experiences, motivations, and pain points. These insights can then inform the design and development of user-centered solutions that meet user needs effectively.

During a user interview, the researcher typically asks a series of open-ended questions to encourage participants to share their thoughts, opinions, and experiences freely. By using a conversational approach and active listening, researchers can delve deeper into participants' responses, uncovering valuable insights beyond simple yes or no answers.

User interviews can be conducted in person, over the phone, or through video calls, depending on the research context and participants' preferences. They often follow a structured interview guide to ensure consistency across interviews and enable comparisons between participants.

The data collected from user interviews is analyzed to identify patterns, themes, and user needs. This analysis helps identify common pain points and opportunities for improvement, informing the design iteration process.

User interviews are a crucial method in UXR as they provide rich qualitative data and enable researchers to gain a deep understanding of users' experiences and needs. By placing users at the center of the design process, user interviews contribute to creating user-centered solutions that ultimately enhance user satisfaction and overall product success.>

User Interviews

User Interviews are a research method commonly used in user experience (UX) research to gather qualitative data from participants. In user research, it involves engaging with individuals, typically users or potential users of a product or service, in a structured conversation to gain insights into their behaviors, attitudes, needs, and goals. This method allows researchers to understand users' experiences, perceptions, and expectations. User interviews usually follow a predetermined set of questions or topics, which are designed to elicit specific information relevant to the research objectives. The questions are typically open-ended, allowing participants to provide detailed and personal responses. These interviews can be conducted in various ways, such as in-person, over the phone, or through video conferencing tools. The primary goal of user interviews is to uncover valuable insights that can inform the design and development of user-centered products or services. By directly engaging with users, researchers can gain a deeper understanding of their motivations, pain points, and preferences. User interviews can help identify usability issues, validate design decisions, and generate ideas for improvement. To conduct effective user interviews, researchers should carefully plan the questions to ensure they provide meaningful and unbiased information. It is essential to create a comfortable and non-judgmental environment for participants, encouraging open and honest responses. Additionally, researchers must actively listen, probe for further details, and avoid leading participants towards desired answers. Overall, user interviews are a crucial tool in the UX research toolkit, enabling researchers to gain valuable insights directly from users' perspectives. By understanding users' needs and desires, designers can create more effective and user-friendly products and services.

User Journey Mapping

User Journey Mapping is a UX research technique used to visually represent the steps, actions, and experiences that users go through when interacting with a product or service. It is a tool that helps UX researchers and designers understand the user's perspective and identify pain points, opportunities, and areas of improvement within the user experience.

The user journey map typically consists of a timeline or flowchart-like structure that depicts the user's interactions and emotions at each touchpoint throughout their journey. It provides a holistic view of the user's experience and enables researchers to identify key moments, decision points, and potential gaps in the user journey.

User Journey Surveys

A user journey survey is a research method used in user experience research (UXR) to collect data on the experiences and behaviors of users as they interact with a specific product, service, or system. It involves gathering feedback from users at various touchpoints throughout their journey, from their initial discovery of the product/service to their ongoing use and potential post-use experiences.

The purpose of conducting a user journey survey is to gain insights into the users' motivations, needs, pain points, and overall satisfaction with the product/service. This helps UX researchers and designers identify areas for improvement and make informed decisions to enhance the user experience.

User Narratives

User narratives, in the context of user research (UXR), refer to detailed descriptions or stories that encapsulate the experiences, needs, motivations, and goals of individuals who interact with a product or service. These narratives provide a holistic understanding of users by capturing their thoughts, behaviors, emotions, and expectations. User narratives are typically derived through qualitative research methods such as interviews, observations, and ethnographic studies. They go beyond demographic information and surface-level data to provide deeper insights into the user's journey, pain points, and desires. Effective user narratives are characterized by rich descriptions that contextualize the user's interactions with the product or service. They paint a vivid picture of the user's environment, the challenges they face, and the opportunities they seek. By exploring the user's perspective, user narratives help UX researchers and designers empathize with users, uncover latent needs, and identify areas for improvement. User narratives are invaluable tools during the design and iteration phases of a product or service. They enable UX teams to make informed decisions, prioritize features, and validate design choices. By grounding the design process in real user stories, user narratives facilitate a user-centered approach that leads to more meaningful and impactful experiences. In summary, user narratives are detailed descriptions or stories that capture the experiences, needs, motivations, and goals of individuals who engage with a product or service. They provide deep insights and help UX researchers and designers empathize with users, leading to user-centered design solutions.

User Needs Analysis

A User Needs Analysis in the context of user-research (UXR) is a systematic process of identifying and understanding the requirements, desires, and expectations of users in relation to a product or service. It involves gathering data and insights directly from users through various research methods, such as interviews, surveys, and observations.

The primary goal of a User Needs Analysis is to gain a deep understanding of users' needs and preferences in order to inform the design and development of user-centered products or services. By conducting this analysis, researchers can uncover insights about users' behaviors, motivations, pain points, and goals.

The process typically begins with defining the research objectives and selecting appropriate research methods. Researchers then recruit and engage with a diverse range of participants to gather data and insights. Qualitative and quantitative data are collected and analyzed to identify common themes and patterns in users' needs and preferences.

Based on the findings of the User Needs Analysis, designers, developers, and other stakeholders can make informed decisions about the features, functionality, and overall design of the product or service. The insights gained from the analysis can also be used to validate and iterate on existing designs and to prioritize future enhancements.

In conclusion, a User Needs Analysis is a crucial step in the user-centered design process, as it helps ensure that products and services are tailored to meet the needs and expectations of the intended users.

User Observation

User observation is a research method used in User Experience Research (UXR) to gain insights into user behavior, needs, and preferences. It involves observing users as they interact with a product, system, or service in their natural environment or in a controlled setting. During user observation, researchers carefully observe and take notes on how users navigate, interact, and complete tasks using the product or service. This method allows researchers to identify usability issues, pain points, and areas for improvement. It also helps uncover user expectations, motivations, and satisfaction levels. User observation typically involves two key components: naturalistic observation and structured observation. In naturalistic observation, researchers observe users in their everyday context to capture real-world behavior and use patterns. This allows for a deeper understanding of user needs and preferences in their natural environment. In structured observation, researchers create specific scenarios or tasks for users to complete while being observed. This method provides a more controlled environment where specific interactions and behaviors can be observed. To conduct user observation, researchers must carefully plan and prepare the observation process. This includes defining research objectives, selecting participants that represent the target user group, creating observation protocols, and ensuring ethical considerations and privacy concerns are addressed. Overall, user observation is a valuable research method in UXR that provides rich qualitative data and helps inform design decisions. It allows researchers to understand users on a deeper level, uncovering valuable insights that can ultimately lead to improved user experiences.

User Pain Points

User pain points are the specific challenges or frustrations users experience when using a product or service. These pain points often arise from areas where the product or service does not meet the user's expectations or needs. Identifying and understanding user pain points is crucial in user research (UXR) as it allows researchers to address these issues and improve the overall user experience.

By conducting user research, such as interviews, surveys, and usability testing, designers and researchers can gather insights into the pain points users face. These pain points can range from issues with usability, functionality, performance, accessibility, or even emotional factors such as confusion or frustration.

Once pain points are identified, UXR professionals can prioritize them based on their impact on the user experience and the product's overall goals. Addressing these pain points may involve making design changes, improving functionality, enhancing accessibility, or providing better onboarding and support materials.

Iterative testing and analysis are key in understanding and resolving user pain points. By continually collecting feedback and observing user behavior, researchers can track the effectiveness of solutions and make further improvements.

User Persona Creation

A user persona is a fictional representation of a specific target user segment or group that is created by user-researchers (UXRs) to better understand the needs, goals, behaviors, and characteristics of users. Personas are developed through data collected from various sources, such as interviews, surveys, and observations, and are often visualized as a profile that contains demographic information, personal details, and key attributes of the target user group.

The purpose of creating user personas is to humanize and personalize the users, allowing UXRs to empathize with their needs and goals. By using personas, UXR teams can prioritize and make informed decisions during the design and development process, as they have a clearer understanding of who they are designing for.

User Persona Validation

A user persona is a fictional, generalized representation of a specific user segment within the target audience. It is created based on real user data gathered during user research, and is used as a tool for designing and developing products that meet the needs and goals of the intended users.

In the context of user research (UXR), user personas serve as a way to summarize and communicate key insights about the target audience. They help to create a shared understanding of who the users are, what their preferences and behaviors are, and what their goals and motivations are.

User Personas

User Personas are fictional characters that represent different user types within a targeted user group or audience. They are created based on extensive research and data collected through user research, interviews, and surveys. The purpose of creating user personas is to develop a deeper understanding of the users' needs, preferences, behaviors, and goals.

User personas provide a human-like face to the target audience and help UX researchers and designers to empathize with and better design for the users. They allow designers to make informed decisions based on user-centric insights and ensure that the end product meets the users' requirements and expectations.

User Profiling

User profiling refers to the process of creating detailed personas or profiles that represent the characteristics, behaviors, needs, and goals of different user groups. It involves gathering and analyzing data to understand users' demographics, psychographics, preferences, and motivations. User profiling is conducted in user research (UXR) to help designers and developers gain a deep understanding of their target audience, enabling them to create user-centered solutions that meet users' expectations and lead to improved user experiences.

Through user profiling, researchers aim to uncover patterns and insights about users, such as their age, gender, education, occupation, interests, and values. They also gather information about users' goals, needs, challenges, and pain points related to the product or service being studied. User profiling often involves collecting data through various qualitative and quantitative research methods, including interviews, surveys, observation, and user testing.

User Prototyping

User prototyping in the context of user research (UXR) refers to the process of creating early, simplified representations of a product or service to gather feedback and test usability. Prototypes are used to evaluate and refine designs, allowing researchers to understand user needs, preferences, and pain points. Prototyping is an iterative process that involves creating multiple versions of a design, from low-fidelity sketches to high-fidelity interactive simulations. It helps researchers and designers to visualize and communicate their ideas, as well as gather insights from users before investing time and resources in development. The purpose of user prototyping is to uncover usability issues, validate design assumptions, and facilitate collaboration among stakeholders. By involving users early in the design process, researchers can identify and address potential problems, leading to a more user-friendly and effective end product. Prototypes can take various forms, such as paper prototypes, digital wireframes, or interactive mock-ups. During the prototyping phase, researchers may conduct usability testing sessions, interviews, or surveys to collect qualitative and quantitative data on user experience. This data helps inform design decisions and iterate on the prototype for further improvements. User prototyping enables researchers to gain valuable insights into user behavior, expectations, and interactions, ultimately guiding the development of user-centered designs. It allows for early detection of usability issues, reducing rework and saving time and costs in the long run. In summary, user prototyping is an integral part of the user research process, providing a valuable means to gather user feedback, refine designs, and create impactful user experiences.>

User Recruitment

User recruitment in the context of user-research (UXR) refers to the process of identifying and selecting individuals who meet specific criteria to participate in research studies that aim to gain insights into user behavior, preferences, and needs. The goal of user recruitment is to create a representative sample of users who can provide valuable feedback and contribute to the development and improvement of products, services, or experiences. During the user recruitment process, researchers typically define target user profiles or personas based on characteristics such as age, gender, occupation, education, and specific product or service usage. These criteria help to ensure that the selected participants match the intended user base, allowing for more accurate and meaningful findings. User recruitment methods can vary depending on the scope and goals of the research study. Common approaches include online surveys, interviews, social media advertisements, and recruitment agencies. Researchers may also leverage existing user databases, such as customer mailing lists or user forums, to reach out to potential participants. Once potential users are identified, researchers typically screen them to assess their eligibility and fit for the study. This may involve conducting interviews, administering questionnaires, or reviewing applications. It is important for researchers to ensure that participants are not biased or have any conflicts of interest that could impact the integrity of the research. Overall, user recruitment is a crucial step in user-research as it allows researchers to engage with real users and gather insights that inform decision-making, drive product improvements, and enhance user experiences.

User Research

User research is a systematic process of understanding the needs, behaviors, motivations, and preferences of users in order to inform the design and development of user-centered products and experiences. It involves gathering and analyzing qualitative and quantitative data to gain insights into user perspectives and behaviors.

During user research, various methods such as interviews, surveys, observations, and usability testing are conducted to collect data directly from users. This data helps uncover user needs, pain points, and goals, as well as identify opportunities for improvement and innovation.

By conducting user research, designers and researchers can gain a deep understanding of the target audience, allowing them to make informed design decisions that better meet user needs. It helps identify usability issues, validate design assumptions, and uncover new opportunities for enhancing the user experience.

The insights obtained through user research are crucial in guiding the design and development process, ensuring that user-centered solutions are created. It helps prioritize features, optimize user interfaces, and improve overall user satisfaction. Additionally, user research can be used to evaluate and validate design solutions, ensuring that they effectively address user needs and align with business goals.

User Researcher

User Researcher in the context of user research (UXR) is a professional who conducts systematic investigations to understand user behaviors, needs, motivations, and preferences. Their primary objective is to gather insights that inform the design and development of user-centered products, services, and experiences.

To achieve this goal, user researchers employ a range of qualitative and quantitative research methods. These may include conducting interviews, surveys, usability testing, user observations, and analysis of user data. They employ a human-centered approach, focusing on understanding users' goals, experiences, and expectations in order to create more intuitive and satisfying interactions.

User Retention

User Retention in the context of user-research (UXR) refers to the ability of a product or service to retain its users over a period of time. It measures the number of users who continue to use a product or service after their initial interaction or purchase.

User retention is a critical metric for businesses as it directly impacts their growth and success. High user retention indicates that users find value in the product or service and are willing to continue using it. It also suggests that users are satisfied with their experience, which can lead to positive word-of-mouth and potential referrals. User research plays a crucial role in understanding the factors that influence user retention. By gathering qualitative and quantitative data, user researchers can identify pain points, motivations, and behaviors that contribute to user churn or long-term engagement. This research helps businesses optimize their products or services to better meet user needs and expectations, ultimately improving user retention rates. User retention can be influenced by various factors, including the overall user experience, the value proposition of the product or service, customer support, and competitive market dynamics. Through continuous monitoring and analysis of user behavior and feedback, businesses can identify areas for improvement and develop strategies to retain and engage their users. In conclusion, user retention is a key metric that determines the success or failure of a product or service. User research plays a vital role in understanding user behavior and preferences, enabling businesses to make informed decisions to enhance user experience and increase user retention rates.

User Reviews Analysis

User Reviews Analysis refers to the process of gathering, analyzing, and interpreting feedback and opinions provided by users of a particular product or service. It is a key component of user research (UXR) in order to understand user experiences, preferences, and perspectives, with the ultimate goal of improving the product or service based on user feedback.

During the analysis phase, user reviews are collected from various sources such as online platforms, social media, or dedicated review websites. The collected reviews are then organized and categorized to identify recurring themes or patterns. This involves identifying common positive and negative sentiments, as well as issues or areas of improvement that users have encountered.

The analysis of user reviews involves both quantitative and qualitative methods. Quantitative analysis focuses on numerical data such as ratings or scores given by users, while qualitative analysis delves into the textual content, sentiments, and specific details provided in the reviews. By combining both approaches, deeper insights can be obtained regarding user sentiments, preferences, and the specific aspects of the product or service that require attention.

The findings from user reviews analysis are invaluable in informing product development and improvement strategies. They help identify pain points, usability issues, and areas of satisfaction or delight for users. This feedback can guide decision-making processes and drive the prioritization of enhancements or updates in order to meet user expectations and enhance the overall user experience.

User Sampling

User sampling is a key methodology in user research (UXR) that involves selecting a subset or sample of users from a larger population to study and gain insights into their behaviors, needs, and preferences. This process allows researchers to gather data and draw conclusions that can be generalized to the larger user population.

The goal of user sampling is to ensure that the selected users represent the diversity and characteristics of the target user population. This helps to minimize biases and increase the validity of the research findings. It is important to carefully define the criteria for user selection to ensure that the sample adequately represents the target audience.

User Satisfaction Surveys

User Satisfaction Surveys are a commonly used method in user-research (UXR) to gather feedback and assess the level of satisfaction and user experience with a product or service. These surveys aim to understand the users' perspective and provide valuable insights to improve the overall user experience.

The surveys typically consist of a series of structured or semi-structured questions that users answer based on their experience with the product or service. The questions can cover various aspects such as ease-of-use, functionality, aesthetics, performance, and customer support. The survey may also include open-ended questions to allow users to provide additional comments or suggestions.

User Satisfaction Surveys are often conducted at different stages of the product or service lifecycle, such as during the initial development phase, after a major update, or periodically to track changes in user perception over time. They can be administered through various channels, including online platforms, emails, or in-person interviews.

The collected data from these surveys is analyzed to identify trends, patterns, and areas of improvement. The insights gained can help inform design decisions, prioritize feature enhancements, and validate the effectiveness of implemented changes. User Satisfaction Surveys are an essential tool for UX researchers and designers to ensure the end-users' needs and expectations are met, ultimately leading to a more user-centered and successful product or service.

User Satisfaction

User Satisfaction, in the context of user-research (UXR), refers to the degree of contentment or fulfillment that a user experiences when interacting with a product or service. It is a measure of how well the product or service fulfills the user's needs, expectations, and goals.

User Satisfaction is a crucial aspect of UX design as it directly impacts the success and adoption of a product or service. Understanding and improving user satisfaction is a primary goal of user-research, as it helps to identify areas of improvement and guide design decisions.

User Scenario

User research (UXR) is a systematic approach to understanding users, their behaviors, needs, and preferences in order to inform the design and development of effective products or services. It involves gathering and analyzing qualitative and quantitative data to gain insights that can guide the decision-making process.

UXR aims to identify user pain points, uncover user goals and motivations, and assess user satisfaction with a product or service. This research can be conducted through various methods such as interviews, surveys, observations, and usability tests. The gathered data is then analyzed to identify patterns, trends, and areas for improvement.

User Scenarios

A user scenario is a formal description of how a specific user interacts with a product or service in a given context. It provides a narrative that outlines the user's goals, actions, and experiences throughout the interaction, helping to understand their needs and behaviors.

As part of user research (UXR), user scenarios are created to gather insights and inform the design and development of user-centered solutions. They are typically derived from qualitative data collected through methods such as interviews, observations, or usability testing.

User Stories

User stories are short, formal definitions that are used in the context of user research (UXR). They serve as a way to capture and communicate the needs and expectations of users, helping to inform and guide the research process.

A user story typically consists of three main elements: the user, their goal, and the value or benefit they hope to gain from achieving that goal. This format allows researchers to focus on understanding the specific needs and motivations of individual users, rather than making assumptions based on broad generalizations.

By using user stories in UXR, researchers can better understand the context in which users will interact with a product or service. This helps guide the research process by identifying the areas that need to be investigated and the specific research questions that need to be answered.

Furthermore, user stories can also be used to prioritize and plan research activities. By grouping similar user stories together, researchers can identify common themes or patterns, allowing them to prioritize research efforts and ensure that the most critical needs are addressed.

In conclusion, user stories provide a structured and concise way to capture the needs and expectations of users in the context of UXR. They help researchers understand the specific goals and motivations of users, guide the research process, and prioritize research efforts to ensure that user needs are effectively addressed.

User Surveys

A user survey is a method used in user-research (UXR) to collect feedback and gather valuable insights from users or potential users of a product or service. It involves the use of questionnaires or interviews to systematically gather information about user preferences, behaviors, attitudes, and needs.

The primary objective of conducting user surveys is to gain a deeper understanding of users' experiences, expectations, and pain points. By collecting quantitative and qualitative data, user surveys provide valuable insights that can inform the design and development of user-centered products and services.

User Tasks

User research (UXR) is a process of understanding the needs, expectations, and behaviors of users in order to inform the design and development of products or services. It involves various qualitative and quantitative methods to gather insights and feedback directly from the target users. The primary goal of user research is to identify user needs and pain points, and to guide the design team in creating user-centered solutions. UXR helps to uncover user preferences, motivations, and behaviors, which can then be translated into actionable design decisions. Qualitative research methods, such as interviews and usability testing, provide in-depth understanding of user experiences and perceptions. These methods allow researchers to observe and analyze user interactions with a product or service, providing valuable insights into usability issues and areas for improvement. Quantitative research methods, such as surveys and analytics, provide statistical data and metrics to measure user behavior. These methods help researchers to gather a large amount of data to identify patterns, trends, and preferences among users. User research is an iterative process that involves continuous feedback and validation from users throughout the product development lifecycle. It helps designers make informed decisions, prioritize features, and optimize the overall user experience. In conclusion, user research is a vital practice in the field of UX design, enabling designers to gain valuable insights into user behaviors and preferences. By understanding the target users, designers can create products and services that meet their needs and expectations, resulting in improved user satisfaction and overall success of the product or service.

User Testing Environment

A User Testing Environment, in the context of user research (UXR), refers to the physical or virtual setting where user testing activities take place. It is a controlled environment carefully designed to simulate real-world conditions, allowing researchers to observe and gather insights on how users interact with a product or interface.

The User Testing Environment aims to create a realistic experience for users while ensuring that the research objectives are met. It provides a safe space where users can freely explore the product, providing valuable feedback and allowing the researchers to identify areas of improvement.

User Testing

User testing, in the context of user-research (UXR), refers to a method used to evaluate the usability and functionality of a product or service. It involves observing and analyzing how users interact with the product or service, in order to identify any usability issues and gather feedback for improvement.

The process of user testing typically involves selecting a representative group of users who match the target audience of the product or service. These users are then given specific tasks to perform using the product or service, while researchers observe and take notes on their actions, feedback, and overall user experience.

During user testing, researchers strive to maintain a neutral and unbiased position, allowing users to freely explore and interact with the product or service without any interference. This approach helps to capture genuine user reactions and uncover potential pain points or difficulties that users may encounter.

The data collected from user testing is analyzed and used to inform design decisions and iterate on the product or service. By observing how users navigate through the interface, complete tasks, and provide feedback, researchers can identify areas of improvement, such as confusing or unclear instructions, difficult-to-use features, or overall inconsistencies in the user interface.

User testing is an essential part of the user-centered design process, as it allows product teams to validate their design choices and ensure that the end product meets the needs and expectations of its intended users. It provides valuable insights into user behavior, preferences, and expectations, allowing designers to make informed decisions and create more intuitive and user-friendly experiences.

User-Centered Design

User-Centered Design (UCD) is an iterative design process that aims to understand the users' needs, preferences, and behaviors through research and usability testing. It focuses on putting the user at the center of the design process to create products, services, or systems that are intuitive, efficient, and enjoyable to use. In the context of user-research (UXR), UCD involves gathering insights about the target users through various qualitative and quantitative research methods. This may include conducting interviews, surveys, and observational studies to gain a deep understanding of the users' goals, tasks, and pain points. The insights gathered from the research inform the design process, ensuring that the end product is tailored to the specific needs and expectations of the users. UCD involves actively involving users throughout the design process, seeking their feedback and involving them in usability testing sessions to evaluate the effectiveness of the design. By employing UCD principles in user-research, designers can create more user-friendly and effective solutions. It helps in identifying potential usability issues early on and allows for adjustments to be made based on user feedback. UCD ultimately aims to improve the overall user experience by creating products that are not only visually appealing but also meet the functional and usability needs of the users.

User.Com

User research, also known as UXR (User Experience Research), refers to the systematic study of users and their interactions with a product or service. It involves gathering qualitative and quantitative data to gain insights into user behavior, needs, preferences, and pain points. UXR aims to inform and improve the design and development process, ensuring that the end product caters to the users' expectations and goals. Through various methodologies, such as surveys, interviews, usability testing, and analytics analysis, UXR uncovers valuable information that helps design teams make informed decisions. By understanding users' motivations, frustrations, and goals, UXR enables organizations to create user-centered solutions that drive engagement, satisfaction, and loyalty. The primary objective of UXR is to bridge the gap between users and technology, ultimately optimizing the user experience. It plays a crucial role in identifying design flaws, refining product features, and optimizing usability. UXR helps identify patterns and trends in user behavior, allowing organizations to make data-driven decisions and innovate based on real user feedback. By conducting user research throughout the design life cycle, organizations can tailor their products and services to meet the specific needs and expectations of their target audience. This not only enhances user satisfaction but also increases the likelihood of achieving business objectives. In summary, user research is a systematic approach to understanding users and their interactions with a product or service. Through the collection and analysis of data, UXR informs decision-making processes, ensures user-centered design, and ultimately enhances the overall user experience.

UserBit

UserBit is a user research (UXR) platform that helps UX researchers and product teams efficiently collect, analyze, and collaborate on user research data. The platform is designed to streamline the entire research process by providing a centralized hub to manage user research projects.

With UserBit, researchers can easily create and organize research tasks, interviews, surveys, and other data collection methods. The platform also offers built-in tools for data analysis, allowing researchers to make sense of their findings and uncover meaningful insights.

One of the key features of UserBit is its powerful tagging system. Researchers can tag their research data with various labels and attributes, making it easier to search and filter the data later on. This tagging system enables researchers to quickly find patterns, identify trends, and draw connections between different research findings.

UserBit also promotes collaboration among team members by allowing them to share research projects, invite others to contribute, and provide feedback on findings. The platform offers a user-friendly interface that encourages cross-functional collaboration, ensuring that everyone involved in the product development process can easily access and leverage the research data.

In summary, UserBit is a comprehensive user research platform that supports researchers and product teams throughout the entire research process. By providing tools for data collection, analysis, and collaboration, UserBit helps teams make data-driven decisions, enhance user experience, and create more successful products.

UserBob

User research, also known as UXR (User Experience Research), is a systematic investigation method used to understand users' needs, behaviors, motivations, and preferences. Its primary goal is to gather insights and data to inform the design and development of products or services that best meet users' expectations and requirements.

UXR involves various qualitative and quantitative research techniques, including interviews, surveys, usability testing, field studies, and analytics. These methods help researchers gain a deep understanding of users by observing their interactions, collecting feedback, and analyzing their behavior.

The findings from user research contribute to the design process by providing actionable insights that guide decision-making. By understanding users' wants and needs, organizations can make informed design choices that improve user satisfaction and enhance the overall user experience.

User research plays a crucial role at different stages of the product development lifecycle. It helps identify target users, develop user personas, evaluate prototypes, measure usability, and validate designs. By involving users early and consistently throughout the design process, user research minimizes the risk of creating products that do not meet user expectations or fail to solve their problems effectively.

UserBrain

User research, also known as user experience research (UXR), refers to the systematic process of understanding users' needs, behaviors, and motivations through various qualitative and quantitative research methods. This discipline aims to uncover insights that help inform and guide the design and development of products or services that meet users' requirements and expectations.

During the user research process, researchers employ a range of techniques such as interviews, surveys, observation, and usability testing to collect relevant data. These methods allow them to gather both qualitative and quantitative data to gain a comprehensive understanding of users' preferences, behaviors, and pain points. By analyzing this data, researchers can identify patterns, generate user personas, create customer journey maps, and gain valuable insights into users' mental models and motivations.

User research plays a crucial role in the iterative design process, as it helps designers and developers make informed decisions based on user needs and preferences. The insights gained from user research can inform the creation of user-centered designs, enhance usability, and contribute to the overall success and satisfaction of the end-users.

UserIQ

UserIQ is a term used in the field of user-research (UXR) to describe the level of understanding a researcher has of their target audience's needs, preferences, and behaviors. It is a measure of how well a researcher can empathize with users and anticipate their expectations in order to design and develop products and services that meet those needs.

UserIQ is often achieved through a combination of qualitative and quantitative research methods. Qualitative research, such as interviews and observations, allows researchers to gain a deep understanding of users' motivations and pain points. Quantitative research, on the other hand, provides statistical data and trends that help researchers identify patterns and make informed decisions.

UserInterviews

A user interview is a qualitative research method used in user experience research (UXR), where researchers directly engage with individuals to gather insights into their experiences, needs, preferences, and behaviors related to a product, service, or system.

During a user interview, a researcher asks open-ended questions to elicit detailed responses from the participant. The goal is to understand the participant's perspective, uncover pain points, discover opportunities for improvement, and gather feedback that can guide the design and development process.

UserReplay

User replay is a research method commonly used in user experience research (UXR) to gather valuable insight and data about user interactions with a particular product or service. It involves observing and recording users as they navigate through the product, performing various tasks and providing feedback. User replay typically takes place in a controlled environment, such as a usability lab, where researchers can closely monitor user behavior and gather accurate and detailed data.

During a user replay session, researchers use various tools and techniques to capture the user's actions, such as screen recording software, eye-tracking devices, or clickstream analysis. This allows researchers to analyze the user's interactions, identify potential usability issues, and gain a deeper understanding of the user's experience. By observing users in action, researchers can uncover valuable insights that may not be apparent through traditional surveys or interviews.

UserReport

A user report in the context of user research (UXR) refers to a document that summarizes findings, insights, and recommendations from a study or analysis conducted with users. This report aims to provide clear and concise information to stakeholders and team members involved in the design, development, or decision-making process of a product or service.

The user report typically includes various sections that help structure and present the research findings effectively. These sections may include an introduction, objectives, research methods, participant profiles, key findings, analysis, and recommendations.

In the introduction, the report provides background information about the research objectives and the methodology used. It also highlights any limitations or constraints that may impact the interpretation of the findings. The objectives section succinctly states the research goals and the purpose of the study.

The participant profiles section outlines the characteristics, demographics, and any specific criteria used to recruit participants. This information helps readers understand the target audience and the diversity of perspectives represented in the study.

Key findings are the core of the user report, presenting the major themes, patterns, or insights derived from the research. These findings are often supported by direct quotes, observations, or data collected during the study. The analysis section delves deeper into the findings, providing explanations, interpretations, and implications for design or decision-making.

Finally, the user report concludes with recommendations based on the research findings. These recommendations aim to guide the next steps in the design process, inform product improvements, or provide insights for future research. The report may also include appendices or additional resources, such as survey results, interview transcripts, or personas, to provide further context or evidence.

UserResearchConsent

A user research consent is a formal agreement between the researcher and the participant that outlines the purpose, process, and potential risks of a user research study. It is a necessary step in ensuring ethical conduct and protecting the rights and well-being of the participants.

The consent form typically includes details such as the study's objectives, the expected duration of participation, the types of data that will be collected, and any potential risks or discomforts the participant may experience. It also outlines the measures taken to ensure confidentiality and data protection.

The consent form serves as an informative document, explaining the research to the participant in a clear and concise manner. It provides an opportunity for the participant to ask questions, seek clarification, and make an informed decision about their involvement in the study.

By signing the consent form, the participant acknowledges that they have understood the information presented and voluntarily agree to participate. Their signature indicates their agreement to the terms and conditions outlined in the form.

The researcher is responsible for obtaining the consent of participants before the study begins and ensuring that it is fully informed consent. This means that participants have a complete understanding of the research, its purpose, and any potential risks or benefits before they agree to participate.

Obtaining and documenting informed consent is essential in user research, as it demonstrates ethical conduct and adheres to legal and professional guidelines. It helps to protect the rights and well-being of participants, establishing a foundation of trust and transparency between the researcher and the participants.

UserTesting.Com

UserTesting.com is a user research platform that provides businesses with valuable insights into the usability and user experience of their digital products and services.

Through UserTesting.com, businesses can conduct remote usability testing by connecting with real users who match their target audience. These users are then given tasks to perform on the website or app being tested, while their actions and verbal feedback are recorded. This provides businesses with first-hand insights into how users interact with their product, what issues they encounter, and where improvements can be made.

By gathering qualitative and quantitative data from users, UserTesting.com helps businesses make data-driven decisions that improve the overall user experience. This user research platform provides a variety of testing options, such as moderated and unmoderated tests, as well as mobile and desktop testing. Additionally, UserTesting.com allows businesses to target specific demographics, ensuring that the feedback received is relevant to their target audience.

In conclusion, UserTesting.com is a valuable tool for businesses seeking to understand and improve the usability and user experience of their digital products and services. It allows businesses to connect with real users, gather valuable insights, and make informed decisions that ultimately lead to a better user experience and increased customer satisfaction.

UserTesting

UserTesting is a user-research method used in the field of User Experience Research (UXR). It involves observing and recording the interactions and experiences of users while they use a product or system. The goal of UserTesting is to gather firsthand feedback and insights to inform the design and development process.

In UserTesting, participants are typically asked to perform specific tasks or use cases while researchers observe their actions, behaviors, and verbal feedback. This can be done remotely or in a controlled lab environment. The researcher may also ask participants questions before, during, or after the test to gather additional information.

Through UserTesting, researchers gain a deep understanding of how users interact with a product, identify pain points or areas of confusion, and uncover opportunities for improvement. This method allows researchers to gather qualitative data, such as user insights, preferences, and opinions, as well as quantitative data, such as task success rates and time on task.

By analyzing the findings from UserTesting, researchers can identify patterns and trends, which can inform decision-making in the design process. These insights help designers and developers identify usability issues, validate design choices, and make informed decisions to optimize the user experience.

UserVoice

UserVoice is a platform commonly used in user research (UXR) to gather and prioritize feedback from users. It enables companies to understand their customers' needs, pain points, and preferences to improve their products and services.

With UserVoice, businesses can create a forum or a feedback portal where customers can submit their suggestions, ideas, and concerns. This platform provides a centralized location for users to share their feedback, offering a space to discuss and vote on different suggestions. Through this process, UserVoice helps companies identify the most critical issues and desired features, giving them valuable insights to guide their product development decisions.

UserZoom

UserZoom is a user-research platform designed to facilitate user experience research (UXR). It provides a comprehensive suite of tools and features that enable researchers to conduct both qualitative and quantitative research studies, with the goal of gaining insights into the needs, behaviors, and preferences of users. The platform offers various research methodologies, including usability testing, remote testing, surveys, card sorting, and tree testing. These methodologies can be adapted to suit different study objectives, allowing researchers to explore different aspects of the user experience. UserZoom provides a user-friendly and intuitive interface, making it easy for researchers to create and manage research studies. The platform also supports participant recruitment and scheduling, ensuring that researchers have access to a diverse pool of participants. With UserZoom, researchers can analyze and visualize data in real-time, allowing for quick and efficient analysis. The platform offers various data visualization tools, such as heatmaps, clickmaps, and task analysis, which help researchers identify patterns and trends in user behavior. The platform also offers collaboration and sharing features, making it easy for researchers to collaborate with colleagues and stakeholders. Research teams can work together to analyze data, create reports, and share findings, ensuring that research insights are effectively communicated and utilized. Overall, UserZoom is a powerful and versatile user-research platform that provides researchers with the tools and features they need to conduct effective and impactful user experience research studies.

Userflow

Userflow is a term used in user research (UXR) to describe the path or sequence of steps that a particular user takes while interacting with a product or service. It aims to understand the user's journey and behavior within the system, identifying any pain points and areas of improvement.

Userflow analysis is an essential method used by UX researchers to gain insights into how users

162

navigate through a website, application, or any digital interface. It helps in understanding the user's goals, motivations, and decision-making process.

Userlane

Please note that it is not possible to provide a definition for "Userlane" in pure HTML format as it is a markup language used for structuring content on the web, not for providing definitions or explanations. However, I can provide the definition of "Userlane" in plain text format for user research (UXR) purposes: Userlane is a digital adoption platform that helps users navigate and interact with software applications by providing step-by-step guidance within the user interface. It is designed to enhance the user experience and facilitate the onboarding process for new users by providing contextual, interactive walkthroughs and support. By using Userlane, UX researchers can gather valuable insights into how users interact with software applications, identify pain points and usability issues, and optimize the user experience. It enables researchers to observe and analyze how users navigate through different interfaces, understand their thought processes, and identify areas for improvement. With Userlane, user researchers can create interactive prototypes, conduct usability testing, and gather data on user behavior, preferences, and performance. It allows them to track user interactions, measure task completion rates, and collect feedback in real-time. Overall, Userlane is a powerful tool for UX researchers to understand user behavior, improve the usability of software applications, and enhance the overall user experience.>

Userlytics

Userlytics is a user research platform used in the field of User Experience Research (UXR). It allows researchers to gather valuable insights into user behavior by conducting various research methodologies remotely, such as usability tests, interviews, and surveys.

With Userlytics, researchers can create and customize tasks and questionnaires to meet their specific research objectives. They can recruit participants from a diverse pool of users and remotely conduct testing sessions through screen and voice recordings. This enables researchers to observe and analyze user interactions with websites, apps, prototypes, or even physical products.

One of the key features of Userlytics is its ability to offer demographic and psychographic segmentation, which helps researchers target specific user groups based on factors like age, gender, education, and interests. This allows for more focused research and the identification of patterns and trends within different user segments.

Furthermore, Userlytics provides a range of analytical tools to assist in data analysis, such as heatmaps, clickstream analysis, and sentiment analysis. These tools help researchers gain deeper insights into user preferences, pain points, and overall user satisfaction.

In conclusion, Userlytics is a comprehensive user research platform that offers remote testing capabilities, demographic segmentation, and advanced analytical tools. It empowers User Experience Researchers to understand user behavior, improve digital experiences, and make data-driven decisions to create more user-centered products and services.

Userpeek

Userpeek is a user-research (UXR) tool that enables researchers to conduct remote usability testing to gather valuable insights about user experiences. It allows researchers to observe and analyze how users interact with websites or applications, identifying potential usability issues and areas for improvement. With Userpeek, researchers can create tasks and scenarios for participants to complete while recording their screen and voice. This remote testing approach eliminates geographical limitations and enables researchers to collect data from a diverse range of users, providing a comprehensive understanding of the user's perspective. The tool provides researchers with a platform to recruit and manage participants, ensuring a diverse set of users that represents the target audience. Userpeek also features a robust analytics dashboard that allows researchers to analyze and interpret the data collected during testing sessions. By using Userpeek, researchers can identify navigation problems, confusing user interface elements, and other obstacles that hinder the user experience. This allows them to make data-driven decisions when designing or optimizing websites or applications, ensuring a user-centric approach. Overall, Userpeek simplifies the user-research process by offering an intuitive and comprehensive tool for conducting remote usability testing. By gaining insights into user behavior, researchers can improve the user experience, increase customer satisfaction, and drive business success.

Userpilot

Userpilot is a user research tool for UX designers and researchers that allows them to gather valuable insights and feedback from their users. It offers a platform to create and conduct user tests, surveys, and interviews, enabling businesses to better understand user behavior and preferences.

Userpilot streamlines the user research process by providing features such as participant recruitment, task tracking, and real-time analytics. With its user-friendly interface, researchers can easily design and deploy tests and surveys, ensuring a seamless user experience for participants. The platform also offers robust data reporting and analysis capabilities, allowing researchers to visualize and interpret the collected data. They can gain insights into user pain points, uncover usability issues, and identify opportunities for improvement. By leveraging these insights, UX designers and researchers can make data-driven decisions to enhance the user experience. Userpilot facilitates collaboration among researchers and stakeholders by providing a centralized platform for sharing research findings and insights. It allows for easy communication and collaboration, ensuring that the entire team is aligned on the research goals and outcomes. Overall, Userpilot empowers UX designers and researchers to conduct effective user research, enabling them to create user-centered products and solutions. By understanding their users' needs and preferences, businesses can deliver seamless and enjoyable experiences, increasing user satisfaction and driving business growth.

VWO

VWO, also known as Visual Website Optimizer, is a user-research software tool primarily used in the field of user experience research (UXR). It enables researchers to conduct various types of experiments and tests on websites to gather insights and optimize user experience.

In the realm of user-research, VWO offers a range of features that aid researchers in understanding user behavior, preferences, and interactions with websites. A key function provided by VWO is A/B testing, wherein different versions of a webpage are presented to users to identify which design or layout performs better in achieving specific goals. This helps researchers make informed decisions on design and content changes to enhance the user experience.

VWO allows researchers to create and test multiple variations of webpages, and provides statistical analysis to determine the significance of the results. It also offers heatmaps, clickmaps, and session recordings, which provide visual representations of user activity and behavior on a website. These insights help researchers identify areas of improvement and optimize the visual and functional aspects of a website.

Additionally, VWO provides features for creating surveys and feedback forms that allow researchers to directly gather user opinions and preferences. This data can be used to understand user needs and expectations, and make informed decisions regarding website improvements.

Overall, VWO is a valuable tool in the field of user-research, enabling researchers to conduct experiments, gather data, and analyze user behavior to optimize website design and enhance the overall user experience.

Validately

Validately is a user research platform designed for the field of User Experience Research (UXR). It provides researchers with a range of tools and features to conduct effective and efficient user research studies.

With Validately, researchers can recruit participants for their studies, either by targeting specific demographics or by using pre-screened panels. The platform also offers the ability to schedule and manage research sessions, whether they are conducted remotely or in-person.

One of the key features of Validately is its usability testing capabilities. Researchers can set up and conduct usability tests on websites, mobile apps, prototypes, or any other digital product. These tests can be moderated or unmoderated, depending on the researcher's preference. The platform also provides tools for capturing user feedback and observations during the testing sessions.

In addition to usability testing, Validately offers other research methods such as card sorting, tree testing, and surveys. These methods allow researchers to gather valuable insights about user preferences, information architecture, and user satisfaction.

The data collected through Validately can be analyzed and synthesized using the platform's built-in analytics and reporting tools. This enables researchers to identify patterns, trends, and usability issues, and to make data-driven recommendations for improving the user experience of digital products.

In summary, Validately is a comprehensive user research platform that provides researchers with the tools and features they need to conduct user research studies effectively and efficiently. It offers a range of research methods, participant recruitment capabilities, usability testing features, and analytics tools, all designed to empower researchers in their quest to improve the user experience of digital products.

Video Interviews

A video interview in the context of user-research (UXR) is a method of conducting user interviews using video conferencing or recording software to capture both audio and visual components of the interview.

Video interviews are typically used in UXR to overcome the limitations of traditional face-to-face interviews, such as geographical constraints, scheduling conflicts, and cost implications. By conducting interviews remotely, researchers can interview participants from different locations, making it easier to gather diverse user perspectives.

Video interviews allow researchers to observe and analyze non-verbal cues, such as facial expressions and body language, which can provide valuable insights into users' emotions and reactions. This additional layer of information helps researchers gain a deeper understanding of users' experiences and can aid in the identification of pain points and usability issues.

Furthermore, video interviews enable researchers to record and review the interviews multiple times, allowing for more accurate data analysis and interpretation. They also serve as a valuable reference for stakeholders who were unable to attend the interviews, ensuring everyone has access to the same user insights.

Overall, video interviews have become an essential tool in the UXR toolkit, enabling researchers to conduct user interviews efficiently and effectively, regardless of participants' geographical location. It allows for a more comprehensive understanding of user experiences, facilitating the design and development of user-centered solutions.

Vidyard

Vidyard is a user-research tool commonly used in the field of UX research (UXR). It is designed to help researchers gather and analyze user data in order to understand user behavior, preferences, and needs. With Vidyard, researchers can conduct user tests, interviews, and surveys, and collect both qualitative and quantitative data.

The tool offers various features that make it useful for UXR professionals. One of its key features is screen recording, which allows researchers to capture users' interactions with a website or application. This helps researchers observe and analyze how users navigate through a product, identify usability issues, and gain insights into user preferences.

In addition to screen recording, Vidyard also provides features such as heatmaps, click maps, and scroll maps. These visualizations help researchers understand how users interact with specific elements on a webpage, such as buttons, links, or forms. By analyzing these maps, researchers can identify areas of improvement and optimize the user experience.

Furthermore, Vidyard offers robust analytics and reporting functionalities. Researchers can track and measure various metrics such as task completion rates, time spent on specific pages, and user satisfaction scores. These insights help researchers make data-driven decisions and prioritize improvements to enhance the user experience.

In conclusion, Vidyard is a powerful user-research tool that enables UXR professionals to gather, analyze, and interpret user data. By using features like screen recording, visualizations, and analytics, researchers can gain deep insights into user behavior and preferences, ultimately leading to the creation of more user-centric products and experiences.

Virtual Reality User Interviews

Virtual Reality User Interviews are a qualitative user research method conducted within a virtual reality environment to gain insights into the user experience (UX) of a product or service. These interviews involve virtual interactions between researchers and participants.

The purpose of Virtual Reality User Interviews is to understand user perceptions, behaviors, and preferences in a simulated, immersive environment. They allow researchers to observe and analyze how users navigate and interact with virtual elements, providing valuable feedback for product development and UX design.

The process of conducting Virtual Reality User Interviews typically includes several stages. First, researchers set up a virtual environment that simulates the product or service being studied. Participants are then immersed in this environment using virtual reality headsets, hand controllers, or other interactive devices.

Researchers guide participants through a set of tasks or scenarios, observing their actions and collecting data on their experiences. They may conduct interviews during or after the virtual experience to gather participants' thoughts, feelings, and perceptions. This combination of quantitative and qualitative data helps researchers identify usability issues, pain points, and areas for improvement.

Virtual Reality User Interviews offer several advantages over traditional face-to-face user interviews. They provide an enhanced level of immersion, allowing participants to interact with virtual objects as they would in a real-world context. This can result in more authentic and realistic user feedback. Additionally, virtual reality enables researchers to manipulate variables, such as virtual environments or product features, to test different scenarios and collect more precise data.

In summary, Virtual Reality User Interviews are a research method that uses virtual reality technology to gain insights into user experiences and preferences. By simulating real-world interactions, these interviews provide valuable data for product development, UX design, and optimization.

Visual Ethnography

Visual ethnography is a qualitative research method used in user research (UXR) to study and understand the behaviors, perceptions, and experiences of individuals within a specific cultural or social context. It involves the use of visual data, such as photographs, videos, and graphical representations, to capture and analyze the dynamics of human interaction, cultural practices, and physical environments.

Through visual ethnography, researchers aim to gain deeper insights into users' needs, preferences, and motivations, as well as the social and cultural factors that influence their

166

interactions with products, services, or environments. By collecting and analyzing visual data, researchers can observe and interpret nonverbal cues, spatial arrangements, and contextual elements that may not be easily captured through traditional qualitative research methods.

Voice Assistant Surveys

A voice assistant survey is a research method used in user experience research (UXR) to collect data and gather insights about users' experiences, preferences, and behaviors with voice assistants, such as Siri, Alexa, or Google Assistant.

This type of survey aims to understand how users interact with voice assistants, their expectations, challenges, and satisfaction levels. It helps researchers identify pain points, discover areas for improvement, and gain a deeper understanding of the user's journey and overall experience when using voice assistants.

Voice Assistant Testing

Voice Assistant Testing is a user research method used to evaluate the performance, usability, and effectiveness of voice-based virtual assistants. It involves conducting systematic assessments to measure how well the voice assistant understands and responds to user inputs, as well as the accuracy and relevance of its generated responses.

During Voice Assistant Testing, researchers design and execute a series of tasks and scenarios to simulate real-world interactions with the voice assistant. These tasks can range from simple requests like setting an alarm or checking the weather to more complex queries that require multiple steps or involve accessing specific information. The goal is to examine how the voice assistant handles different types of queries and to identify areas for improvement.

The testing process typically involves collecting both qualitative and quantitative data. Qualitative data can be gathered through user observations, interviews, and think-aloud protocols, allowing researchers to understand the user experience and any frustrations or challenges encountered. Quantitative data, on the other hand, can be obtained by measuring success rates, response times, and completion rates of tasks.

The insights and findings generated from Voice Assistant Testing are used to refine and optimize the voice assistant's capabilities. This data-driven approach helps identify patterns, identify areas for improvement, and inform iterative design and development processes. Ultimately, Voice Assistant Testing aims to enhance the user experience by ensuring the voice assistant delivers accurate, relevant, and efficient responses, contributing to overall user satisfaction and engagement.

Voice Search Testing

Voice search testing is a method used in user research (UXR) to evaluate the performance and effectiveness of voice recognition systems and voice-controlled applications. It involves conducting experiments and gathering data to measure the accuracy, speed, and user satisfaction of voice search features.

The process of voice search testing typically begins with designing test scenarios that mimic real-world scenarios or specific use cases. These scenarios could include asking the system to perform certain tasks or retrieve specific information. Test participants are then recruited to interact with the voice recognition system or application and complete the assigned tasks using voice commands.

The main objective of voice search testing is to identify and analyze potential issues and limitations in voice recognition performance. This can include evaluating how well the system understands and correctly interprets user voice commands, as well as assessing the system's ability to provide accurate and relevant search results or responses. In addition, voice search testing may also examine factors such as the system's response time, error rates, and user preferences or opinions regarding the voice search experience.

By conducting voice search testing, UX researchers can gain valuable insights into the user experience of voice-controlled applications. The findings from such testing can help inform the design and development of voice recognition systems, enabling developers to improve their accuracy and performance. Additionally, voice search testing can also contribute to enhancing the overall user satisfaction and usability of voice-controlled applications, ensuring a more seamless and efficient user experience.

WalkMe

WalkMe is a digital adoption platform that helps improve user experiences by providing on-screen guidance and support. It is designed to assist users in navigating through complex websites or applications by providing step-by-step instructions and contextual information.

With WalkMe, user-research (UXR) professionals can gain valuable insights into how users interact with their digital platforms. By leveraging WalkMe's features and capabilities, UXR teams can conduct in-depth usability studies, gather user feedback, and analyze user behavior to optimize the user experience.

Webinars

A webinar is a user-research (UXR) method that involves conducting a presentation, lecture, or workshop online, where participants can attend remotely from their own computers or devices. It is a virtual event that allows researchers to share information, insights, and findings with a wide audience, while also facilitating interaction and feedback.

Webinars are commonly used in user research as a means of disseminating research findings, presenting new methodologies or techniques, and engaging with the UX community. They offer a convenient and accessible way for researchers to reach a large number of participants, regardless of their geographical location.

WhatUsersDo

WhatUsersDo is a user research platform that aims to provide insights into user behavior and interactions with digital products or services. It offers a range of research methodologies and tools designed to help businesses understand the needs, preferences, and pain points of their users.

The platform allows researchers to recruit participants who match specific criteria and perform various research activities such as task-based usability tests, focus groups, surveys, and remote interviews. These activities can be conducted remotely, eliminating geographical limitations and enabling access to a diverse pool of participants.

With WhatUsersDo, researchers can design and customize research studies to collect qualitative and quantitative data. Through screen recording and audio capture, researchers can observe and analyze how users navigate through websites or apps, identify areas for improvement, and gain insights on user satisfaction and usability.

The platform provides features for note-taking and collaboration, allowing researchers to easily share findings with stakeholders and team members. It also offers features to generate reports and visualizations that summarize research findings, making it easier for businesses to understand and communicate user insights.

In summary, WhatUsersDo provides a comprehensive user research platform that empowers businesses to gain a deeper understanding of their users' experiences and make informed decisions to improve the design and functionality of their products or services.

Wizard Of Oz Testing

Wizard of Oz testing is a user-research methodology used in UX design to simulate the functions of an interactive system or product that does not yet exist or is not fully developed. It involves creating a facade or prototype that gives the illusion of an operational interface, allowing researchers to observe and collect feedback from users as they interact with the system.

The term "Wizard of Oz" refers to the fantastical element of the testing process, where behind the scenes, a human operator plays the role of the system, responding to user inputs and creating the illusion of automated interactions. This method is particularly useful when testing complex or novel concepts that cannot be easily prototyped or programmed at early stages of development.

By using Wizard of Oz testing, researchers can gain valuable insights into user behavior, preferences, and expectations before investing significant time and resources into actual development. It allows for rapid experimentation and iteration, enabling designers to refine their ideas and improve the user experience before committing to a final design.

Key benefits of Wizard of Oz testing include its flexibility, cost-effectiveness, and low technical requirements compared to traditional testing methods. However, it is crucial to understand that the results obtained through this technique may not fully replicate real-world scenarios, as the presence of a human operator can introduce bias or limitations in response accuracy.

Workshop Facilitation

Workshop facilitation in the context of user-research (UXR) refers to the process of guiding and organizing a collaborative workshop session aimed at gathering valuable insights and feedback from users. This facilitation involves leading and managing a group of participants through various activities and exercises designed to elicit their thoughts, opinions, and experiences related to a product or service.

The facilitator plays a crucial role in creating an open and inclusive environment where participants feel comfortable sharing their thoughts and ideas openly. They guide the workshop by setting the agenda, defining clear objectives, and structuring activities that encourage active participation and engagement from all attendees.

The workshop facilitation process typically begins with an introduction to the purpose and goals of the session, followed by icebreakers or warm-up activities to encourage interaction and build rapport among participants. The facilitator then presents the research topic or problem statement, and participants are encouraged to provide their insights, observations, and suggestions through activities such as individual or group discussions, brainstorming sessions, role-playing exercises, or design critiques.

The facilitator's role is to ensure that the workshop remains focused, that all participants have equal opportunity to contribute, and that the session stays on track within the allotted time frame. They should actively listen, ask probing questions, and facilitate discussions to dig deeper into the user's perspectives and uncover valuable insights. They may also use various facilitation techniques, such as visual aids or interactive tools, to facilitate idea generation and gather feedback effectively.

Workshop

User research, also known as UXR or user experience research, is a systematic and iterative process of understanding the needs, behaviors, and motivations of users in order to design and improve products or services that meet their requirements. The main goal of UXR is to gather insights from users through qualitative and quantitative methods and use these insights to inform decision-making and drive user-centered design.

UXR typically involves various methods such as interviews, usability testing, surveys, and analytics. These methods aim to uncover not only what users say they need or want, but also what they actually do and how they feel about a product or service. By observing and interacting with users, researchers can identify pain points, identify opportunities for innovation, and validate design decisions.

The findings from UXR can help guide the design and development process, ensuring that the end result meets user needs and expectations, improves usability, and ultimately enhances user satisfaction. It can also help prioritize features, improve accessibility and inclusivity, and identify areas for improvement or optimization. UXR is an essential part of the user-centered design process, enabling designers and developers to create products or services that are not only functional and usable, but also enjoyable and meaningful to users.

In conclusion, user research plays a vital role in understanding user needs, behaviors, and motivations, and serves as the foundation for user-centered design. By incorporating UXR into the design process, organizations can create products and services that truly resonate with users and result in a positive user experience.

Workshops

A workshop in the context of user research (UXR) refers to a collaborative session or event where researchers, stakeholders, and other relevant parties come together to explore and address specific research objectives or challenges. It is a structured and interactive session that encourages active participation and knowledge exchange among participants.

The main purpose of a user research workshop is to gather insights, generate ideas, and make informed decisions based on user-centered perspectives. It allows researchers to conduct in-depth investigations, gather qualitative and quantitative data, and gain a holistic understanding of users' needs, preferences, and expectations.

During a user research workshop, various research methods, techniques, and tools may be employed, such as interviews, surveys, usability testing, and empathy mapping. The specific activities and exercises conducted in a workshop depend on the research goals and the stage of the design process.

The benefits of conducting workshops in user research include:

- Facilitating collaboration and cross-functional communication among team members and stakeholders

- Encouraging creativity, innovation, and idea generation to address user needs and pain points

- Generating actionable insights and recommendations that inform the design and development process

- Building empathy and understanding towards users' needs, motivations, and behaviors

In summary, a user research workshop is an organized and participatory session that aims to collect, analyze, and interpret user insights to inform design decisions and improve the overall user experience.

Wyzowl

User research (UXR) is a systematic approach to discover, understand, and uncover insights about users and their experiences with a product or service. It involves gathering qualitative and quantitative data to inform the design and development process, making it more user-centered.

Through various research methods, such as interviews, observations, surveys, and usability testing, UXR seeks to answer questions about user needs, goals, behaviors, and preferences. This helps identify pain points, understand user motivations, and uncover opportunities for improvement.